Before the Dolphins Guild

BEFORE *the*
DOLPHINS GUILD

A STORY OF HEROIC EFFORTS TO SAVE TWO NAVY SUBMARINE
CREWS TRAPPED UNDER THE SEA IN 1915 AND 1916

Jon Humboldt Gates

moonstone
PUBLISHING

FIRST PRINTING 2022

Editor — Katie Sanborn

Cover and book design — Renée Davis

Historical naval advisors — Ric Hedman and Chief David Johnston USN (ret)

Front cover photo — H-Class, National Archives (111-SC-6593) altered by digital illustration

Back cover photo — Emma Freeman, courtesy of Humboldt Bay Maritime Museum

Published By:

P.O. Box 292
Lake Oswego, OR 97034
Info@moonstonepublishing.com

Printed in the United States of America

ISBN #978-1-878136-03-9

In memory of my parents

Irene and Humboldt

who met in the Navy in 1942

Contents

Author's Note

When the submarine *USS H-3* ran aground in the breakers on Samoa Beach in 1916, it happened just a few miles from my grandmother's Victorian home, which stood on an island in Humboldt Bay. I grew up by Humboldt Bay knowing the *H-3* story, mostly through stories my father told me. He'd run a Navy tugboat during World War II in San Francisco and spent a lot of time navigating the coastal waters. He knew the perils.

Years later, after I had completed a collection of maritime stories about crossing the Humboldt Bar at night (*Night Crossings*, 1986), a local Humboldt County historian handed me a first-person account of what happened inside *H-3* that day in December 1916. It was written by Duane Stewart (EM1), a retired Navy submariner who had also been *H-3*'s radioman. Duane felt that historical accounts focused on the rescue efforts outside the sub had neglected what unfolded inside *H-3* during those 10 hours that the crew was trapped under the breakers. His account filled about 50 typed pages of double-spaced notes, anecdotes, and descriptions. In that narration, he also wrote extensively about *H-3*'s chief of the boat, Jack Agraz, and the sub's captain, Lt. Harry Bogusch. That manuscript was the original catalyst that led to this book.

In 2019, I began delving into Duane's notes and doing further research. That's when I discovered the incredible story surrounding the *USS F-4* incident in Hawaii, including Jack Agraz and Harry Bogusch's involvement in that submarine event as well. The story immediately took on greater scope.

Besides scouring hundreds of historical records and articles, I was fortunate to meet John Agraz, a great nephew of Jack Agraz. He and his sister, Jeanette Quick, told me they had a trunk in her attic that had some things about "Uncle Jack" in it. They graciously loaned me family records and documents, some in Spanish, as well as letters, photographs from the sub incidents, and Jack's personal, hand-written diary from his early years in the Navy. That crystalized the telling of this story.

The events in this book focus on the *F-4* and *H-3* incidents and extraordinary actions of Navy and Coast Guard personnel to free the 48 sailors trapped inside the two boats. The *F-4* drama played out off the coast of Honolulu in March 1915 and *H-3* off Northern California's Humboldt County coast in December 1916.

Besides insights from the original, personal documents of those involved, the story is also based on US Navy records, recorded interviews conducted by individuals during and after the events, as well as excerpts from books, magazines, and newspapers spanning 100 years. Use of photographs were offered by museums, historical societies, Naval archives, and personal collections, with many from PigBoats.COM, a private website with an historical archive of information and photographs of submarines from 1900 to 1940. The directors of that website are both retired Navy submariners, and they made significant contributions to the authenticity of this story.

As in the recall of any incident that happened more than a century ago, there are variations of memories and fact among sources. In the overall sketch of these historical maritime events, first-person accounts were prioritized over secondary viewpoints and analysis. Officers who ran the early-era subs often held the rank of lieutenant junior grade, but as an honorary and more streamlined reference in this story, they are frequently referred to as lieutenant, which is a higher rank. In-depth detail from Naval reviews on diving for the *F-4* and on its ultimate recovery and analysis were prioritized over newspaper accounts.

Before the Dolphins Guild is a story about people a century ago who demonstrated incredible courage, willpower and innovation when faced with chaotic and unpredictable events brought on by the sea.

JHG

INTRODUCTION

USS F-3 on Port Townsend Bay, Washington, for performance trials. Behind is the U.S. Revenue Cutter Rush and a four-masted schooner, circa June 15, 1912 (Courtesy of Jefferson County Historical Society)

In the early 1900s submarines were a new and daring technology for modern navies around the world. After centuries of conflict on the earth's surface, war moved into the skies and under the sea. Young men from across America, many from small rural towns, were signing up and willing to take the risks involved to become a submariner. They would learn to dive under the sea in a sealed steel vessel, jammed with electric and chemical battery systems, new armaments and with little navigational capability.

Their training was hands on as well as from exposure to pioneer submariners who passed along their accumulated knowledge through stories and instruction. Every sailor aboard a submarine was a trained technical specialist. Every dive was a testing ground as much as training in the early 1900s. Together the submariners established a new legacy in the Navy, with tribal camaraderie, respect, and commitment to each other.

Early-era US submarines were given names of fish and marine creatures.

The USS F-4 (SS 23) was initially named the Skate and the USS H-3 (SS 30) the Garfish. But in 1911, all US Navy submarines were renamed using a letter and number combination. The letters represented stages of technical development and numbers identified the order in which the boats were authorized for construction. The US Navy made the change to alphanumeric names to align with international protocol of other navies, which considered submarines a minor craft, not deserving of an actual name.

The A-boats were the earliest US subs, starting in 1900. The F-boats and H-boats were later-generation designs, used specifically in the Pacific Ocean in the years 1910 to 1920. By the time the United States entered the Great War in 1917, the submarine force consisted of E, F, G, H, K, L, and N-class boats. The older submarine models became training vessels and were eventually scrapped or sunk as targets. The United States would keep the numeric protocol until 1931, when fleet submarines were again named for fish and marine creatures.

The early undersea experiences of crews from 1900 to 1916 provided the foundation of practices for establishing the US Navy Submarine School in 1917 in Groton, Connecticut. Sailors were screened and handpicked to enter the school. Eventually, sailors graduating from that rigorous academy would apprentice for a year aboard a fleet submarine, learning and memorizing all technological operations of the boat. Apprentices of the guild had to be able to find and identify every switch, valve, breaker, and system on the boat, recite its operation from memory, sketch it on paper, and then operate it flawlessly.

After a year apprenticing aboard a fleet boat, they would be reviewed and questioned by senior rank submariners in an oral exam and ultimately be recommended to the commanding officer for final qualification. If they failed, they were reassigned to the Navy's surface fleet and could never return to submarines. Both officers and enlisted men were subject to this schooling.

In March 1924, nearly a decade after the F-4 and H-3 events, the Dolphins Insignia was introduced by the Navy. It was initially just for officers who graduated from the school as "qualified submariners" but would eventually be awarded to enlisted personnel as well. The Dolphins insignia, a submarine flanked by two dolphins, could be worn only by a qualified submariner. In mythology, dolphins were revered as servants to Poseidon, the Greek God of the sea and patron of sailors.

F-4

A Navy diver was treading water in the middle of the Pacific Ocean off the coast of Honolulu with 300 feet of unpredictable sea under him. A large crowd of people on boats had assembled around him, and their stares were fixed on his motions. The currents swirled below. With little time to prepare himself, he was about to do what nobody in the world had done before. He gripped the side rail of the launch. A sailor lowered the diving helmet over his head and shoulders. The helmet was made of heavy bronze. The weight of it would be the only thing keeping it securely on the diver's shoulders. It had a 300-foot air hose attached to a hand pumping system secured to the deck of the launch. The diver wore long underwear, a light jersey and tennis shoes — no deep-sea pressurized diving suit, fixed helmet, weights, or heavy lead boots.

He checked his breathing line, gripped the steel cable, then slipped below the surface of the 80-degree water. He followed the cable down hand under hand, forcing himself downward feet first, taking in gulps of surface air being piped down the tube. His only thoughts were with the crew trapped at the bottom. He had to get to the *F-4*, help get a cable on the submarine. Bring those sailors back from the ocean floor.

As he descended into the depths, pressure was building rapidly. The air hose was small and limited his deep breathing. He was barrel chested and could consume a lot of air. The sea temperature remained warm even in the deeper waters, but visibility dimmed the deeper he went. Cross currents tugged at him as he descended the cable one hand under the other, methodically. He must not let go of that cable. He might just drift away in the currents.

As he paused, small fish swam up under and into his helmet. They nibbled at his cheeks and neck. He shook his head sharply. The fish swam back out of his helmet but returned in an instant, like flies. They tickled as they sucked at his skin. The air pressure in his helmet was just enough to keep the saltwater below the level of his mouth. He was irritated by the fish. He did not want to swallow one. Not at this depth.

He passed 100 feet. At 150 feet he stopped to allow his body to adjust to the tremendous pressure change. He was going down more slowly on this dive than he had on his previous dives, just a couple days ago. He needed to acclimate.

He continued his descent. He forced himself downward on the cable, hand under hand, pushing himself deeper into the ocean. The air bubbles bubbling out of the loose-fitting base of his helmet floated up toward the surface. The water above him was blue-green, translucent below the bright sky above. He peered into the depths probing for the dark outline of *F-4*. His vision was blurring. The sea below him was darker green. He was looking down into an abyss.

He passed the 196-foot mark, the deepest point of his previous dive a couple of days before. The pressure was intensifying. It was all he could do to resist the crushing weight on his sturdy frame, but he still felt strong, beyond any point of practical reason.

On the surface, the pressure per square inch on a human body was less than half a pound. Down at these depths it was close to 200 times greater. The weight of water on the diver's chest was like a vise, constricting his ability to breathe. But his mind stayed focused.

This was his fifth dive in three days. Each time he was going deeper.

This time he went down more slowly, pacing himself. The 12-man air pump crew on the surface took turns spinning the steel cranks as fast as they could to make sure he had enough air. They worked in teams of four, relieving each other as they tired. They watched the mechanical air pressure gauges like hawks because that was the only thing keeping the diver alive at those depths.

His slower descent kept him under water much longer than prior dives. More exposure to the gut-wrenching forces at work 200 feet below the ocean's surface. He took more than 20 minutes to reach the 200-foot mark. He'd done that in 10 minutes two days before and physically paid the price. He kept going down.

On the surface, Navy rescue crews were stunned by the Navy diver's stamina. He was setting a world record and didn't even know it. People had been talking about him all over the world as they followed the events in Hawaii. Probably even in his hometown of Guadalajara, Mexico.

Jack Agraz was the oldest of three brothers. His father, Juan de Agraz, passed away in 1883, when the diver was just four years old. Jack grew up in Guadalajara with his mother and brothers but traveled north as a young man and joined the US Navy, earning the rank of gunner's mate first class in 1908 in Washington DC. From there he hopped a train out to San Francisco and ended up aboard the USS *Buffalo* on an extended Pacific tour. Since then, he had always sent half his paycheck home to his mother in Guadalajara. He may have wondered if she was reading about the missing submarine. About her son's deep dives off the coast of Honolulu. Virginia de Agraz would undoubtedly have been proud of her son that day.

Everybody hoped Jack Agraz would find the missing sub. He was tenacious and driven, single minded in his commitment to find the boat. But he wasn't thinking about records. He was just trying to reach the 21 men trapped below on *F-4*.

H-3

NORTHERN CALIFORNIA — DECEMBER 14, 1916

A year and half later, the USS *H-3* idled ahead lazily in a dense fog off the Northern California coast at sunrise. The 27 men aboard hadn't seen much more than the submarine's forward deck since leaving the Columbia River bar two days before. Fog dominated the entire trip down the coast. After clearing reefs and rough seas around Cape Blanco in Oregon and Point St. George in Northern California, *H-3*'s crew was looking for the entrance to Humboldt Bay.

The captain's last navigational fix had been on St. George's Reef. They had been navigating by dead reckoning throughout the night, running on diesel engines off the rocky and wild coastline, 300 miles north of San Francisco. Lt. j.g. Eric Zemke, the sub's executive officer and second in command, had been on the bridge most the night but was relieved by the captain in the early morning.

H-3's captain, Lt. j.g. Harry R. Bogusch, was up on the bridge looking out at pea soup fog shortly after 0800 hours, trying to catch a glimpse of the coastline and the entrance to the Humboldt Bar. He'd just finished breakfast in the after battery compartment and taken the watch from Zemke. They'd had hot cakes, bacon, ham, eggs, and coffee.

H-3's chief of the boat, Jack Agraz, was down below having coffee, talking with Duane Stewart, the radio operator, and a few other crew members. They were sitting around the mess table. Agraz was the most seasoned submariner aboard H-3. He reported directly to the captain. But Agraz was eight years older than the captain, and he had been in the Navy more years than either of the younger officers.

Jack wore many hats on the boat. As designated chief of the boat, he was the senior enlisted man and top advisor to the commanding officer regarding the crew. He handled all crew personnel issues for both officers. He was also H-3's chief gunner's mate and diver. They were looking forward to being in the protected waters of Humboldt Bay after all the rough water and engine problems they'd had since leaving Puget Sound, Washington, two weeks before.

The USS H-3 running sea trials in Bellingham Bay, Washington (US Navy, PigBoats.COM)

The mess table was the main social point in the sub. Ten people could squeeze in during mess. At other times, sailors might be playing card games or just sipping coffee at the table. They'd stow the table during diving runs.

The *H-3* crew had nicknamed the boat 'Hoodoo' — possessed by a spirit — for all the unlucky accidents and mishaps it had encountered during its brief time in service on the Pacific Coast. Bogusch was given the command of *H-3* earlier in 1916 after being transferred from Hawaii, where he had served as ensign and then commanding officer of the submarine *F-1* in Honolulu. Jack Agraz had been with Bogusch on *F-1*.

Bogusch was starting to sense that *H-3* was living up to its nickname as one event after another had plagued the sub in the last two weeks. The trip down the coast to Humboldt Bay had started on a chilly December morning in Puget Sound. *H-3* had shoved off along with subs USS *H-1* and USS *H-2* and the 3,225-ton submarine tender, USS *Cheyenne*. The *Cheyenne* was 252 feet long. The flotilla ran into problems right away. *H-3*'s starboard diesel engine failed off Port Angeles in the Strait of Juan de Fuca. The sub was forced to tie up in Neah Bay for repairs. Neah Bay was primarily a Makah Indian fishing village, located on the Makah Reservation, with no roads connecting it to the outer world in 1916. Commercially, it was little more than a dock and trading post and home to only a few hundred people.

The flotilla's mission was under the command of Lt. William Howe, who was also captain of the tender *Cheyenne*. Their mission was to scout for a new submarine base in the Pacific Northwest. The Navy had submarine facilities in Puget Sound, San Pedro and San Francisco Bay. But there was a big gap between San Francisco and Puget Sound. The flotilla planned to scout Astoria on the Columbia River, Coos Bay on the central Oregon coast and Humboldt Bay on the Golden State's rocky, northern coast.

H-3's engine problems weren't anything new. The starboard engine was known as a troublemaker, and it always had been that way. Nobody was surprised that it had failed again. The crew called that starboard engine, "Steve's pet." Chief Machinist's Mate Steve Galazitas kept *H-3*'s twin diesels purring the best he could.

Galazitas knew a lot about diesels. He'd been in the Russian Navy, some crew members said. The Russians were also experimenting with submarines. They'd launched the world's first naval submarine fleet of seven boats in January 1905 from Vladivostok. The crew also learned that Galazitas had altered his name a bit, that his parents still lived in Vladivostok, and that he didn't want people to know that. He didn't say much else about his family.

He'd ended up in Chicago and joined the US Navy as a mechanic. Galazitas spent most of his time at the aft end of the boat, wedged between engines, the twin electric motors, the clutches, air compressors, whirling propeller shafts and overhead steering rods that operated the rudder and aft diving planes.

It took Galazitas and his mechanics all night to repair H-3's starboard engine at Neah Bay, replacing a cylinder liner in the engine block that had sprung a water leak. By dawn, they were ready to move with the rest of the flotilla. The four vessels rounded Cape Flattery that morning, picking up Pacific Ocean swells as they moved down the mostly uninhabited northern Washington coastline. The seas were rough, and the crews were locked inside the three submarines, hatches dogged down, to stay out of the winter squalls and waves washing over the narrow steel decks.

They arrived off Grays Harbor entrance in a dense fog. Rather than try to thread their way across the narrow entrance in the fog, they requested a local bar pilot. The crews stayed in Aberdeen for two days, then shoved off for Astoria, Oregon, near the mouth of the Columbia River.

It was tricky running the subs. Captains had to be careful not to overload the boats with too much weight, such as provisions and fuel. Every ounce had to be compensated for with ballast if the boats were running beneath the surface. On the surface, a sub performed like a standard vessel, but, once submerged, the captain had an exact equation of buoyancy and stability to maintain. Underwater, all the rules changed. It was more like air flight then. Every bit of weight added or subtracted changed the handling of the boat. Where weight was positioned was critical. A few hundred extra pounds here or there could cause a sub to nose downward or upward if the skipper didn't counter it with the angle of the dive planes and by adjusting the balance with the trim system.

The crews on the early submarines operated in a complex environment. Each crew member was a technician with a specific knowledge and responsibility to perform. Crewmen were required to know each other's responsibilities. Every dive tested a crew's capability to manage an array of interconnected technologies, shifting from diesel power to electric motors, building up air pressure, flooding the ballast tanks with seawater, and releasing pressurized air from the ballast tanks in a practiced, choreographed sequence. Every system had to be synchronized to maintain buoyancy control. The captain was at the center of it, but every crewmember played a part.

Every day was a rehearsal and a drill for Lt. Bogusch. There was only so much the Annapolis classroom could have prepared him for. He'd grown up in rural Texas and had never been to sea for an extended period before joining the Navy. He was 29 years old. He'd commanded subs now for little more than a year. Now he had command of the Hoodoo, and they were headed down the Pacific Coast to Humboldt Bay on a survey mission for a new submarine port.

Breaker on the Columbia River Bar around 1900 between two ships in passage (G. E. Plummer, Courtesy of Columbia River Maritime Museum, Astoria, Oregon)

The Columbia River Bar has always been the most dangerous bar crossing in North America. Around 2,000 vessels have sunk in and around that crossing over the years since Robert Gray piloted the first American ship across the Columbia River Bar in 1792. The bar crossing is about three miles wide and six miles in length, with a massive outflow of water from the Columbia River Basin that drains large parts of the Pacific Northwest.

It was clear weather when the three H-boats and the *Cheyenne* arrived off the entrance to the Columbia in early December 1916. The seas were moderate. But as *H-3* made its approach across the bar, both engines quit at once. Another hoodoo moment for the crew. Bogusch decided against switching to the electric motors and radioed Lt. Howe for an emergency towline from the *Cheyenne*. The two vessels proceeded slowly across the long bar crossing. Everything was normal. Then, while dead center on the crossing, wave sets started building from the northwest. The *H-3*'s stern rose up the face of a steepening wave. White water crests toppled, crashing over the sub. The sea swept over the bridge tower hatch before they could get it shut, sending saltwater down the open hatch and inside *H-3*.

That day crossing the Columbia River Bar into Astoria, Duane Stewart thought they were going to sink when the water gushed down the hatch. He was glad that he was wrong on that one. But every crew member was reminded about uncertainties aboard the subs.

⚓

Nearing the Humboldt Bay entrance, the fog eased for just a few minutes, almost in answer to Bogusch's hopes. There was a large swell running. He could feel the sub's 150-foot-long, 358-ton steel hull being lifted and settling back down in a rhythmic pulse as the rollers passed beneath the boat. They'd made a perfect navigational run from St. George Reef.

Just a half mile off the port beam they spotted what Bogusch believed was the sea buoy that marked the entrance to the bay. He'd caught just a glimpse, almost like a shadow. Or could it have been the smoke stack of the *Cheyenne*? Bogusch didn't think so, because the *Cheyenne* was farther out to sea waiting to rendezvous with the other two submarines, *H-1* and *H-2*, before approaching the bar. The other two subs had shoved off from Coos Bay, Oregon, the previous day and were running a few hours behind H-3 and the *Cheyenne*. The actual bar crossing would still be a mile or more due east of the buoy sighting.

The H-class submarines and all of their predecessors posed considerable navigational challenges to their crews and commanders. The boats had large glass-faced depth gauges that looked like enormous barometers that indicated how many feet under water they were, but there was no way to determine the depth of water beneath the hull while submerged. The electronic fathometer wouldn't be invented until 1928. Gyrocompasses were a cutting-edge technology in 1916, though still finicky, and prone to inaccuracy. Radar and GPS were the stuff of science fiction. Celestial navigation was well understood and been practiced since the beginning of seafaring, but it was an art that needed to be practiced regularly to be accurate.

H-3 had a wireless radio that worked on the surface. The only underwater communication device they had was the submarine bell, which was activated by compressed air. The bell signals could travel three to four miles under water. Some early subs communicated on the surface only by semaphore hand flags — or even carrier pigeons, which had a range of 120 to 140 miles.

That morning off the Humboldt Bar, almost on cue, the fog returned, closing in around H-3, drifting silently across the ocean's surface from offshore. Visibility dropped dramatically. Bogusch ordered ahead slow, reducing the boat's speed, probing the mists for a glimpse toward the east, where the Humboldt Coast remained hidden and silent.

The western shores of Humboldt Bay were formed by miles of cascading sand dunes that rose up from the ocean floor, cresting 50 to 100 feet above sea level in an uneven topography then dipping on the east side toward the bay. The bay was 14 miles long, and enormous natural sand barriers protected it from the open ocean. Some of the dunes sprawled more than one mile across.

The bar crossing into Humboldt Bay cut right through the middle of these sand dunes and was a half-mile wide. Dangerous shoals lined the northern side of the entrance. This stretch of the Humboldt coastline had claimed scores of vessels. An unpredictable combination of Pacific swells rolling in from thousands of miles of open ocean, variable currents that hugged the coastline, and dense fog could make navigation risky and unpredictable.

Just six months before, the SS *Bear*, a passenger and cargo steamer with more than 200 people onboard, had gone on the rocks at night, 25 miles south of the Humboldt Bar, near Cape Mendocino, in a dense fog. The ship's captain, who had not seen land since Cape Blanco on his Portland to San Francisco run, had underestimated the onshore currents and thought he was farther offshore. The demolished hull of the steamer was still on the rocks at Sugar Loaf that morning when *H-3* was making its approach to the Humboldt Bar.

Inside H-3 – Crewman at electrical panel in the aft battery compartment looking into the engine room. (PigBoats.COM)

The growling of *H-3*'s twin diesels had been constant since leaving Astoria as the boat cut through the water on a surface run. The crew liked cruising on the engines because it created a strong air flow through the hull. The two large engines that produced almost 1,000 horsepower sucked in a lot of air, creating a pleasant breeze that drove the heat and fumes from the confined stations of the sub. The inner compartments of the boat reeked constantly of diesel oil, tinged by acid wafting up from the large bank of lead-acid batteries located below deck that powered electric motors for underwater runs.

There were few amenities on these early subs, maybe an exposed toilet in a compartment, a few canvas bunks, no showers, little storage space, and gear and supplies stacked against the bulkheads in the different compartments. They had earned the nickname of "Pig Boats" because of the accumulated bad odors. When the ocean was smooth, the sailors often sat outside on the sub's narrow steel deck or rode the conning tower, the highest point of the sub, just to escape the fumes of the interior.

Air entered the submarine through three ventilators that were opened for long surface runs. The ventilators were positioned above watertight compartments. They had maintained the open ventilators along the entire coast run since they were not diving. Air also came in from the conning tower hatch overhead, through a vent in the conning tower that led down to the aft-battery compartment.

The control room was the smallest compartment in the boat and was located dead center under the conning tower. The sub's helm, diving plane controls, ballast control system, and electrical speed controls were all located in this nine-foot-long compartment. It was jammed with pipes, gauges, circular valve wheels, electrical panels, and large vertical steel levers for operating the Kingston valves.

Watertight steel doors at each end of the control room led into two large battery compartments — the forward battery and after battery compartments. Huge battery wells were underneath the battery compartment decks, with berthing and the galley above the wells, along with electrical panels and ventilation fans. The U-shaped main ballast tanks were below and alongside the battery wells, with battery cells sitting at the bottom of the U. Beyond those three compartments were the engine room in the stern and torpedo room in the bow.

Heavy, watertight doors allowed access through the steel bulkheads to each of the five compartments. The conning tower, directly above the control room was smaller yet — a cylindrical-shaped metal space with just enough room for a couple of men to stand. It contained one of the boat's two fixed-position periscopes. The hatch to the upper bridge deck formed its overhead. The bridge itself was exposed to the sea, equipped with a simple metal tube and canvas windbreaker framework that could be removed for dives.

Lt. Bogusch was standing in the bridge deck that morning, near the twin periscope shears, looking for visual navigational references. There were none, just fog in every direction.

The fresh air draft created by diesel intakes didn't do much to keep the boat warm. It was constantly cold and damp inside. Metal surfaces often had beads of condensation. Moisture would drip from the steel framing and pipes. Mattresses were damp with saltwater. So were crew uniforms. Uniforms fell apart quickly from prolonged exposure to battery acid fumes. The crew wore woolen undress blues. Woolen clothes withstood the battery acid better. Dress aboard the subs was much more casual than on the surface ships.

Bogusch ordered the engines stopped and declutched from the shafts. He decided to run the entrance on electric motors that morning. That gave him the maneuvering advantage of being able to quickly back down, as the diesel engines were not capable of being reversed. The starboard diesel had been acting up during the whole trip, from Neah Bay down to Astoria. And both engines had quit on the Columbia River Bar several days before and sent the crew scrambling to emergency stations when they took a rogue breaker over the top of the sub.

Once running on electric motors, the clean, fresh air was gone as the air flow diminished significantly. Inside H-3, the crew breathed noxious fumes from the fuel oil, mixing with acidic battery emissions as the sub continued to rise and descend on the backs of large swells rolling in from the northwest.

The boat's electricians had just finished repairing a faulty ground connection in the sub's after battery compartment. Electrician's Mate First Class Duane Stewart had been working on that detail. The batteries were partially exposed, with floorboards and matting pulled back. The deck hatch cover in the compartment was propped wide open to try to circulate fresh air.

Bogusch ordered the electric motors ahead at a slow speed. He blew the sub's whistle as a warning to other vessels that might be crossing the bar in the fog. H-3 made its approach toward the entrance in the dense fog relying on a magnetic compass on the bridge and a gyrocompass below decks. The skipper cut the sub's speed, then halted the motors to listen for any sounds that might suggest they were nearing the jetties of the entrance to Humboldt Bay. He could hear nothing but the distant sound of the shore break to the east and the sea washing against the vessel's long, steel hull.

H-3 Control Room (US Navy, PigBoats.COM)

Humboldt Bay's south jetty jutted 4,000 feet from the sand dunes into the Pacific Ocean. The north jetty extended about 1,500 feet into the sea. The break-waters were composed of large rock boulders, concrete and steel, carried by railroad cars and dumped into the ocean over the previous 25 years.

Dozens of vessels had sunk on this passage and more than one hundred sailors had lost their lives. After the Columbia River Bar, it was one of the most dangerous bar crossings on the West Coast.

The young captain watched intently from *H-3*'s bridge as the sailor on the steel foredeck threw a lead-weighted line over the side of the sub to check the water's depth. There was plenty of water depth under the boat. The sounding lead was a 14-pound lead weight on the end of a long, thin line. It was the same device the Greeks first used thousands of years ago.

Harry Bogusch believed the lead weight was about as accurate a read as one could get from a submarine having "headway upon her." They were moving very slowly to increase the accuracy of the soundings. The skipper blew the sub's whistle at 60-second intervals as they approached the bay's entrance channel. Visibility was down to less than 200 feet. They were creeping along, moving forward with the quiet hum of the twin electric motors, riding the steep swells.

The leadsman made another throw. The weight descended. Bogusch thought the lead would not yet find bottom on this toss, that it would show at least eight fathoms of water. But to his shock, he saw the lead stop at three fathoms. *H-3* started to rise on a large wave and the sub veered slightly.

Before the leadsman could even call out the sounding, Bogusch ordered both motors into full reverse from his position in the conning tower. But the sub's reverse power was limited. The boat was caught in a ground breaker, which was forming on a shoal and about to engulf the entire submarine.

Down below in the after battery compartment, Jack Agraz, Duane Stewart and a couple other sailors were nonchalantly sitting around the mess table drinking coffee. The table was hung from the overhead. The men sat on folding leg benches that attached on either side of the table. Those were the only seats on the submarine, except for a stool at the radio set in the forward battery compartment.

A few men were up on the bridge with the captain on watch. Breakfast was long over. The electricians were at their control boards that were on the interior steel framing of the sub's hull. They were about to close up the battery well after earlier troubleshooting the faulty ground connection in the after battery compartment.

A subtle motion of the boat caught Jack Agraz's attention. Nobody else at the table noticed it much. Agraz gazed around and listened. "That was different," he said.

When Jack Agraz spoke, everybody listened. He knew a lot about subs and the sea. He'd been aboard them for years. He'd been up and down the coasts of China, Japan and the Philippines aboard ships from the US Asiatic Fleet. From the deck of the *USS Buffalo*, a turn-of-the-century auxiliary cruiser-transport ship, he'd observed the wreck of the *HMS Bedford* in 1901, when the big British warship went 25 miles off course in the middle of the night due to strong currents and crashed onto the Samarang Reef in the South China Sea. Eighteen sailors from the boiler room perished in the wreck.

Jack dove while he was in the Asiatic Fleet. He kept a handwritten diary from those days, listing all the ports he had sailed in and out of and all the ships they had encountered. He'd write about big storms, who fell overboard at sea, where they dropped anchor, took on coal, or how much he got paid extra for diving.

But it was his stories about the *F-4* incident in Hawaii the previous year that would send chills down the spines of younger crew members. Along with Jack Agraz, Lt. Bogusch had been deeply involved in the *F-4* incident as well. They could recall the tense moments of those days off the coast of Honolulu.

"There's change in the boat action," Agraz said, standing up. "That felt like a corkscrew. Boys, trice up the table. The seas are getting restless."

Right after the chief remarked about the boat's action, just before 0830 hours on December 14, *H-3* was lifted by another enormous wave, bigger than the rest. A sneaker. The submarine hung on the crest, beginning to tilt forward. Everybody could feel it. Conversations halted. The sub pitched down the front of the cresting swell, gathering speed and steepness. Tobogganing. Then the steel structure of the boat shuddered as it hit bottom. A second breaker was right behind the first.

The chief felt the sub starting to broach on the first wave as the stern swung from the wave's force. Then with a tremendous push, the second breaker hit. The sub suddenly rolled hard on its starboard beam. Men, mess gear, mess benches, and all the loose gear in the compartment were smashed up against the lockers on the starboard side. Saltwater cascaded down through the main hatch. There had not been time to close it.

Crew members tumbled to the deck, entangled with each other and the loose gear. Duane Stewart landed face down with his coffee cup still clenched in his hand. Jack Agraz right next to him. Circuit breakers blew. Fuses blew. Electrical pops and small explosions were followed by flaming arcs that jumped from behind the boat's electric panels. Insulation caught fire.

Smoke began to form inside of the boat. A small fire broke out in the engine room bilges. The exposed batteries caught fire in the terminal cells. Saltwater rained down through the open deck hatch. A hint of chlorine gas started to stir from the battery cells. H-3 had hit bottom full force crossing the Humboldt Bar. At least that's what the crew thought.

Duane Stewart toppled over, making frantic grabs for the swinging table. But it wasn't there. Electrician's Mate J.B. Rollins and Chief Electrician Jim Anderson were both just coming through the control room door. They tried to grab the door edge. They missed and came hurtling into the mess. At the same time, a large pot of pancake batter was jarred from its rack. The pancake batter and cook flew through the air and landed on top of everybody.

Back in the engine room, Chief Machinist's Mate Steve Galazitas was having a time of it. There was a lot of smoke. They needed fire extinguishers. The engines were already shut down, but debris and water got into the electric motor armatures when the boat rolled hard over, causing shorts and heavy arcing. Electricians were trying to contain the fire. Both drives had to be shut down immediately to prevent a disastrous fire.

Smoke drifted heavily from the forward battery compartment. Saltwater sloshed around on the inside decks above the battery tanks. The sub stayed on its starboard side about 10 seconds. That was it. Another ground breaker lifted

H-3 and dropped it hard on the sea bottom. Stewart felt like he'd just jumped off a 10-foot roof from the impact. This time the sub landed on an even keel. That gave the crew time to get untangled and back on their feet. They immediately secured benches and the table to the overhead framework.

They had just moments to survey the damage before another swell lifted the sub up and pounded it. The impact reverberated through the hull structure. This time it rolled over onto the port side. Several panels of the cork lining were jarred loose and joined the debris already sloshing from side to side in the saltwater that had come through open hatches and ventilators. Stewart could see there was seawater in the control room, too.

The waves kept coming. Saltwater came down through the conning tower hatch and forward battery compartment ventilator. The ventilators were open for a smooth surface run. Not for taking breakers over the top of the sub. Or rolling over in the ocean. A crew member made a dash for the steel ladder leading to the main hatch in the after battery compartment. But before he could get the hatch closed, the boat rolled again. More seawater sluiced through the hatch, knocking the sailor off the ladder.

A second crewman made it up the ladder. He secured a solid grip on the main hatch and brought it down with a heavy clang and spun the locking wheel, securing the seal. That stopped the seawater from entering the aft battery compartment. But the damage was done. Everyone just held on.

With each roll, sailors reached for pipes or any secure handhold to keep from slipping and sliding side to side. Stomachs went hollow. At times the boat rolled in excess of 60 degrees. The compartments were tinged with smoke and acrid fumes of burned insulation and smoldering cloth. One sailor called out, "Chlorine gas!"

With the first roll, Duane Stewart thought the acid must have sloshed out of the lead-acid battery cell tanks below deck and forced its way around the edge of the rubber covering over the planks. The battery tanks were situated beneath the forward and after battery compartments. Duane was standing directly on top

Chief Gunner's Mate Jack Agraz — H-3's chief of the boat and diver (PigBoats.COM)

of the after battery tank, and part of it was exposed from the electrical work that had just been completed.

The boat had 120 cells in the forward and after battery tanks below deck. The cell structures contained more than 2,000 plates of active lead material and 1,800 gallons of sulfuric acid. The entire battery system weighed more than 130,000 pounds. And it could become a bomb if hydrogen gases were ignited.

Chlorine gas was the big worry at that moment for Duane Stewart and the rest the crew. If seawater came in contact with battery acid, it would form a yellow-green cloud of chlorine gas and settle in the lowest part of the boat. It was heavier than air. It was extremely noxious and deadly, even in small concentrations. Duane wasn't as worried about the hydrogen gas. It was odorless and colorless, lighter than air and extremely explosive. But that was a by-product of charging the batteries with the engines. The engines were shut down.

The battery tanks were topped off with sulfuric acid to within three inches of their tops. The tanks were designed to take a 20-degree roll without discharging any acid into the lead-lined tanks. The sub had just taken a 60-degree roll. Incoming saltwater began to mix with the battery chemicals. Duane thought they might have chlorine gas mingling in the compartment. Deep down, he knew it was his fear causing that reaction. But the chlorine odor was there and starting to spread.

F-4

The Four F-boats in Honolulu, Hawaii. F-4 is in the forefront. (NavSource Online: Submarine Photo Archive, from US Naval Historical Center)

On the morning of March 25, 1915, the year before *H-3* hit bottom on the California Coast, Lt. j.g. Alfred L. Ede had been adamant about wanting to take the submarine *F-4* on a dive run out of Honolulu Harbor. Hawaii was still a US territory then and wouldn't become a state for another 44 years. But the US Navy was beginning to base operations there.

Ede's crew was enthusiastic that day because they all got a dollar extra every time they dove, up to fifteen dives a month. As captain of F-4, Ede wanted his 20-man crew to get paid their full allotment. Submariners also received an extra five dollars a month pay for undersea duty. They touted the fact that they were paid more than the surface sailors.

This was Alfred Ede's first submarine command. But he had been the number two officer, an ensign, on F-4 since the boat had been commissioned, so he had a good feel for its operations. In those days, they said he was a "plankowner" on the boat since he'd been part of the commissioning crew. The term plankowner came from the surface Navy, since those ships were historically launched with teakwood decks. Some other crew members had also been aboard since the commissioning. They all knew the boat exceptionally well, having spent every day together around F-4 for the last couple years.

Ensign Timothy Parker, a recent addition to the Hawaiian flotilla, was new to submarines. He'd joined Ede and the F-4 crew that day as an observer, just to ride on the boat and gain some experience. He wasn't officially assigned to F-4 yet. Parker was from Kentucky and, like all young officers, had graduated from the Naval Academy at Annapolis.

The boats often had a mix of new recruits and seasoned veterans. New crew members rotated onto the boats as part of training, and more seasoned veterans would impart their knowledge to the new sailors. Captains always wanted to keep a core group of experienced submariners aboard the boat to maintain confidence and trust in the essential operations of the sub.

Ede had grown up on his family's ranch in Washoe County, Nevada, a few miles outside of Reno. He had never taken an interest in his father's ranch operations or planned to stay in the high alkaline desert. He was thinking about the sea. He went to high school in Reno and was attending the University of Nevada when he took the naval exam for Annapolis. His high score won him a spot at the academy.

He graduated from Annapolis in 1909 and was commissioned an ensign. He first served on the cruiser USS *West Virginia* and later on the destroyer USS *Trux-tun*. But Ede had his eye on the newly emerging submarine force. They were of a different tribe than the conventional surface Navy. The new technologies were intriguing, and the challenge to navigate below the surface with a small crew was compelling. The Navy was looking for coolheaded, smart sailors to operate the underwater boats because the vessels were complex and unproven in many ways.

Ede transferred aboard *F-4*, then took over the command in 1914 when his captain was transferred to another boat. Ede had a reputation of being an iceman in tough conditions. He'd earned the nickname Stoneface at the Naval Academy. Nothing seemed to rattle him. He'd been a boxer and made a name for himself for a short time but gave up boxing for the Navy. Ede frequently trained by running the mile, just to stay in shape. He graduated in the top third of his class at Annapolis and had surprised many of his mates with his French language skills.

Lt. Alfred Ede, commanding officer of F-4 (US Naval Academy Virtual Memorial Hall)

That morning, Ede and the other F-boat officers met for a briefing with Lt. Charles E. Smith, the flotilla commander of the four F-class submarines based in Hawaii. They gathered in the briefing room aboard the tender *USS Alert*, moored in Honolulu Harbor. The *Alert* was an old, iron-hulled steam-powered gunboat built in 1873, recently converted to a sub tender. Lt. Smith had been on the *Alert* since 1912, when it was recommissioned as a tender. He was also captain of the USS *F-1*.

The submariners each gave a briefing on the status of the four boats. Ensign Harry Bogusch from F-1 was at that morning meeting that day in March 1915. Ede reminded Smith about his earlier request to take F-4 on a dive that day. He'd already completed more than 150 dives in his career at that point. The day's dive would boost his crew's dive pay for March. Smith gave his approval.

Ede asked, "Stationary or running dive, sir?" "Running dive," Smith responded.

As F-4 motored out of Honolulu Harbor that morning toward open waters, Ede gave the order to switch over to electric motors for the dive. All hands prepared to take the sub down as they passed Quarantine Dock. It was common for the dives to start inside the harbor. They de-clutched and shut down the diesels. Ede would have ordered, "Flood main ballasts."

F4, F2 alongside the Alert(Pacific Fleet Submarine Museum at Pearl Harbor)

There were three U-shaped main ballast tanks at the bottom of the hull, wrapping around the battery wells and control room. They were divided in half at the keel, giving the boat six separate tanks. To commence a dive, Ede would order the Kingston valves at the bottom of the tanks to be opened. Then he would order air vents at the top of the tanks opened. A great rush of air would be forced through the upper vents as the seawater flooded the tanks, blowing a plume of air and water upward from the upper vents, almost like whale surfacing for air. Once the ballast tanks were full of water, Ede would order the upper air vents closed, and then close the Kingston valves.

F-4 would begin its dive.

Two operators stood next to the captain in the control room and monitored large, circular steel wheels on the port side of the control room. Turning these wheels adjusted the angle of the bow and stern planes, with the bow planes controlling depth and the stern planes controlling the boat's downward angle. Once completely submerged, Ede would adjust the amount of water in the forward, midships and after trim tanks to fine tune the boat's buoyancy and level the boat out. Crewmen would study a bubble-type angle indicator, like a carpenter's level, to determine if the boat was on an even keel or not. Once trimmed properly, they would change depth solely by adjusting the angle of the planes.

Ede and his crewmen would monitor the bubble indicator and two large glass-faced depth gauges. Nobody could see anything outside the steel bulkheads of the boat, and they had no sonar to determine depth or objects on the surface. The periscope offered a limited view of the surface. But once they submerged below periscope depth, they would be flying blind.

Just off F-4's starboard bow that morning at 0900 hours, F-1 was already returning to the harbor after an earlier routine surface run with F-3. Lt. Smith was on the outer bridge of F-1 with his second in command, Ensign Harry Bogusch. They were motoring back toward the harbor when they met F-4 on its way out to sea on its dive run.

Crews would usually take the subs out early morning for an hour or so on practice and training runs and then return to port by mid-morning and tie alongside the Alert. Dives seldom exceeded 100 feet in order to keep boats well within the pressure limitations of the F-Class hull rating, which was 200 feet, or 33 fathoms.

Once the subs returned to the dock, the crew would take care of basic maintenance duties and sometimes have a free afternoon. Some of the submariners brought their wives and children to Hawaii and maintained homes and an active social life in Honolulu. It was a beautiful, calm morning on March 25 when F-4 and F-1 met at the entrance to Honolulu Harbor. The mood among the F-class submarine corps in Hawaii was relaxed in those days. It was two years before the United States entered the Great War, though preparations were underway.

As Smith and Bogusch watched the departing F-4 flawlessly glide beneath the water's surface off the port side of F-1, Smith said to Bogusch that the dive was executed exceptionally well. Smith and Bogusch thought they saw F-4's periscope trained on them — with Alfred Ede watching F-1 — so they waved their officer's caps with a salute for good luck to Ede and his men.

Then F-4 disappeared from their sight.

Ede had had some doubts about his boat. He hadn't talked about it with his flotilla commander, but the crew had been discussing his concerns on and off the boat for the last month or so. Though Ede was confident of his ability to run F-4, he'd written a letter — three days before the March 25 dive — to his brother, Allison Ede, questioning the boat's seaworthiness. Nobody in the Navy knew about that letter — yet.

Alfred wrote to his brother about an explosion aboard the sub just one month before. And there had just been a major engine replacement done in dry dock. There were questions in Ede's mind about how successful those repairs had been. He also told his brother in the letter that on a dive three days before, they were 50 feet below the surface and found water trickling into the boat through a faulty valve. But it was his final comment in the letter that would later stir the most attention. He wrote, "In fact, if the whole boat should suddenly vanish in smoke, I do not think that I'd be terribly astonished."

Ede wasn't the only one with questions about F-4's seaworthiness.

William Nelson was F-4's chief machinist's mate. He had come to America from Sweden and later joined the US Navy. He'd been born in Malmo, Sweden, in 1883 and was 32 years old, one of the older crew members on F-4. Malmo, on the southern coast of Sweden, between the North Sea and Baltic Sea, at that time was a seafaring town with one of the largest shipyards in Europe.

Nelson ran the sub's diesels and auxiliary equipment. Chief Electrician Aliston Grindle and Electrician's Mate First Class George Deeth ran the electric motors. Nelson's station was in the engine room compartment. He had several machinist's mates who worked with him.

F-4 had just two other compartments, including the torpedo compartment in the bow and a battery control room in the center of the boat. That compartment occupied a large area of the sub. It was an older design.

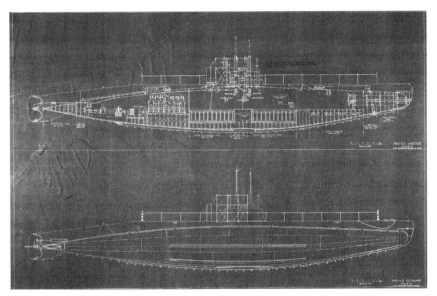

F-Boat design blueprints (Courtesy of Donald M. McPherson – US Navy Historical Center; NavSource.org)

There had been growing criticism about the F-boat design not having enough watertight compartments. If the boat ever took on water, the crew wouldn't be able to isolate the problem, especially in the battery control room. The newer H-boats on the Pacific Coast had five watertight compartments, but even those boats would sink like a rock if they ever flooded any single compartment.

William Nelson felt F-4 had been compromised a month before, when it was damaged by a hydrogen gas explosion during recharging at the docks. And it had also suffered a cracked cylinder head in one of the engines due to excessive vibrations. He talked to his wife, Elsie, about it. Several crewmen from the sub had come over to the Nelsons' home in Honolulu and discussed the incident as well at a private gathering.

"They appeared greatly worried about the blowout, and I saw them shaking their heads," is how the Nelson's landlady put it. "A few days later they went to Pearl Harbor to have the engines repaired, but Mrs. Nelson told me that her husband had said the engines would never be the same again."

Thursday morning at breakfast before going down to the boat and shoving off for their dive, William Nelson had had some concerns. He'd told his wife earlier that F-4's high-pressure air system used for discharging the ballast tanks had been compromised and couldn't generate enough air supply to meet Navy requirements. The morning of the dive, Nelson also told her that he'd had a bad dream the night before. He had a troubled look on his face. He told her that he had dreamed that F-4 had gone down with the whole crew.

By mid-morning on March 25, three F-boats were tied alongside each other and done with the day's duties. F-1 and USS F-3 had returned from their surface runs; USS F-2 hadn't left port due to some repair work. Lt. Smith was back aboard the Alert. The Alert served as a mess hall, officer accommodations and meeting area for the submariners.

But F-4 was still out to sea.

Everybody knew that the subs didn't stay out to sea for extended periods. And that day was no different than any other. Bogusch thought F-4 might be delayed by a technical problem, which wasn't uncommon on the early-design boats. Ede might be adrift somewhere outside the harbor. Or maybe he'd taken the boat farther out to sea on the morning run. The trade winds were mild and the seas calm.

By 1030 hours, F-4 had still not returned. There had been no radio transmissions. The chain of command started to stir. The cadence of activity and concern began to build. The commanding officer of the Alert, Lt. Bruce Canaga, was informed that *F-4* was late. Canaga immediately ordered Ensign Bogusch to take a power launch and crew and head out of the harbor to look for *F-4* and its crew of 21 men. He put the other three F-boats and all available motor launches on stand-by and notified the flotilla commander, Lt. Charles Smith, of the developing situation.

The launch engineer powered up the 26-foot, gas-powered motor launch, and the coxswain guided it out of Honolulu Harbor. Anxiously, Bogusch scanned the horizon. The young officer could feel the warm tropical air as his launch sped along the surface. After a preliminary search, Bogusch could see nothing but the endless horizon of blue-green Hawaiian waters. *F-4* was nowhere in sight, and it had been at sea a couple hours now.

Jack Agraz (lower center) and ten of the F-1 crew on the rear deck, out at sea off Honolulu (Agraz Family Collection)

Bogusch was hailed from afar by the deck watch of a German steamer moored to a pier near the Honolulu Harbor entrance. The ship was a collier, supporting a German naval cruiser that needed repairs and had taken refuge in a neutral seaport to avoid being attacked by Japanese warships that were traversing international waters around Hawaii. The German deck watch had been monitoring *F-4*'s departure out of the harbor that morning with his binoculars. He had seen the sub dive but had not seen it resurface. He'd been scanning what he could see of Mamala Bay for the last hour. Bogusch was alarmed and ordered the coxswain to head back to the Navy dock full speed.

Charles Smith immediately ordered the other three F-boats to commence a search and notified the 14th Naval District command in Pearl Harbor that *F-4* was missing. Lt. Canaga ordered the crew to cast off the lines of the *Alert* and head out for Mamala Bay. The District began contacting tugboats and other support personnel, including the *USS Navajo*, a Navy fleet tug working out of Pearl Harbor.

F-1 and *F-2* got underway and scoured the surface of Mamala Bay, into which Honolulu Harbor emptied on the south side of Oahu. Smith and Bogusch were on the *F-1* bridge, scouting for any surface signs of the sub.

Lt. Francis W. Scanland's *F-3* left the harbor and immediately dove, following the charted course that *F-4* would have taken. Scanland rang the sub's underwater signal bell every 30 seconds. His radioman listened for a signal bell response with a headphone but heard nothing. Smith and Bogusch ran *F-1* in search patterns.

USS Alert and submarine flotilla crew members standing on the deck of an F-boat, Jack Agraz far left (Agraz Family Collection)

Smith took *F-1* down as well and rang the bell repeatedly. All the boats were ringing their bells, again and again. This mechanical signal was the underwater communication system that submarines relied on in 1915. They had no other way to communicate while submerged.

Sensing that time was running against them, Scanland pushed F-3 to the edge and took it down to 200 feet, ringing the underwater communication bell repeatedly. But there was still no response. Dead silence. At 200 feet, they'd reached an F-boat's maximum safe operating depth, at which design engineers drew the line on safety operations. Anything deeper than that would take the boat and crew into uncharted territory and risk hull failure. As Scanland cruised on the electric motors at six knots, 200 feet below the surface, all they heard was silence as they listened for F-4's underwater bell response.

On the surface, F-2 cut through the waters in its search pattern. A crew member on the forward deck yelled out, "Oil!"

That shout immediately put the crew's senses on knife edge. F-2 had crossed into an extensive oil patch across the ocean's surface. It was a chilling discovery and likely meant F-4 was in trouble, maybe even on the bottom. A small trail of air bubbles traced up from the depths. The navigational chart indicated the sea floor was 480 feet below.

Crews traced the drifting patterns of oil and air bubbles that led them back toward shore. That instilled a sense of hope in Lt. Smith, who was leading the search. The underwater seabed rose sharply on the shores of Oahu. They found that the oil and air bubbles coincided at around 300 feet of water. If that is where F-4 was stranded, Smith thought, it might be reachable and the crew stood a chance.

More ships arrived by the hour at the scene of F-4's disappearance. Smith left F-1 and boarded the *Alert*, directing operations in the middle of the flotilla. Ensign Harry Bogusch took over F-1's helm.

Chief Boatswain's Mate Frederick W. Metiers, skipper of the Navy tugboat *Navajo*, was on the bridge when he got the marine radio call that morning in Pearl Harbor that one of the F-boats had failed to surface. They needed the *Navajo*, with drag cables. Metiers immediately changed course to the naval yard, loaded massive steel cable snares aboard the *Navajo* and set out to sea to join the search by early afternoon. The civilian tug *Makaala* arrived mid-afternoon, followed by the tug *Intrepid*. The *Makaala* was owned by the Young Brothers Tug Company in Honolulu. They ordered all six of their vessels to head to sea and join the hunt for *F-4*.

US Navy sailors looking for F-4, peering into the clear Hawaiian waters (Pacific Fleet Submarine Museum at Pearl Harbor)

Cable systems were dropped from the stern of the *Navajo* and *Makaala*. Deck crews secured a 250-foot, heavy chain-link snare between two 650-foot cables that extended to the seafloor. The rigging totaled almost a third of a mile in length. The two tugs started a search pattern, dragging the cable snares along the bottom near where the oil and air bubbles were drifting.

It was the appearance of air bubbles and oil floating to the surface that drove rescuers in their attempts to reach the missing sub. Sailors leaned over the edge of open motor launches and peered into the translucent depths, trying to catch a glimpse of the missing *F-4*. Rescuers noticed two patterns of air bubbles about 100 feet apart. The boat was still releasing air. There was hope.

Lt. Smith's sense of optimism that *F-4* could be okay at the 300-foot depth was probably conjured by an incident three years before, when he had been forced to relieve the previous *F-1* captain, Lt. j.g. James B. Howell, of his command after a deepwater dive that broke all the Navy records and rules.

According to Charles Lockwood, a young ensign aboard an older A-boat at the time, Jimmy Howell was known to some as an enthusiastic and adventuresome submarine commander. Lockwood described a day back in 1912 when Howell was making submerged runs in deep water off the California coast. Smith was not aboard. Navy rules generally advised submariners to train at a depth of 60 feet in 1912 — just enough for their fixed position periscopes to clear hull bottoms of the largest ships. There were too many uncertainties that still existed around the emerging submarine designs to encourage commanders to make deeper dives.

Lt. James Howell (left) and Ensign Harry Bogusch (center) on the F-1 bridge and Naval Constructor H. M. Gleason (right) (SF Chronicle 1915)

That day in 1912, Howell took *F-1* down deeper than any submarine had ever gone before. He was courageous, not afraid to push boundaries. He'd grown up in Wyoming, far from the sea, but he had a passion for subs and adventure.

Howell guided *F-1* downward at six knots. The electric motors turned the screws quietly as they passed through the 100-foot mark and continued to drop.

Then 200-feet. Still descending. The crew was frozen, speechless. They were descending past the F-boat's maximum design depth. Jimmy Howell had a smile on his face. At 250 feet the hull started groaning and creaking under compression and stress. The crew had never heard those sounds coming from the boat before. Howell kept going down.

As Lockwood told it, the only person moving in the sub was a crewmember making coffee. He kept wiping and wiping the same cup. He was staring at the depth gauge the whole time, silently mouthing the numbers. At 275 feet he stopped wiping the mug. At 280 feet he dropped the mug. It shattered. The hull was shrieking, and seawater started to leak in through a bulging seam. They were approaching crush depth. The sub's structure was starting to give way under the enormous pressure.

At 283 feet, Howell gave the order to blow the ballast tanks and surface. The crewmember with the coffee cup later said, "Man, oh man, I sure thought I'd collect six months' pay on that dive!" His comment was riveted with dark humor in reference to Navy policy at the time of granting "six months pay" as compensation to family members if a vessel sank and a sailor was lost.

Though a risk taker, Howell was also a gifted submarine skipper. He had an innate sense on guiding a submarine through a dive. He would call out the angles on the dive planes, feel the tilt of the boat in his core and sense the speed of descent. Keeping the electric motors and the boat's buoyancy dialed in tight, adjusting the trim tanks, leveling dive planes, he maintained tight control.

In 1912, submarines were a new technology, and Howell wanted to take it to the brink. See what it could do. Like a test pilot, he flew the boat into the depths, pressing boundaries to see what the design could take and what it couldn't take. He could hear the hull plates groaning and starting to weaken. He didn't flinch at the edge of disaster. He just rode it.

Jimmy Howell was just what the Navy wanted, a confident talented skipper with an intuitive feel for his boat. But this risk taker was also the Navy's worst nightmare. The Navy wanted things done by the book. They were structured to operate through chains of discipline and established protocols. Howell had a crew of 20 men and the Navy to answer to after that record-setting dive.

Back at base, an excited Lt. Howell sat before his flotilla commander, Lt. Charles Smith, going on about his record dive. "Done what?" Smith demanded in a measured tone, staring intently at the impulsive skipper. He immediately relieved Howell of command as captain of the F-1.

But now, with F-4 possibly on the bottom in 300 feet of water, Smith had to remember that F-boats could actually withstand far greater pressure than the 200-foot test depth that engineers had conservatively estimated for the boats.

The Hunley – an 1864 Confederate Navy Submarine – 19th Century Illustration (US Navy)

The Navy was secretive in the early hours of F-4's disappearance. Not even crew members' families were told what was transpiring, though some had begun to hear rumors and rushed to the piers. By early afternoon, news of F-4's disappearance had started to spread across the waterfront and into Honolulu.

Throughout the day, hundreds of people began gathering at the Honolulu waterfront, the beaches, and the piers. Nothing officially had been said yet, but everybody could see scores of large vessels moving toward Mamala Bay and could recognize the ensuing search patterns. People on the beach used binoculars and telescopes to monitor the vessels swarming over the search area.

The United States Navy had never lost a submarine, though the Confederate Navy had lost a small sub — the *Hunley* — during the Civil War, minutes after sinking a Federal warship near Charleston, South Carolina, in 1864. It was the first sub in the world to ever sink a warship, but then it, too, infamously sank and vanished, taking its eight-man crew to the bottom. It wouldn't be rediscovered for 131 years.

The multitude of people along the shore stood watching the vessels offshore attempting to snare and raise F-4 with grappling cables. Rescue crews improvised with what tools and capabilities they had. There had never been a sea rescue anywhere in the world at these depths. There was no special equipment designed for the task. They did not have training. Every idea was an exercise in spontaneity, ingenuity, and purpose.

As the sun set on the beaches of Hawaii, the crowds onshore and aboard vessels watched the dramatic search move into the night. In the darkness, tugboats continued their cable sweeps of the sea bottom. Vessels illuminated the water and night sky with an array of beacons and ship's lamps. A deep-water dredge, the *California*, was being prepared to move out of Pearl Harbor to the location. It had heavy lift capacity and huge drum spools of cable.

Divers were preparing to go down at first light to try to get a line of sight on F-4. Chief Gunner's Mate Jack Agraz from F-1 and Chief Machinist's Mate George B. Evans from F-3, both trained divers, immediately volunteered. Both men knew they'd be going down deeper than either had ever been.

H-3

SOS

When waves engulfed *H-3*, sailors outside on the bridge were slammed by the full impact of a ground breaker. Every crewmember grabbed for something fixed to hold onto. The wave had come out of nowhere, a serpent rising from the mist. They were looking east, trying to spot the channel. The wave had come barreling out of the fog and steepened from the west. When it broke over the sub, the turbulence ripped loose the flimsy light metalwork and canvas windbreak where Bogusch and a couple crew stood watch. The assembly was intended to be used only for extended surface runs.

The power of the breaker damaged the structure significantly. It tore the deck grating free, ripped loose the wind dodger and stripped the awning away as churning white water followed the break. No one was washed off the sub on that first breaker, but they were drenched to the bone and some had been under water. They all clung to any piece of metalwork they could get a hand hold on: periscopes, air horn piping, framework, cables, stanchions, anything solid.

Bogusch ordered all hands below to take up positions in the control room and conning tower. The first breaker had snapped the forward battery compartment ventilator in half. The broken apparatus was wide open to the ocean. Saltwater rained down into the forward battery compartment. Jack Agraz knew the threat of saltwater pouring into a sub could be devastating if it reached the batteries.

With the sub on its side, the whole interior looked cockeyed to Jack. He lurched forward into the forward battery compartment, pulling himself through the door, clambering over debris, struggling over the frameworks as the boat lay hard over, the ventilator open to the sea. Water was pouring through the open vent. Standing on the inner hull's side bulkhead, Jack grabbed the ventilator valve and cranked it shut. That stopped saltwater from entering the forward battery compartment.

H-3 caught in the breakers on Samoa Beach, California, December 1916 (Agraz Family Collection)

As the first breaker passed and the sub regained an even keel, Lt. Zemke had raced up the ladder into the conning tower to see what in the hell had happened. He'd been dozing off in his canvas bunk in the control room after his all-night watch when they hit bottom. He'd awakened to the unfolding nightmare inside the sub.

The captain told Zemke they'd hit a shoal. He didn't yet know they were on the beach. He thought they were on the Humboldt Bar. The fog was still heavy.

The men were now scrambling to regain control. Inside the boat was a madhouse of electrical shorts, smoke, and sailors trying to stabilize the systems and put out fires.

The control room was the smallest compartment in the sub. Zemke and the crew came sliding down the steel ladder from the conning tower and packed themselves tightly into the control room. About this time Zemke, from Wisconsin, might have been wishing he got that Marine Cavalry assignment. He'd entered the Navy with the intention of joining the Horse Marines. He ended up on H-3 instead.

Midshipman Eric Zemke at the Naval Academy at Annapolis 1913 (United States Naval Academy Yearbook – Class of 1913)

With the sub rolling in sweeping arcs, Bogusch secured the upper hatch and joined the crew in the control room. They were shoulder to shoulder and banging into each other every time the sub rolled. The control room could seem crowded with six men in it under normal conditions. Now there were more than 20.

The air inside the boat was horrendous. Duane Stewart thought the deck guys may have jumped from the frying pan into the fire. Electrical panels were still smoldering, circuit breakers still burned, emitting a strong smell of charred rubber and insulation. All that topped off the underlying stench of diesel oil and battery acid gas. From where Duane sat, it was absolutely overpowering.

The skipper ordered an immediate, complete hull check. Sailors clambered through the smoke into the other four compartments for a preliminary check.

The rolling continued, sending men sprawling at times and crawling along side bulkheads that were now inverted. There was fear that the steel hull could have fractured a seam from the shock of hitting bottom. The skipper wanted to know if seawater was entering the hull.

Within minutes, the crew reported back that the seawater inside the boat appeared to have all come from open hatches and ventilators. The hull structure was believed to be sound.

Bogusch ordered the main ballast tanks partially flooded to try to stabilize the sub and stop it from being tossed around so violently. He also ordered the dive planes fully extended to help stabilize sideward motion. Submerged, the sub could hold 25,000 gallons of seawater in its ballast and trim tanks, which would weigh 100 tons if fully flooded.

A sailor opened the Kingston valves and thousands of gallons of seawater mixed with sand poured through the valves into the ballast tanks along the bottom of the hull. The air hissed as the top side vents allowed the displaced air to exit the tanks. Then he shut the valves. The skipper didn't want the tanks completely filled.

Bogusch hoped the extra weight would steady the vessel and stop throwing the men on top of each other in what felt like an underwater dungeon of gases. The round-bottomed sub had been rocking side to side in more than 50-degree swings, with only the conning tower preventing it from rolling like a log in the surf.

When the disaster hit, Bogusch barked orders and prioritized what needed to get done. He was tall and wiry and tended to talk with his whole body, and his brown eyes often sparkled when he engaged people. His sister would later say that he was the risk taker of the family, never afraid to venture out into places he was unfamiliar with. His peers had said he "talked with his whole soul" and was outspoken, regardless of time and place. And when conditions were right, he had an infectious laugh. Bogusch wasn't laughing now. He was all business.

The lockers on the port side of the after battery compartment dumped all their contents onto the deck. The heavy roll to port did the same to the lockers on the starboard side. There were knives, forks, spoons, and tools being sloshed back and forth. Some of the tableware washed up into the power panels and started another fire. "Doc" Carter, an H-3 electrician from Oklahoma, reached up the first chance he had and pulled the main battery breaker, shutting down the sub's electric power. Everything went dark.

When Doc Carter switched off the sub's main power, only the emergency overhead lights were still on — one small bulb in each compartment. By the time Bogusch made his inspection, the fires were out. But smoldering insulation continued to generate fumes. The crew went after the last of the small electrical fires with fire extinguishers, adding carbon dioxide and nitrogen to the air. With the electricity still off and the hatches and ventilators secured, the toxic smoke was sealed inside the hull. The air in H-3 was now utterly unbearable.

After Bogusch ordered all hands into the control room, the watertight compartment doors were shut and secured. That allowed the skipper to isolate any potential hull failure to a single compartment and to try to stop the smoke and battery gases from wafting through the entire boat. With the control room, he figured they could periodically open the upper hatch and allow fresh air to circulate in that small compartment. Foremost in the skipper's mind were the battery banks below deck. He needed to protect the batteries from saltwater. Chlorine gas would be a deadly threat.

Now with the engines shut down, every system on the boat relied on the batteries. Bogusch hoped they'd hold up. There was also concern that the enormous weight of the battery tanks suspended over the keel might threaten the hull structure from the impact of crashing onto the sea bottom.

When the sub had hit bottom, the skipper had immediately ordered four gunner's mates to the torpedo compartment to assess damage and the condition of the torpedoes. The enormous weight of the torpedoes suspended against the hull was another concern. Just minutes before, everything had been routine, and now Bogusch was running all kinds of survival scenarios through his mind. He needed to protect the crew, contain the fires and gas, secure the torpedoes. He needed to get an emergency SOS message out.

The four gunner's mates in the forward station reported over the voice tube to the captain that all was clear in the torpedo compartment. The "fish" were being held fast by metal straps, so far. They said there was no smoke or gas, but they were concerned about the rolling and the four, 1,600-pound torpedoes banging around against their restraints. The hull was sound. The skipper directed them to stay there. Then he held muster.

Bogusch and Zemke called out each crew member's name. There were 22 men jammed into the control room and conning tower spaces and four in the torpedo compartment. One man was missing: Chief Machinist's Mate Steve Galazitas from the engine room. Nobody had seen Steve since they'd hit bottom.

"Where is Galazitas!" Bogusch hollered, scanning the faces surrounding him in tight quarters. "Chief Galazitas!"

The captain shot a glance over to the chief of the boat, Jack Agraz.

Agraz covered his face with a wet rag and headed for the engine room. He un-dogged the watertight door that separated the control room from the after battery compartment, slipped into the smoke-filled chamber and re-sealed the door behind him. He moved through dim light. The engine room door was locked down tight. Jack turned the steel levers to open the door, feeling his way through near darkness as the sub rolled and twisted in the breakers. The engine room reeked of diesel. Smoke was trapped in there, too. Just one light illuminated the compartment, casting a hazy image of the machinery works.

The chief could make out the long mechanical shapes of the twin diesels, the rows of exposed vertical rocker assemblies along each side of the catwalk between the engines. Everything was shut down in the engine compartment. He could see the cylindrical shapes of both electric motors, beyond the diesels. They were without power. He called out to the chief machinist's mate. He could hear Galazitas's voice from behind the engines, in the shaft alley, beyond the electric drives.

Inside H-3 engine room looking aft (PigBoats.COM Courtesy of Carolyn Fields Snyder)

Galazitas had become dazed by being tossed around in that maze of machinery. He'd hit his head. He struggled to breathe, but only got gasps of smoke and fire extinguisher fumes. He didn't know where he was, but thought he was going forward. Agraz got a hold of him and led him back through the passageways and sealed compartment doors to the control room. Galazitas was disoriented and near suffocation when Agraz brought him into the crowded control room.

Now, 23 men filled the nine-by-14-foot space and small conning tower room above. From where the taller crew members stood, like Jack Agraz at six foot two, they only had about 10 inches of clearance between their heads and the steel overhead. The captain was deeply aware that he had a problem with so many men crammed into such a tight space.

The control room was total congestion. All the boat's mechanical controls were there. It was a cluster of gauges, dive plane wheels, the helm, air and sea valves, piping, and the Kingston valves levers that controlled the incoming and outgoing seawater used in submerging and surfacing. The aft periscope came down into the control room, and there were two foldup bunks for the captain and Eric Zemke. The cook had crates of eggs, meat, flour, bread and other dry goods stowed there as well since they were running for a few days down the coast. And there was the ladder leading up to the lower conning tower hatch.

Inside H-3 engine room looking forward (PigBoats.COM – Courtesy of Carolyn Fields Snyder)

Duane Stewart was looking around at a chaotic situation. But he was glad he was on an H-boat that had five compartments and an extra hatch in the conning tower. The previous designs, like the F-boats, had only three compartments and fewer hatches. They felt like tombs. Stewart was just clinging to the bulkhead trying not to smack into the guy next to him as the sub rolled again in the breakers.

Myriad thoughts raced through Stewart's head in those moments. What about chlorine gas? The torpedoes? The gyro? Now he was waiting to see what might happen next. Beyond the control room, both the forward and after battery compartments were inundated with smoke and battery fumes, with an churning ocean outside, all around them.

The only good thing about the control room was that it was right under the conning tower. They could get air if they could open the hatch. A few men braced themselves inside the conning tower. Gunner's Mate T.H. "Toad" Blabon and Chief Electrician Jim Anderson were up there opening the hatch between wave sets to let in fresh air. The cylindrical conning tower chamber was only seven feet long and about five feet across. The space contained the forward periscope. It also had three thick, glass eye ports offering a very distorted and restricted view to the outside world, one on each side, and one dead ahead. Because the waves were swirling over the glass ports there was no visibility.

With the sub trapped in the chaotic turbulence of the shore break, Bogusch knew he needed to get an SOS out. He ordered Stewart to go to his radio station in the forward battery compartment and send a distress signal. Agraz would go with him. Duane had never had to send an SOS before, but he'd practiced a lot for that very moment. Bogusch told the men that the antenna was still up on the boat despite the rest of the flying bridge gear getting smashed. He said to give their position as north of the Humboldt Bar entrance. Bogusch now realized that they'd missed the harbor entrance altogether and run onto the beach north of the jetties.

Stewart and Agraz headed to the forward battery compartment. The radio set was located on the port side, wedged between the hull and the gyrocompass. Duane wasn't excited about going into that smoky compartment. He hated the idea. But he and Jack placed wet cloths over their noses and opened the door. In they went.

Duane was grateful Jack was with him. They couldn't see anything but a dim glow from one overhead light. Through the toxic haze, the men could barely make out the shapes of valves and pipes. All the mattresses and junk sloshed around when the boat rolled. The ventilator was shut down to keep the seawater out, but there was nowhere for the bad air to escape. Duane knew the SOS had to be sent. His nerves were bolstered by Jack being there, too. They felt their way over to the radio set.

There was just a small lamp, no brighter than a candle, over the desk. Duane knew where everything was by memory. He switched the transmitter to the distress wavelength. Then he pushed the starter button. The juice was still on that circuit. He gently tapped the key, watching the antenna amp meter. The needle showed a normal signal. He was in business.

H-3 forward battery compartment, where the gyroscope and radio were located; watertight door open to torpedo compartment (PigBoats.COM, courtesy Ric Hedman Collection)

Jack held onto Duane to steady him against the rolling. He had one arm around Duane and with the other, he gripped the hull framework as he braced against the ocean surges. That made it possible for Duane to free up his hands and send his first distress call. The rolling boat sometimes left Duane positioned at a 40-degree angle, with Jack bracing him, as he typed Morse Code signals on the wireless. Slowly, Duane got the SOS out. Then he very deliberately sent the boat's call number, followed by the double break. The whole time the sub was pitching back and forth, back and forth.

Duane studied the amp meter on his send. The needle only pegged once. He repeated the word that pegged the needle because he knew that anybody listening would not be able to decipher the word if the needle pegged. He'd gotten the boat's position out on the distress wire. The wireless receiver operators onshore that received the SOS later said that it was remarkable that the key operator on the sub was able to get that message out with such clarity, given the conditions.

After the first outbound signal, Duane tried to get reception on his crystal detector to listen for a response. He couldn't hear anything. So, he threw the switch and sent out another call. Again, he tried to get the crystal receiver working. But he knew those devices were "fluky things at best." Being pinned down in the breakers didn't improve his odds.

Another big ground breaker slammed the sub, jarring the hull. The needle hit the peg and stayed there. Duane knew the antenna had just come down. He shut down the radio, pulled the main switch and told the chief their work was done. The men returned to the control room. Duane reported to the captain that he'd gotten the SOS out, then found a place to hang on.

They were greeted with some good news. Bobby Burns, a gunner's mate from Indiana, had volunteered to be a lookout. Standing at the two periscopes on top of the conning tower in between swells, he said he'd seen the beach for just a minute or two. It was a several hundred yards east. Maybe people would come looking for them, he said. Breaker lines covered the entire distance toward shore to the west and large, outside breakers were forming on the seaward side to the east. They were trapped in the outer edge of it all. Burns hadn't seen any people. But it was cheery news to know that they could see the beach. Burns was soaking wet. He'd been submerged a few times, just clinging to the superstructure. He was freezing.

Breakers started to build up heavily again. The water was washing over the top of the conning tower more often, and the sub was again rolling side to side. Toad Blabon and Jim Anderson found it more and more difficult to lift and lower the conning tower hatch to refresh the compartment's air and did it less often. The crew in the control room found it increasingly difficult to breathe. Opening the upper hatch had allowed some fresh air in, but with it closed, the oxygen levels were deteriorating.

F-4

THE DIVERS GO DOWN

Ensign Charles A. Lockwood was 25 years old when *F-4* disappeared that day off Honolulu. He was stationed at Manila Bay in the Philippines with his first command — the older, smaller submarine *USS A-2*. It was about 60 feet long with a 10-man crew. It was part of the A-class, the first operational class of submarines in the Navy, built just after the turn of the century.

Conflict in the early 1900s had suddenly shifted from surface engagements, which had been the norm since civilization began, up into the skies with airplanes and beneath the seas with submarines. In 1915, just about every sub was a proving ground. The US wasn't in a war yet, but they were rapidly scaling up designs and refining the technical operations to keep pace with the expansion of the Navy's mission. The E-class and F-class were the first US submarines with diesel engines. Diesel fuel was far less combustible than gasoline. Earlier sub designs, from the A-boats to the D-boats, mostly ran on gasoline engines, which were more dangerous to operate because of the explosive potential.

From 1900 to 1915, when *F-4* disappeared, 61 submarines had been damaged or lost by navies around the world. Many of these accidents were attributed to collisions with other vessels, especially when blindly surfacing. The crews had no idea what was on the surface above them because the periscopes were fixed and couldn't telescope upwards on the early boats. Gasoline and battery gas explosions were also frequently cited, along with mechanical mishaps and human error. A number of submarines were damaged or lost when the crew forgot to close a hatch or ventilator before a dive, allowing seawater to flood the boat.

Lockwood had watched from the deck of the *A-2* as another sub, one of the B-boats, raced across the bay toward them that morning. When it arrived in a froth of white water and turbulence sending off waves, the sub's skipper yelled to Lockwood through a megaphone, "Just heard that the *F-4* was lost off Honolulu Harbor Thursday morning, Hawaiian time. They're dragging for her. So far, no luck!"

Lockwood looked around at his nine crewmembers, whose faces became studies of shock, bewilderment and sorrow. They knew some of the crew on the F-boats from their visits to Honolulu. Lockwood knew that Alfred Ede was a good captain. Senior officers had decided that Ede was the best choice to take over *F-4* because of his experience on the boat and the backing of the crew. In their view, Ede had a smooth, unhurried efficiency, a calm, alert personality, and easy-going ways in leadership. These qualities had instilled a confidence and loyalty among the boat's crew.

Later in the evening at dinner aboard the submarine tender *USS Mohican*, a ship that Jack Agraz once served on in the Philippines, Lockwood and his crew sat subdued, not engaging in their usual bantering and boisterous proclamations. Instead, they were soul searching, listless, asking questions. What happened on Ede's boat? Could it happen to us? Lockwood listened to all the theories and conclusions around the table from his crew. How had the ship been lost? Was the crew still alive? Had a battery explosion or chlorine gas snuffed out their lives? Had the sub gone too deep and been crushed by the pressure?

The sailors discounted a fuel explosion because *F-4* ran diesel. The speculation centered more on the explosive qualities of odorless, invisible hydrogen gas mixing with air and being ignited by a spark. Or could thick, green chlorine gas clouds have been generated by saltwater pouring into a leaking battery tank filled with lead and sulphuric acid?

The hydrogen gas phenomena had long haunted submarine crews. Hydrogen was invisible and was created by charging and discharging batteries. It had been blamed for an explosion aboard *F-4* already, earlier in the year.

Lockwood reflected on that emotionally charged discussion aboard the *Mohican* that night. For the first time with *F-4*, the grim specter of total oblivion had made its entry into the US submarine service. Lockwood reflected even at the time that half a dozen nations around the world had already lost 15 subs between 1903 and 1915, but none of them had been American boats. This one hit home.

Lockwood and his crew discussed another event that night, one that had left a deep impression on them all. It was from a letter written in 1910 by Lt. Sakuma Tsutomu, a submarine captain in the Imperial Japanese Navy, in the

Charles A. Lockwood, United States Naval Academy Class of 1912; Lockwood was ensign aboard A-2 when F-4 sank. He later became vice admiral of the US Navy and commander of the Submarine Force Pacific Fleet in World War II (US Naval Academy Yearbook)

last minutes of his life, after his sub became stranded on the bottom of the sea. The letter had been widely published after its discovery and was re-published by one of the Hawaiian newspapers a day after the *F-4* went missing.

Lt. Sakuma Tsutomu wrote:

"...we submerged too far and when we attempted to shut the sluice-valve, the chain gave way. Then we tried to close the valve by hand, but it was too late ... the boat sank at an angle of twenty-five degrees. The switchboard being underwater, the electric lights gave out. Offensive gas developed and respiration became difficult."

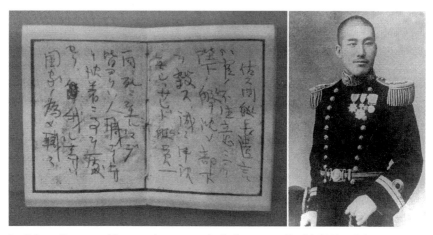

Lt. Sakuma Tsutomo and his journal, written in the final moments of his life (Wikipedia)

"The above has been written under the light of the conning tower. When it was 11:45 o'clock. It is my opinion, that men embarking in submarines must possess the qualities of coolness and nerve and must be extremely painstaking; they must be brave and daring in their handling of the boat. People may laugh at this opinion in view of my failure, but the statement is true ... We are now soaked by the water that has made its way in. Our clothes are very wet, and we feel cold. I have always expected death whenever I left my home and therefore my will is already in the drawer at Karasaki. I beg respectfully to say to His Majesty that none of the families left by my subordinates shall suffer. The only matter I am anxious about now is ... atmospheric pressure is increasing, and I feel as if my tympanum were breaking. At 12:30 my respiration is extraordinarily difficult. I am breathing gasoline. I am intoxicated with gasoline. It is 12:40 o'clock ..."

That night aboard the *Mohican* in Manila Bay, Lockwood would later say, "Thus we sat until far into the night aboard our ancient tender, and dwelt on point by point, possibility on possibility, like beads on a rosary of peril. Being a brand-new submarine skipper, I kept my mouth shut and my ears open. ... But on that March night in 1915, as darkness gave way to dawn and I still lay sleepless on my bunk, all I could do was to project my thoughts eastward from Manila Bay to Mamala Bay off Honolulu; to try to pry through time and distance for some sort of answer to my prayers that, by now, the *F-4* had been found, hauled into shallow water, and her men set free."

By dawn the second day, *F-4* had been below surface for 20 hours. Despite rumors of discovery, nobody could confirm the boat's exact position, but hopes were running high that the rescue teams assembled would be able to locate the sub and bring the crew back to the surface. Across the waterfront in Honolulu, in the Navy yards and among top brass and officers, everybody raced to figure out how to locate the sub and save the crew.

Tugboats had worked through the night nonstop. They were still dragging the large cables across the sea bottom, with chain tethered between the vessel's sterns with 650-foot steel wires, trying to snare something solid between the boats. They would occasionally snag coral or other underwater formations. Navy officers involved in the search had not slept at all since *F-4*'s disappearance.

Lt. Smith was in charge of the rescue aboard the *Alert*, Bogusch was on *F-1*, and Jack Agraz was getting ready to dive with his buddy George Evans off *F-3*. They were facing depths that no person had ever reached without wearing a pressurized dive suit. And the sub weighed 435 tons submerged. They had no idea how they'd lift it. But none of that mattered. First, they had to find it.

In Honolulu people were throwing out all kinds of ideas how to find the sub.

Some suggested going up in a hot air balloon to spot its dark shape from above. Another plan was to take photos from a camera on a kite looking down. A couple of vessels left the harbor, towing an electric buzzer that mechanics on the tender *Alert* had improvised, working all night long. The system was fabricated using a couple nails in a framework at the end of a 600-foot-long telephone wire hooked to a battery. The device would be dragged along the bottom of the seabed. If it touched something metal, it would buzz.

That morning Rear Adm. Charles B. T. Moore — the top Navy commander in Hawaii — made inquiries about getting a float plane to scan the seabed from above. But he was informed that the only two available planes had recently been sold in an auction to civilians and the new owners had taken them apart to rebuild them. It would take several days at least to reassemble the aircraft. There were no other aircraft in Hawaii in March 1915. All travel to the islands was by ship.

With nothing working so far, Lt. Smith called on Jack Agraz and George Evans from F-1 and F-3 to dive in the search area to look for F-4. Dozens of sailors on the surface had been scanning the depths from the rails of open boats with primitive glass viewing boxes that extended just below the surface, eliminating reflections, but had seen nothing. Evans and Agraz donned basic submarine dive gear, a loose-fitting USN Mk2 helmet with an air hose attached. They wore long-underwear bottoms, undershirts and tennis shoes. There were no pressurized deep-sea diving suits available in Hawaii at the time or heavy dive boots

Jack Agraz had always been a strong swimmer and had become passionate about diving in the Navy. He and George were dive buddies. They'd been stationed aboard the *Mohican* in the US Asiatic Fleet until 1913, when both were transferred to Hawaii to join the F-class subs. In the Philippines, where the waters were warm, they'd grown accustomed to diving without pressurized dive suits or weights, just the lighter jerseys. Most of their dives with the Asiatic Fleet were less than 100 feet. No diver in the world had ever reached 300 feet. They were using the older diving helmets that day — without pressure suits; the helmets balanced loosely on the divers' shoulders, held in place by their weight. Air bubbles would escape around the base of the loose-fitting helmet.

Evans went down first.

The dives that George Evans and Jack Agraz did that day off Honolulu left rescuers onboard the flotilla circling the dive site in awe. Even though the sub had not really been located, both divers would try to get a glimpse of it in the deep, clear waters. When they'd go down, everybody just went silent. The tension would mount by the minute. The divers descended into depths people could hardly imagine. It was sheer will power and daring. Neither of the two men paused a minute to question how these unprecedented dives might impact their personal health.

Agraz surfacing after a dive. The helmet has been pulled aboard the launch, and men are reaching into the water to assist the diver aboard. (Pacific Fleet Submarine Museum at Pearl Harbor)

Each diver would go down into the void, trying to trace a path of drifting oil and air bubbles still coming from far below. Neither had ever been down more than 100 feet, but that did not stop them. They kept pushing themselves way beyond limits.

George Evans reached 186 feet that day. It was by far the deepest he'd ever been. George was another sailor that hailed from the Midwest. He'd grown up in a farming region at Galesburg, Illinois. When he joined the Navy, he took up diving. After coming up from his deepest dive, George described breathing in those deep waters as animalistic. "You just breathe like a horse with heaves," he'd said. He described having his mouth wide open and inhaling in deep gasps to counter the enormous pressure on his chest. He couldn't breathe through his nose at all.

When it was Jack's turn to go down, he was excited by the air bubbles he saw coming to the surface. He jumped into the sea and started down the cable as fast as he could go. Hand under hand, forcing himself down the cable feet first. He went down almost 200 feet in six minutes. It was too much.

Jack recounted that dive. "I got down there and noticed something was wrong. I couldn't see a thing. I moved my hand up inside my helmet and wiped my eyes off, and still I couldn't see anything. Then I put my hand outside and wiped off the glass, and I couldn't see then, either. My head felt like it was going around, and everything was black.

"I thought maybe it was something in the water," Jack said. "And so I went down a few more feet. And it wasn't any better. I could breathe, so I knew it wasn't something wrong with the line. The air felt as pure as it would up above. So I decided I was in bad shape and had them haul me up."

Jack was severely weakened when he returned to the surface, after having been down 190 feet. But the blackness had gone away, and he could see daylight again. The crew reached out to grab Jack and haul him into the boat. Exhausted, he slumped to the deck.

Neither diver had seen the ocean bottom or any sign of the submarine on those dives. It was believed then that nobody in the world had been that deep before without a pressurized diving suit to protect against the tremendous pressures below.

The surface rescue crew had manned the hand pumps frantically to force air down the long rubber tube to Agraz and Evans. Both divers had descended quickly — too quickly, they would discover. The speed of their descents into

crushing depths and the equally fast returns had left them exhausted, nauseated and disoriented. Neither diver paused to think about the risk or the physi-
ological impact of their actions. They would just lie on the deck and recover their
strength to go again.

George Evans and Jack Agraz aboard an F-class submarine in Hawaii 1915 (Agraz Family Collection)

When Jack Agraz and George Evans were diving for F-4 in 1915, nitrogen
narcosis was an unknown factor. That would be discovered 20 years later. George
and Jack were breathing surface air pumped down to them. The surface air was
naturally loaded with nitrogen. Once a diver descended more than 100 feet, the
pressure increase would cause nitrogen to disrupt neurological senses. The
deeper the dive, the more powerful the narcosis.

At 100 feet, the divers would feel mild impairment, at 200 feet severe
disorientation. Pressure at 300 feet could cause unconsciousness or death.
Breathing normal air and diving deep could induce reversible neurological disorders later referred to as The Martini Effect, because narcosis could induce
euphoria at times, or extreme anxiety and even terror. That day off Honolulu,
Agraz and Evans were having the equivalent of half a dozen martinis every
time they went down.

After his last dive, Evans was in very bad shape, almost unconscious when he returned to the surface. They took him back to shore to recover in Honolulu. Agraz had also felt the deep physical impact but refused to quit. Some of the sailors tried to persuade him to give it up. But he wanted to go down again. Lt. Smith gave Agraz a direct order to cease diving.

H-3

First Sightings

Walter Pratt was chief electrician at the Hammond Lumber Company mill on Humboldt Bay's Samoa Peninsula. He'd been going about his day in the little mill town when he heard a distress whistle out on the ocean, across the peninsula. But he couldn't see the source of it. Then three young boys who had been to the beach came running into the town saying there was something that looked like a whale trapped in the breakers. The three kids were the first ones to spot *H-3*.

Walter telephoned the life-saving station from the mill office to alert them about the whistle and what the children had seen. Then he hurried across the dunes with the boys. That's when he spotted the sub. He stood on the Samoa Beach scarcely believing what he was witnessing. Far from the shore, out where the largest wave sets were breaking, a submarine lay in the surf. It was early morning and still hard to see because of the fog. The waves were smashing up against the sub, rolling it around and sometimes washing over it.

Walter told the children to run down the beach and help guide the surf rescue team to the sub's location. It would be difficult to spot in the drifting fog. The lifesaving station was a couple miles away, built along the western edge of the bay near the harbor entrance. One of the young lads was a Boy Scout, and he hurried back home to Samoa to put on his uniform and bring his semaphore signal flags back to the beach. He wanted to communicate with the submarine crew if they appeared on deck.

H-3's SOS had been picked up by a wireless operator in Eureka on the bay's eastern shore, and they'd relayed the information to the Coast Guard's Humboldt Bay Life Saving Station near the harbor entrance and to the *Cheyenne*, which was standing offshore. Coast Guard Station Keeper and Senior Surfman Lawrence Ellison received the transmission at the station.

Ellison hadn't heard the sub's distress whistle from the station because of the overpowering sound of the surf, but he did receive the wireless message. He immediately formed a small rescue team and began trudging across the sand dunes and north up the beach, transporting a steel Lyle gun and line on a wheeled cart. The cart's wheels sank into the sand, slowing their progress. Ellison would attempt to shoot a line from the beach to the sub with the Lyle gun to set a breeches buoy — a 19th century rope-based rescue system, resembling a modern day zipline. It took them two hours to reach the scene of the wreck.

Although fog was starting to lift by then, the sub was barely visible, heeled over on its side a few hundred yards from shore and washed over by breakers. Nobody could be seen on the sub, and the hatches were locked down. One minute the rescuers could see H-3, then it would disappear under the break.

Ellison studied the situation. Nothing he'd done in his career quite prepared him for this moment. He'd been the Humboldt Bay Station Keeper since 1908, before the Coast Guard even existed. He'd rescued scores of people from the decks of beleaguered wooden vessels, sinking vessels, and from the water itself. But never from inside a windowless, sealed steel tube rolling around in breakers. They didn't even know he was out there.

The Life Saving Station skipper wondered what was going on inside the sub. Maybe the machinery was coming apart, breaking loose from the framework, pounding against the hull's inner bulkheads, causing injuries, or worse. He saw wreckage washing onto the shore from the framework and canvas shell of the sub's superstructure.

As he watched and plotted, the veteran life saver heard a low moaning coming from the stricken vessel's whistle as it rolled side to side. The boat swung back and forth, a horizontal pendulum in the rhythm of the waves. The wall of fog slowly drifted back onto the beach.

H-2, H-3, and H-1 in Bremerton, Washington (PigBoats.COM; Ric Hedman Collection)

The *Cheyenne* was 25 miles west of the Humboldt Bar when Howe's radio operator received a wireless transmission relayed from a station in Eureka, California, that *H-3* was foundering in the breakers north of the Humboldt Bar. The message wasn't from the sub, but from a Marconi wireless operator in Eureka, the largest town on Humboldt Bay. The operator was instructed to forward Duane Stewart's distress signal to the *Cheyenne*. The Coast Guard station at

Humboldt Bay also received the distress relay.

The *Cheyenne* had been offshore waiting for the *H-2* and *H-3* boats to arrive from Coos Bay and for the fog to lift so the flotilla could cross the Humboldt Bar and rendezvous inside the bay. Big festivities had been planned. The public had been invited to view the three submarines and the *Cheyenne* at the Eureka waterfront. It would be the first time that submarines had entered Humboldt Bay. The local paper had carried the story on the front page the day before. Now they had a new front-page story in the making.

Howe gave the order to ring up all ahead full, and the *Cheyenne* started moving at 13 knots toward *H-3*. It was a two-hour run from offshore.

The flotilla commander arrived off the end of the north jetty at about 1030 hours and could see the sub trapped inside the outer breaker line to the north. Bogusch had missed the harbor entrance by a long shot. Howe radioed the *H-1* and *H-2* crews and ordered them to proceed to San Francisco. He didn't want the other two boats exposed to the Humboldt Bar crossing. There would be no waterfront submarine tours in Eureka.

Howe believed he could still tow *H-3* out of the surf, but they had to get the men off the sub first. In a decisive moment, he directed the helmsmen and engineers to back the *Cheyenne* in toward the outer line of breakers. The *Cheyenne*'s leadsman took repeated soundings from the stern as the 3,000-ton ship slowly backed toward the break. The swells got steeper and closer together as they approached the shore break. When the sailor called out six fathoms, Howe ordered the ship to full stop.

They were rising and falling on the large rollers, dangerously close to the outer breaker line. The *Cheyenne*'s hull extended 13 feet below the surface. That left about 20 feet of clearance from the bottom. Some of the big swells were closing that distance precipitously close as it rose and settled heavily in the combers. That was far enough, Howe determined. They were still 200 yards from the sub.

The *Cheyenne* was a very dangerous ship to maneuver, especially in rough seas and close quarters. It was an antiquated warship design, based on a Civil

War-era concept, obsolete before it was even launched in 1904. The ship was designed with most of its hull underwater to protect it from incoming shells, akin to the *USS Monitor* — from the Civil War. When underway the *Cheyenne* had little more than a foot of freeboard, allowing waves to wash freely over its decks. It was more like a submarine in that regard. The Navy was quick to relegate the *Cheyenne* to a submarine tender due to its design failures as a war ship.

H-2 alongside H-1 in Coos Bay, Oregon, before departing for Humboldt Bay, December 1916 (PigBoats.COM, Courtesy Rick Larson)

Howe didn't think they could shoot a line from the *Cheyenne*. Nobody was on *H-3*'s deck. They probably didn't even know the *Cheyenne* was there, so he lowered a lifeboat. Howe put his best oarsmen in the open lifeboat, and, carrying a heavy line, the men rowed over the swells toward the sub. They wanted to board *H-3*, get the line secured and try to pull the sub off the shoals before more damage could occur. The effort failed.

Breakers smothered the sub. The *Cheyenne* couldn't get close to it, or beyond the outer wall of breakers. *H-3*'s crew had the hatches battened down. It would be too risky to take a lifeboat into that turbulence. They might not be able to get back out. The commander changed plans. The rescue would be done from the beach.

Howe moved the *Cheyenne* offshore about a mile and swung south to make an approach to the Humboldt Bar. It was about noon. The men aboard *H-3* had been subjected to severe pounding for almost four hours now. The sub had been hit by hundreds of breakers during that time.

Lt. Howe wanted to get his ship into the bay and his men on the beach to rescue the *H-3* crew, to get them out of the boat. He was worried about the risk of chlorine gas and, no doubt, injuries. He pushed *Cheyenne* towards the entrance channel with a full head of steam.

❧

Inside *H-3*, just as he had the previous year when he dove for *F-4* in Hawaii, Chief Jack Agraz became the morale builder for the beleaguered crewmen. Despite being trapped under the breakers for hours, Jack never let on that he was worried about the outcome. He went from compartment to compartment, sailor to sailor, telling crew members to hang on, stay awake, stay focused — they were going to get out of this. His encouragement was as relentless as the breakers.

To Duane Stewart and others aboard *H-3*, that made a world of difference. Stewart had never experienced such an emergency. He knew they were in a bad shape, with no power, the sub getting battered on the sea bottom, limited air supplies, and the constant threat of chlorine gas. Jack Agraz shrugged it off and kept moving.

Serving eight years in the Navy's Asiatic Pacific Fleet had honed Jack's sea skills. The *H-3* crew knew about Jack's *F-4* dives and a little bit about his Asiatic Fleet stories. But Jack didn't talk a lot about his exploits unless it served some purpose. He could scare the hell out of some of the green sailors with his frank tales of the *F-4* dives and what went through his head 200 feet below the surface.

He would claim that anybody could do what he did that day off Honolulu. Everybody knew that wasn't true.

Young sailors, often from small inland towns, were eager to learn the ways of the sea. Jack would describe harbors, waterfronts and shore leave at Nagasaki, Yokohama and Hong Kong — places the young crew had never seen. He could detail the dives and the mistakes made, the risks. New recruits learned from hearing about real world experiences from veterans like Jack. About situations you couldn't even imagine happening. The way things unfold. How people react. The things you couldn't learn in a book. Captains wanted most of their crew to be experienced seamen. The ones you could count on. The ones that knew what to do in an instant. That's why Bogusch had made Jack Agraz chief of the boat.

⚓

Jack had been trapped under the sea before. He'd learned how to maintain his composure and trust his instincts. While in the Asiatic Fleet, he'd been stationed in the Philippines aboard the *Mohican*, the same tender that Ensign Charles Lockwood was later stationed aboard when F-4 went down.

Jack had been tasked with a solo dive to fix a faulty air valve that had caused a floating dry dock to sink in 90 feet of water in Subic Bay in the Philippines. Jack was down inside a dark inner chamber of the submerged dry dock trying to reset the valve with a prybar. The bar slipped. The valve closed suddenly, clamping down on both of Jack's hands.

He strained to pull his hands out of the valve, but they were stuck. He was trapped almost 100 feet under the sea in a small dark compartment. He couldn't tug on his signal line since both hands were stuck in the valve. Realizing that he'd never be able to open the valve himself, Jack just relaxed. He lowered his heavy bronze dive helmet to rest on the valve to relieve the weight and preserve his energy. He thought, "They'll send someone down to see what has happened when they get no signal from me."

Jack stood immobile in the dark compartment listening to the sound of air being pumped into his helmet from above. His breathing slowed. He wondered how long it would take for somebody to notice that he wasn't responding. Time slowed. There were no distractions, just the whoosh of precious air. The dive officer on the surface watched the air bubbles coming up from Jack's position down on the seafloor. There was no motion. The dive officer flipped the signal line. No response.

"Something's wrong!" he shouted to the surface crew. "I can't get any signal from him. Get a man down quick to help him!"

Another diver slipped on a helmet with a separate air hose and immediately slid down the shot rope, making sure not to tangle his lines with Jack's. He followed the lines and found Jack motionless, inside the dark chamber. Jack was bent over, his helmet resting against the valve. He wasn't moving. The diver ran his hands along Jack's arms in the darkness and discovered his hands stuck inside the valve. He grabbed the steel bar and pried the valve open, freeing Jack. A quick tug on the signal line got both of them hauled up 90 feet, to the surface.

But that wasn't the end of it.

Several days later, working on the same sunken dry dock, Jack was in another inner compartment when the surface crew turned on a large suction pump to discharge the seawater. The suction pipe was near Jack's worksite. This time another diver was nearby. The powerful suction pulled Jack off his feet and sucked him up against the pipe opening, wrenching off his dive helmet and air hose. Jack spread out his arms and legs to resist being pulled into the pipe and managed to break free. The other diver grabbed Jack's helmet and airline and put it back over his head. Jack just kept working until the task was completed. After surfacing he said to the other diver, "I had a sort of close call down there today, didn't I?"

F-4

BRASSWORK

Forty-eight hours after *F-4* disappeared, former submarine commander James Howell appeared in the newspapers. He was a featured speaker at San Francisco's Commonwealth Club on March 27, two days after *F-4* went down. Howell had quit the Navy after he lost his *F-1* command and joined an engineering firm in San Francisco. Though out of the Navy, Howell was still known as a former submarine commander of the US Navy and the holder of the world's deepest submarine dive record. Nobody had been down 283 feet since Howell took *F-1* on that daredevil ride in 1912 off the coast of California. People wanted to hear what he had to say.

That night at the Commonwealth Club, Howell described how the *F-1* hull castings had begun to leak under the strain of the deep-sea pressure on his record dive. Saltwater was entering the boat, he told the audience. He went on to describe, in his own opinion, what could have happened to *F-4* on that last dive. This would stir up a frenzy at Navy command.

"With reports from the various officers (aboard) that all was in readiness, Lieutenant Ede probably ordered the automatic plow set for 70 feet," Howell said. "And the dive began."

The "plow" Howell was referring to was the automatic surfacing mechanism that F-boats used. It was routinely set at 60-70 feet. If a boat went deeper than the plow setting, air discharge systems automatically kicked in, purging the seawater from the ballast tanks and causing the boat to surface immediately. It was the failsafe against unplanned deeper dives.

Howell described to the Commonwealth Club audience what might have happened next once the plow depth was exceeded. "With increasing (downward) momentum the boat passed the 70-foot mark then reached 100 feet. The automatic plow must have clicked. The crew waited," he said. "150 feet! 'Blow auxiliary forward and middle main ballast,' Lieutenant Ede probably ordered. Then 250 feet! The momentum could not be stopped. Something had gone wrong. Too much water had entered the (auxiliary and trim) tanks at the beginning of the dive."

Prone to action and sensationalism, Jimmy Howell graphically described what could have happened next: "250 feet! The rivets and seams began to leak. The torpedo hatch casting gave way. ... 300 feet! The tanks tore away from the skin of the vessel and saltwater rushed over the batteries. A short circuit. Darkness ... The air became terrible. The crew became unconscious and as the little vessel reached the bottom they passed into eternity."

Howell added that had F-4 been recovered in 24 hours there would have been a chance some of the trapped men might have been rescued. Some of the crew might have saved themselves by crowding into the torpedo room, he suggested. Men able to get into this compartment might have been able to live for a day or more, despite little air space.

In the end, Howell blamed poor seamanship for the accident. "I do not believe that battery trouble or engine trouble caused F-4 to sink," he said. "The trouble was inexperience. In the case of the F-4, I believe the vessel got away from the commander. When a submarine gets into deep water, the chance of stopping its descent decreases as it gets lower."

The Navy was incredulous at Howell's comments at the Commonwealth Club. His declarations were carried all over the country by different newspapers. Commanders were also livid. Howell wasn't even in the Navy anymore. Lt. Kirby B. Crittenden, the commander of the Navy's first submarine division called Jimmy Howell's claims "a totally unwarranted and vicious attack and absolute falsehood." He added, "I consider it bad taste for anyone, even a person who has had such wonderful experiences in submarines as Lt. Howell, to publicly discuss at present time, the probable causes of the accident."

On Saturday, the Navy was telling people that hope was dwindling for the F-4 crew. The sub had been on the sea bottom now for two days. Under ideal conditions the boat might hold two to three days of air supply for the crew, maybe less, as long as the hull was intact. F-4's chief machinist's mate, William Nelson, had told his wife before the voyage that in the event of an accident the amount of breathable air would be limited. But air bubbles still emerged at the surface, as did the spreading violet and green oil slick. It now had drifted almost six miles.

Crews of the other F-boats and the submarine commanders tried to stay hopeful. They thought the crew might be releasing the oil intentionally to lighten the boat. The sub held about a thousand gallons of diesel oil in its fuel tanks. Jettisoning that fuel could increase buoyancy.

The tugboats and rescue crews had been operating nonstop through night and day, towing deep-water cables across the ocean floor in a grid beneath the oil slick, trying to snare the sub. Each cast of the cables and chains of the search pattern below the surface took an hour.

When the cables were hoisted aboard at one point, sailors noticed fresh signs of gray paint on the spreader lines use to position the snare cables. It was the same type of paint used on submarines. They believed they were near F-4. They just had to get ahold of it. The rescuers were heartened, and the cables were cast again. Each cast was improvised. They'd never before attempted to snare a boat that was 300 feet down.

Then on Saturday night, the tugs Navajo and Intrepid snagged something down deep. Boatswain Metiers had been on the bridge of the Navajo directing every pass with the cable rigging. Having been on duty around the clock now for three days, he was weary, but now he had snared something very large on the sea bottom, less than 300 feet down. The 650-foot-long drag cables snapped tight when their sling snared the object. The excitement of the contact drove rescue teams to more fervent action. The tugboats secured more underwater rigging and strengthened their snare.

Dredge California dropping cables to F-4 (PigBoats.COM)

In the commotion, Metiers' tug lost its hold on the object below. He hauled the drag rig back aboard the Navajo to recast it. As the giant cable and chain harness was winched aboard, a stunned deck crew saw a piece of brasswork jammed in the chain. It was a section of periscope. Lt. Charles Smith, the flotilla commander, identified the brasswork as part of F-4. Between the paint and this brass metal work, they were sure they'd found the missing sub.

Charles Smith directed the dredge *California* to a position over the snare. They dropped an anchor cable to mark the spot. Everyone was on edge. They'd latched onto something big. There was still time to rescue the crew. But it would take a miracle.

Crews aboard the dredge *California* had been working the rigging all night long, reeling in and then slacking off lines, with the big drum turning slowly. The dredge shook and vibrated severely from tension on the cables. All night, the dredge lifted and fell with the rhythm of the swell, complicating the catch below.

Chief Jack Agraz inside F-1 at the dive plane control wheels (Agraz Family Collection)

Jack Agraz and George Evans had given it their all on Friday, trying to get a line on *F-4* — to no avail. The dives the two men performed would be talked about for years, but Jack's deepest dive was yet to come.

The rescue flotilla moved into place on Sunday morning, March 27, circling around the wire cable pulled tight off the deck of the *California*. Close to 20 boats now maneuvered in a half circle around the dredge's cable. A launch arrived carrying Hawaii Territorial Legislature members, another launch brought out Honolulu Harbor officials and the chairman of the harbor commission.

The cable went straight down into the sea and disappeared in the depths.

Everyone on the ocean that day knew that Jack Agraz was about to embark on an extraordinary mission of great risk. As usual, Jack was unemotional, just focused and matter of fact. One reporter at the scene thought he looked like a heavyweight wrestler in his tights, because of his strong upper body and the theatrical drama surrounding the moment.

All eyes were on Agraz as he stepped from the dredge into the diver's boat and was pulled around in front of the cable. He slipped into the water. A sailor prepared the brass dive helmet. The 12-man air-pumping crew readied to hand pump air down the 300-foot-long hose to Jack. There were three crews of four pumpers so they could relieve each other. They would have to keep a vigorous pace. The air hose was very long so that Jack would have plenty of hose to probe the depths.

Jack Agraz was over six feet tall and in his early 30s. He weighed 210 pounds, all bone and muscle, as people described him. He had broad shoulders and a deep chest, and his thick dark hair highlighted his Mexican ancestry. He was a looming figure aboard the cramped quarters of the submarine. His peers said Jack wasn't afraid of anything and that he had one of the most determined mindsets in the Navy.

Jack was born Juan de Agraz Hinojosa in the mountains of Mexico in 1879. His father, Doctor Juan de Agraz, had married the young Virginia Hinojosa in his hometown of Autlan, an agricultural region in the state of Jalisco located at a high elevation in the western foothills of the Sierra Madre Occidental. Jack's father had earned a military medical degree in Guadalajara two years before marrying Virginia but had chosen to start his family in Autlan, where Jack was born.

Jack's father had been a military doctor in Guadalajara and personal physician to Porfirio Diaz, the Mexican president and general who held office during a tumultuous period of almost 30 years at the turn of the 19th century.

Jack's father passed away four years after Jack was born. The family moved back to Guadalajara, where Jack grew up with his two younger brothers, Emilio and Salvador. The three brothers would go on to distinguish themselves in very different careers.

Jack set out for adventure, crossing the northern border and joining the US Navy in 1904. He'd been stationed on various ships in the Asiatic Fleet for most his career. When he crossed the border, he'd changed his birth name from Juan to John. Everybody called him Jack, but his Navy records listed him as John Agraz.

He and his younger brother Emilio liked to push themselves. They were both tenacious in their pursuits. In California, Emilio Agraz Hinojosa was establishing himself as a great bicycle racer while Jack was diving in the Navy. Emilio set a one-mile world record pedaling a Racycle, a fixed-gear racing bike, at the Los Angeles Coliseum Track on July 21, 1909, covering the distance in just over sixty seconds.

Emilio was a national contender at velodromes and multi-day bike races across the country, drawing thousands of spectators, and his name was constantly in the spotlight. In one brutally contested bike race around San Francisco Bay, Emilio was on the way to anchoring a win for his team, when a rival bike team member stepped out from behind a tree along the course and shot Emilio with a rifle in an attempt to stop his win. Emilio didn't slow down. He kept riding hard. He finished the ride, winning the stage and the event for his team, with blood streaming and a bullet lodged in his leg. He passed out at the finish line.

Jack had been shot once, too, but accidentally during gunnery practice in the Philippines. He didn't write much about it in his journal, just that he spent three months in the hospital recovering. The notion of service was well embedded in the Agraz family. Jack's second brother, Salvador Agraz Hinojosa, also served as an officer in the Mexican Army and was Mexican Consul in San Antonio, Texas.

But Jack was a long way from Guadalajara now. He was treading water in the middle of the Pacific Ocean. The air was warm and sultry on the surface as the rescue attempt unfolded for hours. One Navy officer later recounted Jack's efforts in the Hawaiian waters: "It was just guts and stubbornness and regards for his ship mates that sent him that deep. Jack was our morale builder."

H-3

Against All Odds

Lt. Bogusch had to change strategies, fast. They were getting hammered by the breakers, and the constant rolling was taking a toll on his men. When he was out on the bridge, he could see the powerful first line of high breakers that rose between the sub and the open sea. Still sealed inside the sub with his crew, he had not seen the *Cheyenne*'s approach and attempt to launch a lifeboat.

He didn't think any rescue boat could safely make it through that gauntlet, let alone go back out against it. Those were ground breakers. When they toppled, they carried hundreds of tons of crushing power, driving the turbulence into the sea bottom. Bogusch could also see the swells of wave sets passing the submarine, regrouping and rising again toward the shoreline. It seemed to him that any rescue effort was going to come from the beach, not the sea.

He needed to move the sub closer to shore, into shallower water where the waves weren't as powerful. With both engines and the electrical system out of commission, they had no propulsion; they would have to surf the breakers in towards the beach. The skipper also knew that the flood tide was about to commence, deepening the water around the boat and helping their advance. Seas were building again, and Bogusch saw his chance.

H-3 drifting in toward the beach in the wave sets after discharging ballast water (ibiblio.com)

Bogusch ordered the main ballast tanks blown, using precious air supplies. This would make the sub ride higher in the water and allow the surge to carry it east, toward the shore. Air pressure forced tons of seawater from the ballast tanks, and the boat became more buoyant. But the rolling worsened immediately as *H-3* bobbed unevenly in the surge. Wave trains would lift the sub and send it forward, grinding the steel hull against the sandy bottom as it slid, sometimes crashing hard against the sea bottom. Then the sub would settle heavily back onto the seafloor, sometimes toppling over on its side. They had no rudder control.

The crew could hear the air purging seawater from the ballast tanks and feel the increased action of the boat. They gripped whatever they could, struggling to keep from sliding back and forth across the deck inside *H-3*. Chief Agraz hauled mattresses from the forward battery compartment and gave them out to sit on, which helped. But oxygen was becoming a real problem.

The waves roared onto shore in uneven, rhythmic surges one after another, varying in height by 10 feet or more. Some of the outside breakers reached 20 feet. The biggest wave sets sometimes arrived in groups of three, followed by more moderate swells. Just when the crew would sense things easing, another large set would erupt and send them sprawling. They'd endured over four hours of this relentless surge as innumerable breakers hit the sub.

During a lull in wave sets, Bogusch ordered a few crewmen out on deck with fire axes to chop away the remaining framework of the wind fairing structure that blocked the passageway. The captain wanted a clear passageway. Agraz led a team of sailors out of the top hatch. They took their unsteady positions and swung heavy axes to break loose the twisted and crumpled tubing from the deck. Everyone had one eye on the axe strikes and the other on the horizon. They tossed the damaged metal framework overboard, freeing up the hatch and passageway.

The next big wave set was forming on the seaward side of the boat. Bogusch ordered the crew below. The men moved quickly. The skipper was the last man down the hatch. The 27 submariners were again sealed inside H-3.

Submarine commanders like Lt. Harry Bogusch and Lt. Eric Zemke wore multiple hats, and every decision they made affected the entire crew and the boat. The captain had to keep chlorine gas from forming no matter what. He had to keep his men safe. He was the commanding officer first, but he also was the Navigator, the Engineering Officer, the Electrical Officer, and the Gunnery Officer. He had oversight of every system in the boat.

Harry Robert Bogusch, United States Naval Academy Year Book – Class of 1911 (US Naval Academy)

Training at Annapolis involved a broad range of skills, including navigation, battery technology, tactical maneuvers, torpedo and mine drills, machine design and assembly, as well as designs and models of airplanes. The notion of airplanes would stick in the back of Harry's mind for years to come. He imagined that flying an airplane would be much like guiding a sub underwater with the interplay of both vertical and horizontal fins and the fine balancing of trim controls guiding the glide patterns. He liked the sensation of gliding into turns under the sea.

The submariner's command structure was much different than the large surface ships that operated with hundreds of crewmen. On the larger ships, many of the crewmen didn't know the other crew members. Formality and naval protocol were rigidly enforced. Their roles were compartmentalized, with interactions among the various stations and divisions being infrequent.

The submariners functioned as a tight, cohesive unit. Everyone had a job to do, but because they were all technically inclined, they often knew each other's jobs in case they needed to step in for somebody. They intermingled in very close quarters, elbow to elbow, and relied on each other every step of the way. Though still a core part of their existence as sailors, formalities of dress and protocol were often put aside among the enlisted men, and even the social divide between crew and officers blurred on the subs.

They would descend into the sea, sealed together in an airtight capsule, breathing the same precious air together. They worked in extremely close quarters. Intimacy required respect. Everyone on the boat knew each other by their first name. They shared joint shore leaves, overlapping friendships and social connections. The hardships they endured together forged camaraderie.

Aside from the specialty trades of electrician, mechanic, and gunnery, part of the training to become a submariner leading up to 1916 was informal, through storytelling. Sailors would share sea stories, situations, humor, and scuttlebutt from other subs. There were lessons in the stories. Captains always wanted to maintain a core group of experienced men at key positions — men who could trust each other, know their duties without fail, maintain discipline, understand the boat and the sea, and who could react instantly. They could influence the new recruits and teach them.

Bogusch's involvement with the F-4 submarine event in Hawaii had proven a defining moment in his young naval career, as it had for Jack. Both men put in long hours and many weeks on that epic incident and had proven themselves in different ways. Bogusch had been given command of the submarine F-1 after F-4 went down. His mentor, Lt. Charles E. Smith, chose to step aside and focus his efforts on running the flotilla and recovering F-4. Harry Bogusch would also play a key role investigating the F-4 event.

Like Jack, Harry was also born in Mexico. Harry's family was in Mexico City when Harry arrived on November 10, 1887. Jack had been born eight years before, about 400 miles away, near Guadalajara.

Harry had a relentless determination from an early age. When he graduated from high school in the rural town of Mason, Texas, in the foothills west of Austin, he decided he would join the Navy. In his mind, that meant Annapolis.

That summer at a July 4th barbecue celebration in Mason, Harry walked up to the district congressman and asked him if he'd support his nomination to attend the Naval Academy. The congressman was a little surprised by the youth's directness. He had nothing to offer but promised he'd contact Harry if something opened up. The congressman might have gone along his way at the barbecue that day and just forgotten the conversation. Harry didn't.

Instead, he badgered his parents to send him to a Washington DC prep school where he could be in close proximity to the Naval Academy. They arranged it. In DC, he went to the Capitol Building, sought out a United States Senator from Texas and doubled down on his appointment request. Soon after, Harry received a letter in the mail. He had been offered the unenviable slot of fourth alternate for a single cadet position.

For Harry to even have a shot, all three of the other candidates would have to fail their entrance exams. His folks tried to get him to drop the idea. They thought it would only end in disappointment since he was just a kid from Texas hill country and didn't have big money or political connections.

When the day of the exams came, the other three candidates did fail their exams. Harry passed his with high marks. He was accepted to Annapolis, against the odds, and graduated with honors in 1911.

At graduation, Bogusch successfully led the Annapolis Twelfth Company in a competitive tactical drill between all the graduating Midshipmen — the featured commencement event — and took top honors. He was presented a ceremonial sword and colors of the brigade for leading his company to the highest rating. He'd also been on the Naval Academy Rowing Team, something that would come in handy years later on the coast of Northern California.

F-4

GOING DEEP

Jack Agraz gave a nod to his crew and slipped beneath the surface of the ocean without a sound. For 22 minutes, he descended without weights, hand under hand, forcing his way straight down the cable. He was going much more slowly this time than on the Friday dives, only two days before. Everyone on the surface felt tension building with each minute. When Jack passed through 50 feet, people on the surface started to lose sight of him in the hazy depths. He became a vague, dark shape and then completely disappeared at 100 feet.

Jack was fighting off the same disorientation he had experienced on Friday. At 150 feet, Jack again couldn't see very well. He thought he might see better if he took the helmet off. It seemed like a good idea. Narcosis was setting in. It was funny how the depths played with your mind. He slowly removed the heavy brass dive helmet. Now he was 150 feet down without air or head protection. Jack looked around. But as on his prior dive when he tried to wipe down the glass, he couldn't see any better. His vision was blurred. He was holding his breath for what seemed a very long time, but it was only seconds.

He put the helmet back on. The air pressure from the hand pumps above forced the seawater out of the loose-fitting helmet with a whoosh. The water level dropped in the helmet to around his neck. Jack could breathe again. He took a deep breath through his mouth. The tropical surface air was refreshing.

Then Jack had another idea. He wanted to look straight down into the sea, get a better look at what was below him. The narcosis was building up, clouding his judgment. He gripped the cable and just let his feet float upwards, holding onto his helmet, until he was inverted. His tennis shoes were very light. As he spun around upside down for a better look straight down the cable into the ocean depths, the seawater came rushing back into the helmet. His helmet filled with saltwater again. He held his breath and stared straight down into a green void.

Jack felt relaxed. He wasn't panicking despite his dive helmet filling with seawater. He changed grip on the wire cable and righted himself. The air pressure again, slowly forcing all the water out of the helmet. The crews on the surface were cranking furiously. Jack knew if he hadn't been able to get his feet back below him it would have been lights out. But he'd proven to himself that he could work in different positions at that depth and still survive. He thought that might be handy when setting underwater rigging on the sub.

He continued down the cable, hand under hand, feet first, approaching 200 feet again as he'd done on Friday. The surface crew kept uncoiling the air hose as he descended. The air supply team spun the metal wheels as fast as they could. They needed to keep that air flow steady.

The month before, Jack had read in a magazine about a fellow in the Navy on the East Coast who'd gone down 274 feet and felt fine. But that man had worn two pressurized dive suits with an air pocket between them to protect him against the pressure. He also had strapped a small mattress device to his chest and abdomen for protection. The diver practiced for a month before going that deep. He practiced going in and out of a pressure chamber to test the stress of being at that depth. Jack hadn't had the time to practice. He'd just jumped into the ocean and gone down 200 feet without the slightest idea what would happen. His mind stayed riveted on the F-4 crew below.

Jack wondered what it would feel like to have all that gear. He wore just a light summer jersey. The pressure on his chest was like being crushed by concrete blocks, intensifying by the foot. He willed himself deeper. When he reached 200 feet he looked up toward the surface, which appeared a translucent blue. Occasionally, a fish would swim past and eye him. Some larger fish circled farther above.

He wasn't blacking out as he had on Friday. As he peered down, the visibility was only about 40 feet, and the water below was dark green and very hazy. He could feel the tug of currents sweeping through the sea at different levels. Jack could not know that the oxygen and nitrogen of the surface air was starting to break down in his body and creep into his consciousness because of pressure at 200 feet.

On the surface, the crowd waited anxiously. Everybody was concentrating on Jack Agraz and F-4 below. As the diver signal line played out and the air hose with it, Ensign Paul Bates called out the depth from the deck of the Navy power launch.

Jack felt confident that day. It was his fifth dive since Friday. He later thought that he could work at 250 feet with this gear. He continued down the cable another 15 feet but hit the end of his tether. He saw the shape of something below him. He gave the signal line a tug. He wanted to go further down.

"He is asking for more line, sir!" Ensign Bates yelled to his commanding officer, Lt. Charles Smith, who was aboard the launch.

"How deep is he?" shouted Smith.

"I make it 215 feet, sir!" Bates responded.

"Holy Moses, man!" Smith barked. "He's crazy! Don't give him another inch! Signal him to start up at once!"

Jack felt the sharp tug on the signal line, pulled from the deck, more than

200 feet above him. He knew the commander wanted him back on the surface. He took one last look down toward the sea bottom to confirm what he'd seen, then started slowly going hand over hand up the dredge cable, toward the surface. He knew what he had to tell Lt. Smith.

On that return to the surface, Jack went far more slowly than he had on Friday. He'd crawled down the cable this time, taking more than 20 minutes to reach the 215 foot mark. He would take his time on the return as well. He felt much better at the slower pace, going hand over hand up the cable. The adrenalin that propelled him Friday had given way to a more methodical dive.

Those were tense moments until Jack finally broke the surface after an hour underwater. There was a loud cheer from the surrounding onlookers aboard launches. Jack let go of the deep-water cable and swam to the dive launch. Eager hands wrestled the metal dive helmet from his head. Crewmen reached out to help him. He brushed them off, pushed their hands away and pulled himself out of the water without assistance. People were stunned at his stamina.

One Navy officer said what Jack just did would have killed the average person. Another longtime seafarer on the deck of the *California* that day said, "There isn't another man in 10,000 who could do that."

Jack's breath came back in gasps for fresh air. His metabolism readjusted to the surface pressure and atmospheric change. He took just a few minutes to recover. Jack was in better condition on this dive than Friday. The slower pace and longer period of pressure adjustment had paid off. Someone told him he'd just set a world dive record for an unprotected descent — no pressurized suit. Jack managed a slight smile, but his mind was still down there on the ocean floor. He had to tell Lt. Smith what he'd seen.

He now knew a dark truth about the rescue attempt to reach the *F-4* crew.

Jack regrouped quickly from his record-setting Honolulu dive. He went directly to Smith and told him what he'd seen down on the seafloor. "There's nothing down there, sir, but an anchor that your chain's foul of," he'd said. "There is no submarine."

The cheers that had greeted Jack's return to the surface, suddenly died down to a murmur. People on the surrounding launches were left with their mouths half open as if the air had been taken away from them. Everyone thought they'd found F-4. Nobody called out questions. Just a stunned silence swept over the waters. The disappointment was palpable.

Jack Agraz and crew inside the F-1 in Honolulu (Agraz Family Collection)

Jack had shrugged off the pats on the back and accolades for his courageous effort. Now the crowd understood why. He had not found the missing sub. When he'd reached 215 feet, he could see only the dim outline of an enormous ship's sea anchor caught in the drag cables, still attached to a rusty length of chain. The thing weighed tons. Barnacles were growing on it. It turned out to be the port side anchor of the battleship *USS Oregon*. The anchor had been lost in 1901 off the Oahu coast.

There was no submarine.

The surge of hope and enthusiasm that Jack had carried with him into the depths of the sea gave way to a sober dismay among the rescue teams. They had nothing. Nevertheless, they were resolute in their mission and would not give up. Everybody went back to work within minutes of Jack's dive. The tugboats reset their drag cables and resumed search patterns. Lt. Smith was not deterred. "We'll get that anchor onto a scow and out of our way," he said. "Then begin dragging again."

That evening when the sun set over the sea, the mission had reached a turning point. F-4 had been underwater now for four days. The steady trickle of oil and air bubbles that had driven rescuers' early attempts had ceased. Navy communiqués now told people what they had hoped not to hear: The crew was lost.

The surface crews kept at their tasks into the night, however. Captains, hoarse from nonstop actions and little sleep, communicated through megaphones. Before dawn, crewmen lay down on the decks, exhausted. They had no beds or blankets. They'd had little food in the last four days. They might sleep for an hour in any place and position they happened to be in until daylight. Then they would continue their efforts.

By Sunday evening, exhaustion overtook the Navajo's skipper, Boatswain Frederick Metiers, when he collapsed on the deck of the tugboat. He hadn't slept since Wednesday night. He'd geared up with his crew and headed directly out to sea from Honolulu when he got the call that F-4 had failed to surface. They were dragging steel cable snares along the ocean bottom by midday. He never let up his pace. It was around the clock, all day and night into Sunday. The galley crew brought him endless cups of coffee. He ate sandwiches standing up while directing the dragging operations.

His legs and hips had become numb, almost paralyzed, from standing on the deck for close to 80 hours. When he went down, it was from sleep deprivation. He collapsed hard onto the deck. The strain overtook him: Jack coming up without even a sighting of the sub, the false strikes, the idea of those young men down at the bottom of the sea, and all of it without a break. His crewmen helped him back to his quarters aboard the Navajo on Sunday evening, and, for the first time in four days, Metiers slept. By Monday morning, he was back on the bridge directing the deep-water rigging, trying to find and snare F-4.

On shore, crowds on the waterfront and piers swelled. Thousands stood on the docks on the eastern side of the harbor in the hot sun. There were so many automobiles moving around that a dust cloud had formed along the dirt roads. They couldn't see anything but the distant flotilla and the lights reflected on the sea at night. But they had to be there. They all hoped together that the men would be saved. They were willing to stand for hours, people from all walks of life, just for a piece of information about the fate of the F-4 crew.

Lt. Alfred L. Ede was 27 years old. He was now at the bottom of the sea with his crew. Although the Navy had said the crew was lost, nobody really knew if they were just holding on or truly gone. Ede had led a storied life, a University of Nevada and Annapolis graduate, connected to Nevada society through his family and his wife's family. Alfred's sister had married the governor's son, linking him to one of the most prominent families of the state. Before entering politics, Governor John Sparks had been a well-known cattleman as the cattle industry replaced mining across Nevada. He had been a friend of Ede's father, who also had agricultural interests in the state.

The world had not yet heard about Ede's letter to his brother about the condition of F-4, but another letter concerning the condition of the boat broke into circulation in Portland, Oregon, that had been written by George Deeth, an electrician aboard the boat.

George Deeth was down at the bottom of the sea now too with Alfred Ede and the other men. He was 23 years old the day F-4 took that dive. He'd grown up in the tiny rural town of Liberal, Oregon, along the banks of the Molalla River, near the foothills of the Cascade Mountains. His dad, Luther, had passed away just a few months before F-4 disappeared. Now his family had to face the prospect that George might also be gone.

Two weeks before the dive, Deeth had written a letter to a friend. He told his friend that he believed that F-4 was the unluckiest boat in the flotilla. He described the recent battery explosion that had wrecked the inside of the sub and thought it was from a buildup of hydrogen gas. The explosion had thrown

Deeth and a few other crew members hard against the steel hull, leaving them bruised and shaken.

Deeth had been working at a small desk inside the sub's main compartment when the explosion erupted — a sudden flash, followed by a huge bang and a deep concussion. Deeth was flung into the air. A flying projectile struck him in the legs. He smashed into the overhead of the boat and hit the deck hard. His ears were ringing. He hadn't remembered much.

The crew had been using the twin diesel engines to charge the batteries while running a blower to discharge the hydrogen gas byproduct of charging. Because it is odorless, hydrogen gas cannot be detected by smell. It was one of the most dangerous and unpredictable procedures the early submariners had to deal with. Somebody on the sub that day accidently created a dead short with a screwdriver, which caused the spark.

That's all it took. Bang.

Deeth also wrote in the letter about engine problems aboard F-4. They'd just replaced one of the diesels. He thought the engine had uneven mounting blocks that had caused cylinder heads to crack and mounts to break from excessive vibration.

Newspapers were rife with conflicting stories, unsubstantiated claims, and potential scenarios of what might have happened. Rumors sprang up. At the waterfront, a man claimed he knew from good sources that 19 crewmen were dead and two alive. The two were talking by telephone from the sub. After almost decking the liar, a Navy sailor yelled, "How can you peddle such stuff? You're making a joke of this thing. You know nothing ... spreading rumors like that when they may find their way to ears that would believe them only to suffer new disappointment and added pain." Nevermind that there was no telephone on the sub.

Then Alfred Ede's letter was revealed to the press by his brother. Controversy boiled over from Alfred's and George's letters after they were both syndicated across the country. Some wives of the lost F-4 sailors spoke to the press, sharing their stories, their worries and heartbreak. The Navy had a huge public relations crisis on their hands. With each release, they were compelled to counter with the official side of the story.

Once George Deeth's letter hit the press, the Navy adamantly defended the boat's condition. A Navy review board admitted the hydrogen blast the previous month had ripped the battery deck apart and broken several cell separators but said the boat had not sustained structural damage and that repairs had been adequate. A Pearl Harbor Naval officer told the press that all four of the F-boats in Hawaii had been inspected a month before for operational stability and all had passed inspection without issue.

The mood in Honolulu went dark on Monday, March 29.

Everything had suddenly changed over the weekend. F-4 had been underwater too long. No contact with the sub or crew had been established. Jack's 215-foot dive had been the final ray of hope on Sunday morning, and that faded in the shadow of an old ship's lost anchor and then vanished as the sun set on the Oahu coast Sunday evening.

Pacific Commercial Advertiser Newspaper, Honolulu, Hawaii (Newspapers.com)

It was an emotional blow to everyone on the waterfront and across Honolulu — and to the nation. Every newspaper had been carrying the story and conveying the hope of reaching the stranded sailors aboard *F-4*. The papers were already filled with grim stories of the Great War in Europe and of Pancho Villa's actions below the US southern border in the Mexican Revolution. Armies were crossing borders, ships were being blown out of the water, political stalemates developed and ultimatums were being issued.

Amid the news of warfare, the *F-4* story had generated hope. It brought people together. They needed something uplifting in their lives, a miracle. Now, the grim realization set in that Lt. Alfred Ede and his crew of 20 sailors would not be coming home. There would be no miracle.

The tugboats hauled up the snarled mess of drag cables and the barnacle-encrusted anchor of the *Oregon* and went back to port to reset their rigging. Rescuers took the evening off after their around-the-clock efforts. The mission was being reset.

The Navy Department in Washington DC cabled Adm. Moore in Hawaii Monday morning instructing him to shift the focus from a rescue mission to a salvage operation. Secretary of the Navy Josephus Daniels, Assistant Secretary of the Navy Franklin D. Roosevelt, and President Woodrow Wilson stated that they would bring *F-4* up from the bottom "no matter what the cost." Navy funds were appropriated. Lt. Charles E. Smith would lead the salvage effort.

Adm. Moore asked Lt. Cmdr. Julius Augustus Furer, a naval engineer and architect based at Pearl Harbor, to help Smith's unprecedented task of raising *F-4* from the sea bottom. Hailing out of

Julius Augustus Furer, USN Construction Corps. Furer graduated at the top of his class at Annapolis in 1901. Photo taken after the F-4 salvage when Furer had been promoted to captain. He eventually became rear admiral and was one of the most decorated naval engineers in the US Navy (NH 49461, Naval History and Heritage Command)

Wisconsin, Julius Furer, who had graduated at the top of his class at the Naval Academy in 1901, had an enormous talent for solving complex mechanical issues.

Along with Lt. Cmdr. Furer, Master Rigger Fred Busse would join the recovery effort and Bogusch was chosen to work with Smith's team. Agraz and Evans stood by ready to help with the next underwater phase.

A subdued work force hit the decks as the salvage operation got underway.

Tuesday morning, another dragline strike was made on the sea bottom. It was in 300 feet of water, near where the oil slick and air bubbles had been surfacing. The tugs had snared something very large in their cable harness as they moved away from shore toward the open sea. The cables snapped tight. The cadence of activity accelerated immediately. Tugboat crews passed off their rigging to other vessels, loaded a new dragline and made their approach from the sea toward shore this time. They snared the object again. Now they had it from what appeared to be both ends. There was a growing sense that they'd finally found *F-4*, even though hope for the crew was gone.

They positioned the *California* dredge over the cables and began winching up the load. The dredge strained under the tremendous weight as it began to reel in the object. If it was *F-4* they had on the cables it would weigh in excess of 300 tons. The *California*'s lift capacity was far less than that. They wanted to lift the boat slightly and slide it up the sea slope, if possible. That was Lt. Cmdr. Furer's plan.

Furer had ordered a 150-ton floating crane from Pearl Harbor, but it would take several days to prepare the platform and move it out to sea. The *California* dredge was a long shot, but it was all they had. As the recovery unfolded, the Navy faced the reality that they had been building a submarine fleet for 15 years but had absolutely no means to recover a stranded vessel or crew from the sea floor. They had never needed to.

Left: David Bushnell's Turtle submarine built in 1776 during the American Revolutionary War (Courtesy of commons.wikimedia.org); Right: Turtle illustration, artist unknown (Vintage Image Photos, Germantown, TN)

Americans had invented the world's first Navy submarine in 1775 during the War of Independence from Britain when they launched the *Turtle* out of a small bay in Connecticut. The strange little tortoise-shaped submersible was an ingenious invention, controlled by a hand-cranked propeller and using a keg of gun powder as its payload. The keg would be attached to the bottom of the targeted ship. The *Turtle* was deployed several times but never managed to sink a British ship. Tides would carry the *Turtle* away from its mark. Its usage ended when it was hoisted onto the deck of an American vessel to be moved and a British warship sent that ship to the bottom, taking the *Turtle* with it. However, it was the first submersible to use seawater in ballast tanks in order to submerge and surface, a concept still deployed almost 250 years later.

H-3

Thunder Rains Down

Gunner's Mate Bobby Burns climbed the steel ladder into the conning tower again and waited for the wave sets to settle down during the flood tide. He re-opened the hatch and got his head above the tower. He could see the beach. He came back into the control room and told the crew that they'd been spotted. Burns had seen two boys on the beach. One of them had waved semaphore-signal flags trying to send a message to the sub from shore. Bobby had signaled back.

The boys started running down the beach to the south. The fog came in again, but when it lifted the boys were back. The one with the signal flags waved frantically, trying to spell out "help coming," or that's what Burns thought. He also saw an adult on the beach with the boys. Then the wave sets grew larger, crashing over the conning tower. The captain recalled Burns. His news cheered the crew. Help was coming.

Duane Stewart was getting groggy as hours ticked by. On one wild roll, he and Clyde "Batlin" Wyatt were wrenched loose from their holds and came down heavy on a case of eggs in the control room. The ensuing mess was laughable to everybody but Wyatt. He'd had about enough. The sub was still being rolled over during the larger wave sets. Men found it difficult to keep hold of secure objects. They kept getting piled up on top of each other on the port and starboard rolls. Their ribs and limbs were badly bruised.

Duane began to be demoralized and could see conditions wearing on others, too. There was no relief, and they'd been trapped now for hours, sitting inside the sub, with bad air and incessant jolts. Some sailors exhibited signs of shock and fatigue from the lack of oxygen and accumulation of noxious fumes. Some felt nauseated and dizzy. Battery acid had soaked into their clothes.

Duane kept thinking about the batteries and saltwater. He hoped the chlorine gas wouldn't get worse. There were 1,800 gallons of acid sloshing around below decks. Duane knew the boat was designed to keep the acid in the tanks up to a 20-degree roll. But they'd been rolling more than that. He figured some of the acid had already spilled out. A sub would never roll that much in the open sea.

At least the batteries were new. Duane and the rest of the crew had labored long hours to replace the H-3 batteries a few months before, at a cost of $60,000. Replacing them had been a real ordeal. There was no large vault door in the sub that could be opened to lift an entire battery tank out at once with a winch. They had to dismantle the batteries one by one, piece by piece, gallon by gallon and carry each item up the steel ladder and out through the main hatch. A crewman could manage about 60 pounds of material on each trip, carrying metal plates or containers of acid. Then they had to carry the replacement materials back down through the hatch, down the ladder, into the boat. It took a few thousand human trips to complete the entire battery replacement.

The skipper was still blowing the sub's air whistle every few minutes, but the sound was getting weaker and less frequent. The air tanks were being depleted.

On Samoa Beach, Coast Guard Station Keeper Lawrence Ellison positioned the Lyle gun with careful aim toward the sub, which had swung around broadside to the waves. It gave him a bigger target. Bang. The gun bounced back six feet on recoil. The metal projectile and messenger line at its end arced high over the waves into the fog with the line trailing behind it, uncoiling rapidly. It landed over the stern. He'd made a direct hit. He waited, but nothing happened. Nobody appeared from the sub. They didn't know there was now a line from shore across their outer deck.

Lyle gun being fired on the beach (left); rescue cart (right) with lines and Lyle gun similar to Humboldt Bay Coast Guard equipment in 1916; (US Coast Guard/Wikiwand)

A large crowd had been gathering on the beach since late morning. It was now several hundred strong. As word spread in the surrounding towns that a submarine was in the breakers on Samoa Beach, people dropped whatever they were doing, left their homes, left their shops, and set out to find a way over to Samoa Beach. Those who were looking on at the unfolding event were captivated by Ellison's Lyle gun. Some cheered when he fired it, while others just watched in silent concern.

The wave pressure was relentless. Ellison thought that maybe some of the crew had been knocked out from gas or were just struggling to hold their position as the vessel rolled. He decided to shoot another line. He made another direct hit.

Duane could hear some commotion up in the conning tower compartment above the jammed control room. The captain and the chief were up there looking through the glass ports and had spotted some activity. Toad Blabon, Bobby Burns and Jim Anderson were crowded in there, too.

People on the beach watched as the hatch was thrown open. A lone figure emerged from the tower area of the submarine and ran down the deck toward the line over the stern. The line appeared snagged. The sailor couldn't get it free. He struggled and looked very small on the deck of the sub surrounded by breakers out in the ocean.

The sailor turned and dashed back toward the conning tower. The crowd on the beach was riveted by the lone sailor running on the deck. It was their first full glimpse of a crewman from *H-3*. Another big wave set was closing in fast. The sailor scampered up the conning tower and dove back into the hatch as a massive wave exploded against the sub broadside. Crewmen in the tower slammed the hatch down hard at the last, chaotic moment. Then nothing.

Jack Agraz had been lucky again. He'd just made it back inside.

The breaker hit the sub with the impact of a freight train, rolling *H-3* onto its port side. Crewmen in the five-by-seven-foot conning tower fell on each other as the boat rolled. The hatch had come down hard. Mayhem was unleashed inside *H-3* again.

Just when Duane Stewart was thinking that it was a miracle no one had been hurt yet, Toad Blabon came falling down the hatchway into the control room with three fingers missing from his left hand. He was on the steel ladder at the hatch in the conning tower when Jack made his move out onto the deck. When Jack dove back into the hatch ahead of the breaker, Toad was there with Jim Anderson trying to shut the hatch after him.

Toad's timing couldn't have been worse. While he was still hanging onto the ladder, the breaker hit, and the boat rolled hard over. Toad gripped a rung on the ladder with one hand and the other firmly on the steel knife edge for the hatch opening to steady his balance. The wave impact dislodged the steel ladder from its fixed position, leaving Toad dangling from the hatch opening by one hand.

At the same moment the impact jarred loose the keeper on the main hatch cover. The heavy cover slammed down. Jim Anderson tried to stop the hatch, but got his hand crushed, too. Toad Blabon came tumbling down into the control room right into the middle of the crew, minus the three fingers. Blood was everywhere. He held his hand up high with a tight grip around his wrist. Cursed every blue word he knew.

Jack grabbed a rag, tore it and tied a tourniquet around Toad's wrist. Then he put Toad on Tom Scarving's lap. Scarving was sitting behind one of the Kingston levers and was in a secure position. Bogusch and Zemke came to Toad's aid as well. Bogusch dropped from the conning tower into the midst of the crew. He grabbed a medical kit and doused the stubs of Toad's fingers with iodine and salts. The pain was unbearable, but Toad endured it. The skipper treated Jim Anderson's injured hand as well, then broke out the medicinal whiskey. Toad took a big slug and began to quiet. He was probably going into shock. Every sailor in the control room wanted a slug of that whiskey right at that moment.

The ship's clock had been smashed by the falling steel ladder, and now everybody was losing track of time. Duane was disoriented by the constant rolling and pounding. The air quality was getting worse with more than 20 men packed into the control room. Oxygen levels were deteriorating.

Back on the beach, Ellison and the crowd watched anxiously. Waves were breaking over the top of the sub again. The hatch stayed shut. Nobody came out. The veteran life-saving skipper thought carefully about his next move. He needed to get the rescue in motion. He ordered his crew to bring the surfboat from the station. This was going to be a daunting task. But it might be the last chance to get the men out of the sub before dark.

The surfboat weighed over half a ton. It was 25 feet long and held nine men. It was two miles down the beach from the sub, on the other side of the peninsula, separated by a mile and a half of soft, rolling sand dunes. They usually launched a motorized boat into the bay from the station ramp, but Ellison knew they'd never get to the sub through the outer line of breakers. He sent word to get a team of four horses to the station immediately to pull the surfboat boat over the dunes to the ocean beach. This would take hours.

At the lifesaving station, Ellison's crew trundled out the surfboat. They piled eight sets of oars and more rescue gear into the double-ended wooden boat and harnessed a team of four work horses to it. They set off across the dunes, the horses straining in the soft sand. The horses snorted, huffed, sweated and blew heavily out of their nostrils, dragging the heavy surfboat over the rolling dunes toward the beach. Some of the dunes were over 40 feet high. There was no solid footing, just deep sand. The 10-man crew led by Werner Sweins and Gustaf Christensen, two rugged Norsemen, trudged alongside the carriage and aided the struggling horses at times by leaning into the carriage, using their shoulders to push it over the dunes.

Horse-drawn surfboat (Soundings – Real Boats, Real Boaters; American Red Cross Collection; Library of Congress)

As Ellison studied the unusual shape of the submarine, with its round hull and narrow steel deck, he noticed that it was starting to ride higher in the water and surf toward shore. Bogusch had blown the tanks, allowing the boat to rise off the bottom and be pushed by the waves. And with a flood tide just beginning, the sub would be able to surge toward the beach out of range of the larger offshore breakers. Ellison bided his time and waited.

By mid-afternoon, the sub had moved a hundred yards closer to the beach.

The closer-in waves were not as powerful as the outer breaker line, but the sub still was captive to the unrelenting energy of the surf. The crew had endured more than 1,000 breakers by this point, in constant motion since early morning. They were undoubtedly paying a toll.

Ellison shot another line over the deck from the Lyle gun. The upper hatch opened again. The chief climbed out. This time he had a couple sailors with him. The boat was on even keel. They recovered the line and secured it to the sub's conning tower. The crowd on the beach cheered wildly at the sight of the crew and a line fastened to shore. Everybody sensed that the rescue was about to begin.

Bobby Burns appeared in the tower with signal flags and tried to semaphore those on the beach. That was the first communication from *H-3* since Duane Stewart sent his SOS in the morning. People on the beach thought that Burns said two sailors were injured and that escaping gases were threatening the crew.

Another large wave set started forming outside the surf line to the west. People on the shore watched the seas towering upwards with growing anxiety. Bogusch was watching from the conning tower. This was going to be another big set of heavy ground breakers. The skipper ordered everybody below decks. The hatch was sealed.

Thunder rained down on the sub. The boat twisted and rolled again in the grip of the sea, snapping the line to the sub like a bullwhip. A couple local volunteers from the crowd had secured the rescue line to a large log on the beach but had not allowed any slack for the tension. The crowd on the beach groaned, some threw their hands up in the air. One woman prayed at the edge of the crowd, looking up into the sky for an answer from God. Skipper Ellison pulled the frayed line back to shore. The line gun wasn't going to work. It would all be up to the surfboat crew now. But they were not in sight yet. Ellison stood on the beach and waited for his men to arrive with the boat.

Lt. William Howe had been on the move at full-ahead on the *Cheyenne* since receiving the wireless message from their position 25 miles offshore that *H-3* was in the breakers. After his own failed attempt to get a line on the sub from out at sea, he had headed for Humboldt Bay, but was wary of the bar crossing. All the bars he and the flotilla crossed in the last week along the Washington-Oregon coast were treacherous. Besides the big shore break and fog, riptides along the beaches were variable and unpredictable. Large tidal flows from the bays and rivers also factored into the risks. The *Cheyenne* had struggled at Grays Harbor and the Columbia River Bar. Now Howe was about to discover the nuances of the Humboldt Bar.

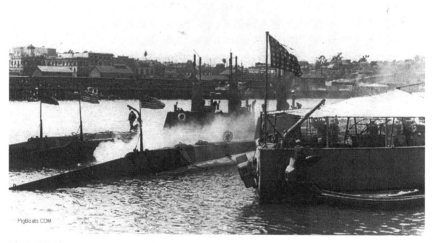

The USS Cheyenne, H-1, H-2, and H-3 boats in California (PigBoats.COM; Ric Hedman Collection)

As they approached the entrance at noon, they hit a nasty cross current that was running down the coast. Just two weeks before, the 200 foot steamer *F.A. Kilburn*, loaded with passengers and produce, had been caught in this unchartable current hugging the jetty ends and had ended up crashing into the south jetty rocks, twice. It didn't sink, but it was heavily damaged.

From the *Cheyenne*'s command bridge, Howe felt the cross current hit the ship's bow hard as they approached the jaws of the jetties. The current was a narrow band running north to south. One minute it wasn't there. Then the next moment it caught the bow and was pivoting the ship off course in the narrow entrance, toward the south jetty. Howe felt the 320-foot *Cheyenne* start to veer and instinctively telegraphed one engine full-reverse, one full-ahead and spun the helm hard over. The *Cheyenne* slowly straightened out and passed through the channel.

They dropped anchor near the western shore of Humboldt Bay. More than a hundred sailors hurried around the decks, loading blankets, medical gear, tents, dry clothes, and food. They lowered lifeboats into the bay and rowed to shore, leaving just a skeleton crew aboard the ship.

The submarine was in the breakers just on the other side of the peninsula dunes. As Howe and his crew marched over the sand dunes, Howe was worried about so much time passing. And he was worried about the risk of chlorine gas forming after he'd seen how severely the sub was being pummeled by the breakers. Howe and his men transported all the gear across the dunes and down the beach to where the sub lay in the breakers, hard over. It was a long, arduous slog through the rolling soft sands. Howe needed to get the crew out of the boat. That was his most immediate mission. And he was focused on it.

F-4

THOSE LEFT BEHIND

All day long on March 25 in Honolulu, under the blazing tropical sun, hundreds of people circulated through the city and down to the waterfront in a nonstop procession.

The disappearance of *F-4* hit people in Honolulu very hard. Six *F-4* crewmen were married. Some had children. One had twins. As the news began spreading into the city like a rising dark tide, it eventually reached the homes of *F-4* families. The Navy chose not to comment on the unknown events surrounding the boat's disappearance and did not contact the families.

By nightfall, 10,000 people had made the pilgrimage to the shores looking out to sea, a solemn stream of pedestrians and automobiles, paying respects, coming and going.

Some people came alone, families came with children, and larger groups would appear near the shores. Every boat that came back to shore from the flotilla would be approached and queried for new information. Was there any news?

Have they raised the submarine? There was absolutely nothing festive in the gathering. People were hopeful but grim as the ordeal wore on.

The beach road was clogged with vehicle traffic into the night, one Model T pulling out, the next taking its place, chugging up and down the roads and streets. The later it got into the evening, the more painful the expressions became.

The phones rang into the night at newspaper offices. They rang at three o'clock in the morning. More often it was a woman's voice, disguised curiosity at first, giving way to frustration and then despair. "Then there's nothing?" one would say. "Just nothing that they know?" To which the response was, "Absolutely nothing." A sob or outpouring of grief might follow on the wire before the line disconnected.

That morning, Frances Pierard was sitting with her 16-month-old twins and her sister in a small cottage on Beretania Street when the news that F-4 had failed to surface came from a friend. Her husband, Frank Pierard, was the boat's chief gunner's mate. Frances's younger sister, Mae, rested in Frances's arms, staring vacantly. Mae had just married Archie Lunger on February 6. Archie was a gunner's mate on F-4 with Frank. They were both onboard the day the boat disappeared.

In the early hours following F-4's disappearance, Frances had sobbed quietly, "Oh, if I only knew Frank and Archie weren't suffering, that they had met a sudden and easy death, it would be such a relief."

She and Frank had married five years before when he signed on with the F-4 when it was stationed in California. Sometime later, after twins Maude and Ernest were born, they'd moved to Hawaii with the flotilla transfer. Two months before, she'd invited her younger sister, Mae, to Hawaii to visit, and Mae had met Archie. They were married by a local minister at the minister's Honolulu home. "We were so happy out here in Honolulu," Frances reflected.

The day she received the news about F-4's disappearance, Frances tried to distract herself from the enormous emotional weight by taking photographs of her twins in the yard as they played with their toys and laughed. A neighbor who was with Frances and the children later in the afternoon said, "Sorrow and sadness cannot last in the presence of darling children like these."

Amid the outpouring of condolences and kindness, Frances was beginning to think about what her life would be like with Frank gone. She had no money saved. They had lived off Frank's Navy paycheck and dive dollars week to week. They'd been married in Iowa, where Frances and Mae were from, but Frances didn't want to go back to the Midwest. There was nothing there for her anymore. She, Mae and the wives of two other sailors who were aboard F-4 decided that they needed to stay in Honolulu at least until the boat was recovered, then maybe go back to California. Beyond that, they did not know what they would do.

❦

The heartbreaking news continued to reverberate throughout the tight-knit community. The officers and their wives had established close friendships and a social network. Many lived in the same neighborhood or on the same street. Alfred and Margaret Ede and their two children lived a few doors down from Harry and Grace Bogusch.

Grace was from Indianapolis, so the tropical neighborhoods of Honolulu were exotic. She and Harry had wanted to marry right after his graduation in 1911, but the Navy discouraged Annapolis graduates from getting married until they'd spent two years in the service. But Harry was determined to marry Grace and fought the ruling, writing letters, contacting school administrators and officers, making his case. He prevailed in the end, and his command consented.

Harry and Grace entertained often at their home on Lunalilo Street. They sometimes hosted bridge parties, and Grace would decorate the cottage with yellow chrysanthemums and Shasta daisies. They'd have the windows wide open, the scent of flowers drifting with the tropical breezes. They would give special

Top row: Margaret A. Ede was from Reno, Nevada. Her father had been the Nevada State Treasurer (Hawaii's newspaper – The Pacific Commercial Advertiser April 1915); Center row: Four F-4 crew members going on shore leave together: Albert F. Jennie EM2 of Festus, Missouri; Chief Electrician Harley Colwell of Seattle, Washington; Horace L. Moore GM1; Clark G. Buck GM2 of Tacoma, Washington. (PigBoats.COM); Bottom row: F-4's Alfred Ede, Frank Pierard and William Nelson (US Naval Academy Virtual Memorial Hall);

prizes like a Japanese sewing bag, cigarettes, candy and playing cards to the players with the highest scores in the bridge tournaments. It was a friendly competition. The Bogusches' guests included Charles Smith and his wife, Alfred and Margaret Ede, Francis and Mildred Scanland, Bruce Canaga, and many other wives and friends from the flotilla at Hawaii.

Margaret Ede was at their small home on Lunalilo Street with their two-and-a-half-year-old daughter, Margaret, and 18-month-old son, Alfred Jr., when the news reached her. It didn't come from the Navy. Somebody came running to her home to tell her what they'd heard on the waterfront — that F-4 had disappeared. Her emotions were unrestrained. Margaret took a deep breath as it all came rushing in on her. She collapsed under the shock of it. As friends rushed to her side, she rallied, with her children around her, hoping for the best but preparing for the worst. She was dealt further emotional blows when somebody mistakenly claimed F-4 had only gone to Hilo and was coming back.

The news of F-4's loss also resonated across the state of Nevada. Like Alfred, Margaret was also from Reno. Her father had been Nevada State Treasurer and her family was also well connected across the state. She and Alfred had been in Honolulu about eight months on that morning when he left their Lunalilo home for the boat after breakfast.

Mrs. Helen Moore, the wife of Rear Adm. Moore, the commanding officer of Naval Station Pearl Harbor, tried to assist the families by offering transport, organizing fundraisers and reaching out across the various communities. Helen was president of the Navy Relief Society and immediately dedicated herself to helping F-4 families. She arranged for donations to be gathered by the Honolulu Ad Club, a civic organization with considerable reach into the business community.

Every merchant in Honolulu was approached. Ad Club Members donated directly. Benefit baseball games were organized across the city. Private citizens chipped in, and soldiers and sailors donated out of their meager savings. The three remaining F-boat crews raised over $400 from their own pockets. Joe Roberts, a ship's cook aboard the *Alert*, donated $50 to the families. He'd cooked the daily meals for the 21 men and knew them all by first name.

A stranger appeared at the Navy wharf and handed the officer in charge a $25 check and another $25 from his employees. More personal donations followed from people who had never known the sailors. Streetcar employees raised more than $100. The Hawaiian community rallied with donations. Japanese business leaders met at the local Yokohama Bank, voting unanimously to solicit funds for F-4 families from Japanese citizens across the region. Donations streamed in from across the islands.

Elsie and William Nelson had a nice life in Honolulu, too. William would go to the sub every day, and Elsie taught dance lessons at the home they rented. By Sunday, three days after the sub disappeared, Elsie was convinced her husband was dead along with the rest the crew. Grief-stricken, she couldn't stand the strain of waiting in Honolulu for word of the sub's fate. The entire city was focused on and talking about F-4. Not long after F-4 disappeared, Elsie boarded a Matson Liner in Honolulu and sailed to San Francisco in an attempt to escape her grief. When passengers learned one of F-4 widows was aboard, discussing the disaster was treated as taboo.

In a newspaper interview in Los Angeles some days later, Elsie said William had informed flotilla command that the motors were not good. Her comments resonated from the front page of several papers and forced the Navy to respond. The Hawaiian papers covered her recollection that William had had a dream the night before he sailed, that F-4 went to the bottom with the whole crew.

Frederick Gilman, gunner's mate first class, had also just married in November. He and his wife lived on the same street as the Pierards. Gilman wanted to be assigned to a sub. The pay was better than in the surface fleet, and the technical aspects of subs fascinated him. He'd been stationed aboard the *Alert* for several months but wanted a change. It was a new century, and submarines were the pioneers beneath the seas. He'd been watching the F-boats gliding in and out of the harbor for a few months and knew some of the sailors.

A friend of Gilman's on the *Alert* recalled, "Two months ago, Gilman was about to be transferred to the submarine flotilla. I advised him to go on the F-4 because I thought she was the best of them all. He followed my advice. Now..."

The news of a lost family member among the crew sometimes took a few days to reach a distant home. The Navy still had not reached out to family members. Gunner's Mate First Class Henry A. Withers, a close friend of Frank Pierard and Archie Lunger, came from San Diego, California. Henry's sister-in-law had always liked Henry and would never forget the deep sadness she felt when her husband, Henry's brother, came walking up the driveway in the middle of the day. Something was wrong. She braced herself for it. Her husband owned a butcher's shop in town. He would never have just walked out of that shop in the middle of the day. She knew right away that something urgent or terrible had happened. She said she would always remember Henry.

James Hoggett was an electrician's mate on the crew of F-4. But he wasn't on the boat that day. He had received routine temporary duty at the Naval Station that morning. He didn't think much about it at the time other than he would not get his dive dollar. One newspaper claimed that Hoggett missed the boat because he lingered too long at the Naval Station talking to people and then went to the wrong dock. Hoggett was stunned by the article and emphatic that wasn't the case. "People will think I was walking around in a daze," he'd said. "I was not. I had an hour's work to do at the station. That being my duty for the day. And I was there on duty when the *F-4* left."

Hoggett had joined the Navy in 1908, from Macedonia, Missouri, a tiny town in the middle of the country down a forgotten backroad — a town that ceased to exist some years later. Hoggett's father had been an officer during the Civil War in a Missouri Regiment so joining the military was held in high esteem in the family. The Navy was James' ticket out of Macedonia. He ended up aboard *F-4*. When news of the boat going down swept the waterfront, Hoggett went to work nonstop at the head of the rescue effort looking for his missing shipmates. He didn't feel lucky at all. The event would

James M. Hoggett — the only member of the F-4 crew to survive (Pacific Fleet Submarine Museum at Pearl Harbor)

change his life forever. He survived a motorcycle accident in Hawaii shortly after the *F-4* disappeared. Hoggett would volunteer time and again, joining in the most daring and dangerous situations that he could find, especially when the US entered the Great War. And he would always survive.

H-3

CURSE OF THE HOODOO

Both *H-3* and *F-4* had reputations among crew members as unlucky boats. *H-3* was nicknamed The Hoodoo and *F-4* had had its own string of incidents, with some crewmen calling it a Hoodoo boat as well. Most of the problems were either caused by mechanical failures or navigational errors. Both of the boats had a running tab on engine repairs.

In one incident, *H-3*'s previous skipper, Lt. William F. Newton, powered *H-3* up from a dive in San Diego Bay. When the boat broke the surface it plowed straight ahead onto an unmarked mudflat. The channel buoy was missing. When the tide went out, the sub toppled over onto its side and lay there all day in the mud like a beached whale for everybody to gawk at until the Navy could pull it off the shoal at high tide a day later. Likewise, *F-4* had been run up on the beach for all to see as well in Puget Sound, northwest of Seattle.

Duane Stewart knew well *H-3*'s long list of troubles. Besides the engine failures, it almost sank stern first into Puget Sound on a shakedown run. Then a shipyard worker accidently left a pair of coveralls near a seawater intake and plugged up a valve to the ballast tanks, throwing the sub off balance when it submerged. Duane wasn't on H-3 during those events, but he did recall the sub's 300-pound anchor suddenly breaking loose from the keel during a submerged run he was on. The electric drives were quiet and didn't vibrate the boat like the noisy diesels. The gut-wrenching jolt and sudden unraveling of heavy anchor chain sent a shockwave through the boat that startled everybody.

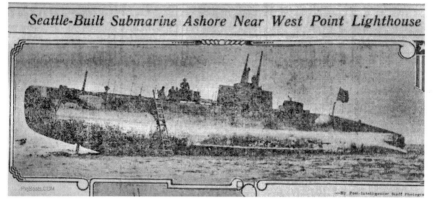

F-4 on the beach northwest of Seattle (Seattle Post Intelligencer Newspaper, March 14, 1913, from Beneath the Surface – Bill Lightfoot)

But for Lt. William Howe, seeing H-3 in the breakers on the California coast had to be a premier déjà vu moment. He'd been on the bridge of the *Cheyenne* the last time H-3 hit the beach. That accident happened at Big Sur in the summer of 1915, just a few months after F-4 disappeared.

Howe was commanding the *Cheyenne*, accompanying the three H-boats up the coast from San Diego to the Panama-Pacific Exposition and July Fourth celebrations in San Francisco Bay. Lt. William Newton was in command of the H-3 that day. Harry Bogusch and Jack Agraz were still involved with the F-4 recovery in Hawaii. That evening, as the heat of the California valleys started to wane, a strong onshore flow carried the coastal fog bank in toward the beaches and up against the tall rocky bluffs of Big Sur. Visibility plunged.

The ocean was smooth and glossy that evening with occasional long swells that would slip under the sub and lift it gently. Newton kept H-3 locked in on the same northerly gyrocompass heading all day. *H-3* was running a few hours ahead of the *Cheyenne* and the other two subs. Newton slowed their speed but kept a steady course in the dense evening fog. The compass heading was accurate, but the winds and coastal currents were conspiring to move *H-3* blindly toward shore.

William Newton did not realize this until it was too late.

Just after sunset, the bow watch saw two enormous rocks appear in the mist, jutting above the ocean's surface. He had no time to even shout a warning. The sub plowed onto the rocks with a deep, metallic grinding sound. Then came to a dead stop. Newton tried to back *H-3* off the rocks with a full bell on the electric motors, but the boat was stuck hard. He immediately sent a wireless message to Howe aboard the *Cheyenne* and to the Mare Island Navy Yard in San Francisco Bay, which caused a big stir among the admirals.

H-3 on the rocks at Big Sur, June 1915 (National Archives photo courtesy of PigBoats.COM)

Howe arrived at the scene with the *Cheyenne* in the middle of the night. Half a dozen other Navy and merchant ships had been poised to respond, but the sub was not badly damaged, just stuck. Howe waved them away. He sent the other two H-boats ahead to the San Francisco events, just as he would at Humboldt

Bay 18 months later. He was confident that his crew would be able to pull *H-3* off the rocks at Big Sur. The *Cheyenne* weighed more than 3,000 tons and had 2,400 horsepower.

Sunrise revealed a shocking tableau. At low tide, the entire sub was suspended between rocks. While they waited for the tide to turn, Lt. Newton and his crew slept, ate cold food or sat out on the deck. At high tide, sailors rigged a towing hauser from the *Cheyenne* to the stern of *H-3*. Howe ordered up full power. *Cheyenne*'s twin propellers stirred up a cauldron of white water, putting enormous tension on the tow line. Wedged solidly in the rocks, *H-3* didn't budge. William Newton was concerned. Then a big swell rolled in and lifted the 150-foot sub from the rocks. The *Cheyenne*'s power broke the submarine free.

But then a second wave smacked *H-3* broadside, slamming it back against the rocks before Newton could start the engines. The impact damaged more hull plates. Five sailors rolled off the deck into the ocean. Two didn't know how to swim. In a tense moment, with the prop wash of the *Cheyenne*, a high-tension tow line, multiple men overboard, and the sub up against the rocks, Newton directed crewmen to get lifelines to the five men in the water and pull them back aboard. Lt. Howe's *Cheyenne* was finally able to pull *H-3* into deep water, Newton got the engines started, and both vessels continued up the coast to San Francisco. But *H-3* was damaged and would have to go into dry dock for repairs.

As captain of *H-3*, William Newton probably felt lucky that day at Big Sur to have gotten the sub off the rocks with so little damage and no injuries to the crew. But another, larger event lay waiting for him on the beaches of Northern California.

F-4

INNOVATION AND DREAMS

In Hawaii, minds were at work on how to get a person down to the ocean floor, at 300 feet, to direct underwater rigging. Within hours of F-4's disappearance, C.W. Parks, a Naval engineer in Honolulu, designed and began fabricating a diving bell. He'd never even imagined such a device before F-4 disappeared. Now they were working around the clock fabricating it at Honolulu Iron Works.

Jack Agraz and George Evans were back on the front page of Hawaiian newspapers, climbing in and out of the diving bell while it was still being fabricated. Jack volunteered to be sealed into the device and lowered by cable to the sea floor. Nobody had ever deliberately gone down into the sea 300 feet inside anything before, other than in science fiction. Jack Agraz wanted to try it.

Parks' diving tube was made from an inch-and-a-half-thick iron plate. It was seven feet high, more than four feet in diameter and weighed six tons. It looked like an iron, cylindrical steam boiler. There were four circular portholes that could withstand four to five tons of pressure. The hatch cover was fabricated from a heavy-duty municipal sewer manhole cover bolted onto the iron chamber.

A journalist for the *Hawaiian Gazette* described what might be ahead for Jack: "Standing in his bell, he will peer out his four glass portholes into the green seawater. Beyond him, shining through the depths and flickering amid coral branches and the age-old accumulations of the ocean floor, will be powerful electric lights which will illuminate the bottom and show the gray shape of the stricken *F-4*."

C.W. Parks' diving bell – Jack Agraz standing on top of the diving bell checking fittings (Upper left photo); Naval Constructor C.W. Parks, designer of the diving bell on the left (Upper right); Boatswain Frederick Metiers of the Navy tug Navajo (Lower left photo); George Evans second from left, standing next to Jack Agraz on the right (Lower right photo); (Hawaii Star Bulletin Staff Photo, Newspapers.com)

Lt. Smith and Lt. Cmdr. Furer were concerned about the speed at which the diving bell was being readied for the task. It had been only 10 days since *F-4* failed to surface. They wanted tests conducted. The diving bell was lowered into Honolulu Harbor. It was left in 35 feet of water overnight, with nobody inside. The next morning it was hoisted up from the bay, and the inspectors found minor seepage. They wanted to test it in deep water.

Meanwhile, Julius Furer knew early on that the *California* dredge would never be able to raise F-4, so he brought in a more powerful dredge, the *Gaylord*. It had heavier winches, more lifting power, and a lighting system for night work, though it, too, had its limitations when it came to the sheer force and rigging needed to raise a submarine from the ocean floor. With his eye on the bigger picture, Furer had the Honolulu Iron Works working around the clock building cable drums, drive shafts and other industrial components. He planned to install that gear, along with twin, steam-powered winches — known as steam donkeys — on two 600-ton, flat-bottomed pontoon floats. The twin pontoons would be capable of supporting the sub's enormous weight under water.

Honolulu Iron Works (Star Bulletin 1900, Images of Old Hawaii)

Furer also fabricated cable reeling hardware out of old sugar mill drive shafts, pressing heavy steel plates onto the ends and riveting them together. His team unearthed four heavy wire cables, each about 1,000 feet long, almost nine inches in diameter and weighing seven tons each. He would have to wind those stiff lifting cables around the fabricated drums. Furer described the steel cables as "not much more flexible than iron bars" to a salvage expert sometime later.

Salvagers were coming to help with the F-4 recovery in every possible way. Besides the dredges, the submarine divers, the scows, and the diving bell, the Navy had ordered the armored cruiser USS *Maryland* to stand by in San Francisco to transport the Navy's top five deep-sea divers, who would travel by train from the East Coast to meet the cruiser, then continue on to Honolulu. Underneath all the hustle to get to the site of F-4, there was a fierce competition going on. Everybody was trying to get to the sub first. World records were going to be set. Questions were going to be answered.

Harry Bogusch and Ensign Paul Bates spent a day taking detailed soundings of the exact depth and position where they could lower the diving bell. Lt. Smith took the diving bell out to the *California* dredge and lowered it in 200 feet of water over night. The tremendous pressure flattened some of the gaskets, allowing a couple of inches of water to seep in. They towed it back to shore and re-torqued all the bolts.

Every day, newspapers were saying Agraz or Evans would be going down in the steel diving bell, sometimes referred to as the diving tube. Every day there was another postponement. They conducted another test in the harbor with Agraz inside the bell. He spent seven minutes on the bottom of Honolulu Harbor and emerged confident of the design.

Commanders of the *F-4* recovery effort, Charles Smith and Julius Furer, took the device offshore and lowered it again, down to 320 feet for the night. Nobody was inside the bell. The next morning only trace amounts of water had seeped in. Jack Agraz told everybody that he was ready to go.

When Jack wasn't climbing in and out of the diving bell, inspecting its construction and viability, he was diving. He wanted another shot at *F-4*. The Navy came up with a pressurized dive suit for him and he wore it down to 175 feet. He came up sputtering. "No more of that for me," he declared. "I'm going down with just the helmet. The same as I've been doing. I can't move in that thing, and the pressure gets worse than when I had nothing to protect me."

Transporting C.W. Parks's innovative diving bell from Honolulu Iron Works to the Naval Dock for testing, just one week after F-4 failed to surface (The Pacific Commercial Advertiser, March 31, 1915)

Jack's diving gear had been upgraded with a telephone headset for commu-

Jack Agraz surfacing from a deep dive in Hawaii (Agraz Family Collection)

nication with the surface. Lt. Smith was talking with Jack on one dive until Jack went beyond the 100 foot mark. Then Jack couldn't hear Smith anymore, and he thought Smith couldn't hear him, either. Jack started singing in Spanish and whistling to himself inside the dive helmet as he descended. Smith was surprised but laughed at the serenade he was getting over the receiver.

The water appeared clearer than it had on Jack's deeper dive 10 days before. From his vantage point at the deepest part of his descent as he followed the two wires down into the depths, Jack caught a glimpse of an object far below his position. It was just a hazy dark outline. It had to be F-4. It was pointed on an east-west heading, on the sea floor. He could make out the shape of the stern but couldn't see any of the cables that had snared the boat. It was a ghostly sight. Twenty-one men that he knew personally and saw on a daily basis were entombed inside that hull.

When Jack got back to the surface he was already planning his next dive. It would be down 230 feet, then maybe 280. He thought that was doable. When Charles Smith was told of Jack's plans, he shook his head and said he wouldn't let Jack risk his life.

That same day, the Navy Department in Washington DC wired Lt. Smith and ordered him to stop testing the diving bell. They had the top five Navy deep-sea divers aboard the *Maryland* headed for Honolulu.

Ninety-year-old Mrs. Nellie McDonald sat in the breakfast parlor in Denver reading her newspaper about F-4 disappearing off the coast of Honolulu. It was the headline story in Denver and just about every other city and town in America that day. Nellie read every inch of it. She was shocked by the fate of all those young men. She read down the list of all the sailors who were aboard the missing boat. Something about reading their names, seeing their hometowns and their ranks of accomplishment in the Navy made it more personal. She stopped abruptly at one name. A chill swept over her. There it was, a young sailor from

Tacoma, Washington, Clark G. Buck, gunner's mate second class. He was on F-4.

He was Nellie's nephew.

She put the paper down and stared out the window, remembering Clark G. Buck Sr. and her nephew, Clark G. Buck Jr., and the dark dream she'd had the night before. She was shaken but reflective as all the pieces came together that morning sitting in her breakfast parlor. After some thought, she got a piece of paper from a drawer and began a letter to her sister-in-law in Tacoma.

Nellie first reminisced in the letter to Amanda, going back 47 years to 1868, when a young Clark G. Buck boarded a whaling ship in Newport, Rhode Island. The ship was bound for the Pacific. It was going to be a real adventure. Clark would sail with a crew of men around Cape Horn and up the coast of South America to the Hawaiian Islands. The storms of Tierra del Fuego and Drake Passage were legendary. Seas could reach 100 feet in that part of the world, with hurricane-force winds and water at near-freezing temperatures in places.

The voyage would take months, sailing the prevailing winds and currents all day and night traversing 15,000 nautical miles. On the clear nights the stars would spread from horizon to horizon in all directions from the ship. Clark G. Buck finally made it to Honolulu. He wrote his family a letter from the Hawaiian seaport in 1868 describing his journey just before they set sail for another leg of the whaling expedition. That was the last they ever heard from him. His whaling ship foundered off the coast of Honolulu Harbor in heavy seas and went down with all hands aboard. The wreckage was somewhere on the seafloor nearby F-4.

What struck Nellie was that Clark Buck Jr.'s passage aboard F-4 had a similar point of origin as his uncle's departure in 1868 on the whaler. Gunner's Mate Buck shipped out from the Naval Station at Newport, Rhode Island, just as the uncle for whom he was named. But Clark Buck Jr.'s journey to the Pacific began with an overland rail journey to San Francisco and then by ship to Honolulu, where he joined F-4's crew. Being in the Navy, it made for a good story that you were named for an uncle who went down with his ship hunting for whales in the Pacific Ocean half a century before. And just like his namesake, Clark Jr. wrote his last letter home from Honolulu, just before departing on *F-4*.

Amanda Schrog sat stunned in Tacoma reading her sister-in-law Nellie's letter. She hadn't even thought about family history when she heard about the fate of *F-4*. She was just hoping that Clark, her son, would be rescued. That was her only thought. *He's going to be okay.*

Amanda continued to read, with a foreboding sense of the supernatural. Nellie wrote that the night before *F-4* disappeared, she dreamed of seeing a submarine go down. The vision of the sinking was so clear that Nellie could see one man pacing alone inside the submarine while all the other crewmen lay about motionless on the deck. The next morning, she read about the missing *F-4*.

Amanda didn't know what to think about the letter. She was still waiting to hear from the United States Navy about her son being aboard the *F-4*, trapped under 300 feet of water. They had said nothing to her. All of her information was coming from the newspapers.

In an interview with a newspaper reporter, Amanda said, "George had never learned to drink, swear, smoke or chew. He was a member of the YMCA and carried his card with him wherever he went. It was his intention to make the Navy his life work." Amanda was solemn about the whole event. "I do not expect to hear anything official," she said, "until the vessel is raised. Of course, I have to give up hope. But he was a sailor and he died at his post."

H-3

FROM BAD TO WORSE

Conditions in *H-3*'s control room were deteriorating by the minute. The captain ordered a machinist's mate to bleed air into the control room from the high-pressure air banks. The quality of compressed air in the tanks was not good. It was never intended to be used for the crew. It was to power air systems in the sub. When the air entered the sealed compartment with the hatch closed, it boosted atmospheric pressure until everyone could feel the force in their ears, inside their head and as extra pressure on their attempts to breathe. Then, when the hatch was thrown open, the pressurized air would burst out of the sealed compartment. But the worst air, the contaminated chlorine air and the carbon dioxide, was heavier than oxygen and would settle at the bottom of the boat and the walking decks where the crew were jammed together. They had no blowers to force the bad air outside.

Toad Blabon suffered more than anyone. The pain in his hand and arm burned intensely. The lack of fresh air added to his agony. The crew knew he was suffering and were trying to keep his hand elevated, keep him from shivering violently and going into shock. Tom Scarving had his arms around Toad so he wouldn't be thrown around by the rolling submarine. Toad laid there in the control room against Scarving and grinned through a locked jaw. He didn't say many words. He was just riding the pain out, feeling the effects of the whiskey.

Chief Electrician Jim Anderson wasn't feeling very well, either. His hand was severely injured, likely broken, when the hatch cover slammed down, but he hadn't lost any fingers. He remained wedged into the control room with the others, hoping for those occasional wisps of fresh air when somebody could open the upper hatch for a few minutes.

Anderson was in charge of the gyrocompass. Now that he was injured, Duane Stewart wondered what would happen to the gyro. Duane recalled listening to Jim talk about that spinning device. Duane never knew if Jim made operating it sound more dangerous than it really was just to make sure crew members wouldn't fiddle with it or get too close to it. Jim had said if the flywheel ever went haywire, like from excessive rolling, then watch out: It might "tumble" as Jim would describe it. It could explode like a ball of shrapnel if it came off its axis.

Stewart figured if the gyro ever did go berserk, they'd be done for. It had still been spinning madly when he and Jack had gone to the forward battery compartment to send the SOS earlier in the day. Underneath it all, Duane knew that fear was making him imagine the things that could go wrong, like chlorine gas and gyrocompasses.

Gyroscopes were a new navigational technology. Elmer A. Sperry, an American engineer, introduced the gyrocompass in 1910

Elmer A. Sperry at the helm of a ship using his gyrocompass invention (Hagley Museum and Library via MarineLink.com)

to replace magnetic compasses, which were useless around concentrations of steel and electricity in submarines and airplanes. Sperry's gyrocompass changed the navigation game as fleets all over the world adopted the technology. The F-boats and H-boats were some of the first US Navy vessels to get the gyrocompass.

The device captured the earth's axis rotation and established a true north bearing from any point above or below the surface, as opposed to the traditional magnetic compass with its five types of correction that was slave to the influence of steel and electric fields. Although the gyro was a vast improvement for indicating a vessel's true direction of travel, it provided no indication of true position.

The captain called the torpedo room on the voice tube. The four gunner's mates there reported the air was good — no smoke or gas — better than all the other compartments in the boat. Bogusch asked if they could handle four more crewmen. They confirmed. The skipper looked around at the densely huddled men holding onto frameworks. He pointed to Nick Carter, Duane Stewart and two other sailors: "You men I've pointed out. Prepare to go to the torpedo compartment in twos." The chief would lead them through the boat.

Jack Agraz, Duane Stewart, and Nick Carter placed wet rags over their noses, then opened the steel door into the forward battery compartment. Nick worked with Duane on the sub's electrical systems. He was as woozy as Duane was at that point, causing him to slur his Oklahoma accent. Conditions in the forward battery compartment remained awful. The narrow passage between the bunks was still jammed with mattresses, dirty boxes, and buckets. The ventilators remained closed, concentrating the smoke and fumes in the terrible air. They had to feel their way through. There was just one dim overhead light in that compartment and one light by the door to the torpedo room. Duane hung onto bunk frames with one hand and clamped the rag over his nose with the other. He tried not to breathe. He and Nick stumbled along behind Jack.

Duane hated going into the forward battery compartment again. He'd already spent 15 minutes in there with Jack, sending the SOS. Duane was concerned what might happen to the gyrocompass if it was subjected to excessive rolls, like the ones H-3 had been enduring. He was worried about everything at that point. The sub at times had pitched more than 60 degrees and come down hard on the conning tower. Gyrocompasses seemed to have a mind of their own. Duane was leery of the thing, though as he stepped past it, he noticed it had stopped spinning.

When Jack, Duane, and Nick reached the torpedo compartment door, Jack banged on it with a spanner. One of the gunner's mates inside the torpedo room unsealed the eight "dogs" that secured the door into the frame, then swung it open. They all felt relief the moment they stepped inside. The air was almost clean. No smoke or gas.

Duane was pleased at first, but then he started to look around. There was no way out of this compartment except the way they had come in or through two battened-down overhead hatches, exposed to the outer deck, which was awash under the breakers. As a last resort, they could crawl out the torpedo tubes if they had to, but that was a dreadful thought. The only air they had were a couple of reserve banks of compressed air that had not been used yet. The ventilator had been shut to keep the seawater out.

Jack went back to the control room and brought the other two crewmen forward. One of them was Batlin Wyatt, who had landed in all the eggs earlier. He was glad to get into the torpedo compartment and out of the control room. Eight men were now in the torpedo room, each hanging on against the rolling and pounding. But no one was fighting for a good breath of air at least. Jack looked around and told the newcomers to find a good place to brace against the rolling, to make themselves as comfortable as possible.

The torpedo tubes came back into the compartment a good six feet, leaving room between them and the hull on both sides, as well as a space between the upper two tubes and the overhead. That space formed a kind of V. Jack suggested placing two men between the tubes and the hull, two on each side of the tubes and one man up in the V. Then he went back into the forward battery compartment to get mattresses. They were soaked with saltwater and acid from the batteries but were better than the steel deck.

Example of the torpedo room (F-2) (PigBoats.COM, courtesy of Mike Dilley)

The men wedged on top of the horizontal storage lockers and torpedo loading skids didn't need the mattresses. Duane and a couple of the guys on the skids had lashed themselves to the inner hull braces. They had taken lines from the block and tackle used to load the torpedoes into the tubes. Duane had tied those knots tightly around himself. The lines caused a lot of chafing, but it was better than having to hang on at all times. They felt like hostages, tied up and captive under the weight of water.

On his next trip to the forward torpedo compartment, Jack told everybody that they had secured a line aboard the sub with the surf rescue team on the beach. Using a Lyle gun, the rescuers had shot a line out to *H-3*. Jack was soaked, he'd been out on deck securing the line. The good news cheered up the men, and Duane felt more hopeful. But the air quality in the torpedo compartment had deteriorated significantly. With eight crewmen in there, carbon dioxide was building up, with nowhere to escape. Oxygen levels were getting low, and the hatches were still locked down. Duane, Nick, and the others had trouble staying awake, even with the hope of getting out of the sub.

Then Jack came back and said the line to the sub had snapped — but that the seas were easing up and rescuers were on their way.

At least that's what Bobby Burns had told Jack after his signal flag semaphore exchanges with the kid on the beach. What Jack didn't say was that with the waves still breaking over the sub, the surfboat probably couldn't get within 10 feet of *H-3*'s deck. Duane just hung on and thought about that surfboat. He thought it would be like having a large rescue ship alongside the sub. Duane's mind felt like it was floating, filled with carbon dioxide and battery gas. Maybe he could just walk down the gang plank and step aboard the surfboat. Then go to shore. He was hallucinating.

Duane, Nick Carter, Batlin Wyatt, and the other crewmen in the torpedo room tried to stay conscious, strapped in between the unarmed torpedoes. Gunner's Mates LK Johnson, L. Peterson and W. Robinson had been there since the beginning of the ordeal. Toad Blabon and Bobby Burns were the other two gunner's mates under Jack Agraz. They'd been in the conning tower the entire time, while Jack was working through the whole boat.

The unarmed torpedoes still bothered Duane. Even though they were just practice weapons, each of the four steel and bronze torpedoes weighed more than 1,600 pounds and were almost 18 feet long. If one of those got out of its chocks, it could be as destructive and deadly as a battering ram.

As larger breakers hit the sub, the boat sometimes rolled over completely onto its side, forcing the men to change grips and alter positions, even Duane and the others who were lashed onto the framing. Sometimes they'd lose a grip and fall into one another. The bruises were compounding. When hard over on the sub's side, two torpedoes were suspended above them at an angle. Their entire 1,600 pounds of destructive potential was restrained just by the metal straps. Duane doubted those straps were designed to be used upside down.

The men had been tumbling around up forward for a few hours when Jack made one of his trips to see how they were holding up. He told them the fog had lifted slightly, that he could see the beach and plenty of people. And that he had seen a surfboat being trundled up the beach by horses.

But the tide was still too high to allow a person to stand on the conning tower. As a parting shot, Jack joked, "It's chow time, but there won't be any for a while." Duane slumped back. No fresh water and no food. He began wondering if the extra five dollars was worth it and the extra one dollar per dive when you came up safely. He wondered if they would get any dive money for this day.

The air quality continued to deteriorate in the torpedo room as the levels of carbon dioxide increased. Duane, Nick, Batlin, and the others became increasingly sleepy. They struggled to stay awake as the oxygen was being depleted. One of the gunner's mates valved in air from the pressurized tanks now and then. But it did little good. Each time he'd crack the valve and let a flood of air into the sealed compartment it drove up the air pressure and added to the sense of delirium. Duane just wanted to sleep. But Jack kept reappearing to keep watch on everybody.

Duane wondered how Jack could keep up his pace. Jack had never hinted at being concerned about the outcome of the situation. Duane was giving up. He didn't understand how Jack kept going. Jack told Duane that keeping his men safe motivated him.

Everybody knew Jack loved being in the submarine service. He liked the close quarters and spartan style of the tightly knit crews. There was discipline but less formality than on the surface ships. He liked the experimental nature of the sub work and the sense of danger that enveloped submariners as they descended together into the depths. He liked to dive and had a friendly disdain for the surface ships and their formalities of station and command.

Jack also maintained a subtle sense of humor about situations around him. Everything had a calculated outcome in his mind. David Masters, an early 20th century salvage diver and author later recalled an incident that occurred when Jack was still overseas in the Philippines, in the Asiatic Fleet, before Jack had transferred to the Hawaiian submarine flotilla. He wrote that Jack was diving on an underwater project for the Navy with another diver. They were going down every day to the sea floor to work on the footings of a dock. The water was a little murky, so the surface support crews couldn't see the divers clearly.

Jack and his fellow diver thought it would be funny to switch helmets and gear underwater and shock their support crews when they were pulled up. The two divers rehearsed the exchange on dry land so that they would know exactly what to do. When the day came, the two were working 60 feet below the surface in close proximity. They stirred up the mud by walking toward each other, further clouding the water.

Both divers grinned at each other through their glass portals. Jack gave the signal and took off his helmet, holding his breath, handing the helmet to his counterpart. The second diver removed his dive helmet, took Jack's helmet but fumbled the transfer, dropping the helmet intended for Jack into a thick seabed of mud. Jack stood there 60 feet underwater considering what to do next — bolt for the surface or try to recover the helmet from the mud?

The other diver was momentarily paralyzed by his mistake, but Jack paused only a second. He reached down into the mud and recovered the helmet, brushing the mud away while still holding his breath, then placed the helmet back over his head and let the air flow slowly purge the helmet of seawater until he could resume breathing. Then they switched tether and signal lines.

When Jack and his fellow diver returned to the surface the dive crews were visibly shocked at uncovering a different diver than they had sent down. That joke became legendary.

F-4

FDR AND THOMAS EDISON WEIGH IN

After *F-4* disappeared, Assistant Secretary of the Navy Franklin D. Roosevelt was in San Pedro Harbor near Los Angeles. Unannounced, he went to the Navy submarine station and ordered the skipper of the *USS K-7*, a more advanced submarine than the F-boats, to take him to the bottom of San Pedro Bay. The *K-7* captain took FDR down 60 feet for half an hour, explaining the operations of the sub. Roosevelt believed that the submarine would be an important part of the Navy's future. He wanted to demonstrate his support to all the crews involved and send a message to the nation. He pledged to boost spending for new submarine designs and safety features.

FDR's passion for submarines may have been influenced by his distant cousin, former President Teddy Roosevelt. Teddy Roosevelt was the first American president to descend in a submarine. Always an adventurer, Teddy Roosevelt rode one of the original Plunger Class subs, later called A-boats, down into the depths of Oyster Bay near Long Island, New York, in 1905. He spent almost an hour at the bottom of the bay after taking the helm of the vessel.

A few months after his underwater adventure, realizing the risks inherent in these new vessels, he issued an executive order to raise submariners' pay by $5 a month and add an extra $1 per dive, up to 15 dives per month. Like FDR, Teddy Roosevelt had also been Assistant Secretary of the Navy, under President William McKinley, and wrote a popular and well respected historical work entitled *The Naval War of 1812.*

An A-boat, Plunger Class. In 1905, Teddy Roosevelt was the first US President to go down in a submarine, riding a plunger class boat into the depths of Oyster Bay, New York (PigBoats.COM)

In the days and weeks following the realization that the crew had been lost, Franklin Roosevelt as well as President Woodrow Wilson and Secretary of the Navy Josephus Daniels spoke to major news syndicates and political gatherings about the F-4 event and their resolve to find out what happened: Why had the US Navy lost its first submarine and an entire crew? The findings could save lives in the future and serve to advance the safety and design of later submarines.

FDR and Thomas Edison (Library of Congress)

The loss of F-4 had provoked an outpouring of communications and hope all across the country and around the world for rescuing the crew. Leaders in Japan, Germany, and other nations sent condolences. Germany's Kaiser Wilhelm II sent his sympathies for the crew and their relatives and families, even though his U-Boats were attacking and sinking unprecedented numbers of mostly commercial ships off the European coast that year — including, a few months later, the *Lusitania*. When F-4 disappeared, the Japanese Navy cruiser *Izumo* was anchored in Honolulu Harbor on a special mission. They were already involved in the Great War and hunting German ships. Japanese Adm. Moriyama was aboard the *Izumo* on that trip. Adm. Moriyama collected $100 from his ship's crew and presented it to Adm. Moore for the F-4 families.

Submarines were an emerging technology to reckon with worldwide. They had changed the rules of naval engagement, and many people did not know what to make of them. In 1915, some traditionalists viewed German U-Boats as sea pirates, renegades, or a wolf pack, stalking unprotected merchant ships, surfacing, releasing chaos, then disappearing beneath the sea. They saw no honor in it and viewed the undersea warriors as marauders.

As more articles appeared about the F-4 disaster, citizens, politicians, and the press were asking the Navy more and more questions. Secretary of the Navy Daniels just flatly said F-4 had been in good condition. "If there was anything wrong with F-4," he said, "no one except her officers knew it."

Being flotilla commander and head of the recovery effort, Lt. Smith was on the front line of questions. When he was shown Ede's letter and other statements by a Hawaiian newspaper reporter, he was matter of fact. He called the statements "Tommyrot ... whenever an accident like this occurs. There always are persons who arise and say that they knew something was wrong all the time or that they had dreams and premonitions."

The reporter pushed Smith about the boat's recent engine replacement and the hydrogen battery explosion. The reporter was asking simple questions about complex issues and systems that he had little technical comprehension of, so Smith kept his answers brief and to the point. He wasn't going to speculate since the Navy had no idea what had happened aboard F-4 at that point.

After hearing about air pressure limitations, the reporter probed the lieutenant with a question about how much air F-4 had onboard. "No one knows how much air [it] had," Smith responded. He made it clear that it was the captain who was responsible for maintaining adequate air reserves. "I presume [they] went out without a full supply, as [it] was pumping before [the sub] left the harbor. However, [they] should have always had enough to relieve [it] of water in [the] submerging tanks. That doesn't require much. One bank would be enough; and all submarines are supposed to have one full bank at all times."

The F-boats had five air pressure banks that could generate more than 2,000 pounds per square inch of pressure. The truth was nobody really knew how much air F-4 had in its tanks before diving that day.

Edison's submarine and mining lamps battery plant in 1915 (Thomas Edison National Historical Park)

Adding to the mounting public relations storm the Navy was facing, Thomas Edison, an American folk hero by 1915, stepped into the F-4 fray and claimed that the crew had been killed by chlorine gas. Most Americans equated Edison with the lightbulb, but few knew he was also a battery expert. He'd spent years testing new battery technologies. On his alkaline battery project alone, he conducted thousands of experiments over five years leading up to 1915. Edison was granted 147 battery patents. His original goal was to power electric automobiles. He believed that would be the future. But combustion engines and Henry Ford's assembly lines quashed that idea. Now Edison wanted to power submarines.

Edison was interviewed at his West Orange, New Jersey, laboratory on March 26, the day after F-4 disappeared and offered a very adamant, if biased, view of what happened off the Honolulu coast. "What I cannot understand," Edison said, "is why they allow a submarine to hold tons of sulphuric acid."

Edison derisively pointed out that sulphuric acid containment cells in the submarine batteries were lined with corrosion-vulnerable lead and rubber and surrounded by ballast tanks that flood with seawater to submerge the boat. He believed that the acid from the cells had leaked through the rubber lining and battery tank metal, attacking the steel plating of the ballast tanks, weakening them.

"When the seawater is admitted to the main ballast tanks, the weakened [metal] gives way and the water floods the battery tank," he claimed. "When the seawater mixes with sulphuric acid in a lead battery, hydrochloric acid is formed. This attacks the lead plates and creates chlorine gas. ... I can picture those poor fellows — first stupefied by chlorine gas — making vain efforts to take the steps that could raise their ship, but in a few minutes they are helpless."

In the interview, Edison pulled no punches and went on to quote Secretary of the Navy Daniels, who had outlined a similar scenario prior to *F-4* going down when he appeared before the Naval Committee of the House of Representatives to describe the biggest technological challenge facing submarines. In his testimony, Daniels said the sulphuric acid-based storage batteries posed the biggest risks.

In his interview, after criticizing the sub's battery technology, Edison plugged his own alkaline submarine battery as superior, even though it was much more expensive. "It costs much more because nickel is many times more [expensive] than lead," he said. "But the battery lasts longer, is more efficient and better in every respect." His biggest claim was that it eliminated the risk of chlorine gas. But even Edison's battery would later prove to have a fatal flaw for submarines.

Thomas Edison and Jimmy Howell weren't the only ones speculating on what happened aboard *F-4*. The *New York Tribune* ran an article on April 11, 1915, after interviewing an "informant" who claimed he'd spent seven years on subs and now worked for a submarine construction firm. The informant wouldn't give his real name.

He claimed that the inner shell of the diesel fuel tanks had collapsed after the sub hit a reef, at 270 feet below the surface. He said the outer shell of the sub was five times stronger than the inner fuel tank walls that were made from weaker metal. Once these "inside plates" were exposed to the tremendous deepwater pressure, they collapsed.

Piling on his dubious assertions, he declared, "I cannot explain why commander Ede was at such a depth. He may have been trying to set a deep sea [dive] record." He claimed the crew would have lived for "many hours after the disaster" and that the sub's log would prove that.

Nobody had even been down to the F-4 at this point. Nobody knew anything. But that didn't stop newspapers from publishing "expert" accounts of what might have taken place aboard the sub. That sold newspapers.

In New York City's Brooklyn Navy Yard, Stephen Drellishak's wedding plans were about to be interrupted. Drellishak was one of the Navy's top deep-sea divers and an ex-boat racer. He'd just set a world record on November 3, 1914, for a pressurized-suit deep-sea dive, at 274 feet. Drellishak and his fellow divers had been following the F-4 events in newspapers and Navy briefings. Drellishak and his fiancée, Alice, had made plans a year earlier to get married and had set the date for the first week in April. That's when Drellishak got the call from the Navy Department. They wanted him in Honolulu immediately, at the request of Rear Adm. Moore.

The Navy wouldn't wait for Drellishak's wedding plans. This was a secret directive. The Navy didn't want the world to know that they were sending their top divers into the Pacific Ocean to a depth never before attained. So, the couple went down to the local borough hall and were married in a civil ceremony on the spot, no frills. Then Drellishak boarded a fast train to San Francisco with his fellow divers and a few tons of cutting-edge, deep-sea diving equipment. They were going to Honolulu. The five Navy divers sped across the country to meet the armored cruiser *Maryland* in San Francisco Bay.

Alice was left behind to cancel all the wedding invitations and plans that she and Drellishak had made over the past year. Her explanations to friends created consternation for the Navy when they ended up in the newspapers, revealing that the top Navy divers were going after *F-4*. The secret was out.

Two weeks after *F-4* disappeared, the *Maryland* glided into Honolulu Harbor to deliver its cargo — the top five US Navy deep-sea diving specialists and their support crew. They'd arrived from their East Coast base, outfitted with the latest dive technology, including pressurized suits, power-driven compressors, and a new reducing valve that would allow for deeper, longer dives. The Navy intended to bring *F-4* to the surface against all odds.

The divers' helmets were equipped with two-way telephones, replacing the primitive diver hand signal-line that Agraz and Evans had been using on their initial dives for *F-4*. And for extra safety, a large, multi-ton steel decompression chamber — like a tiny sleeping compartment on a train — had been brought aboard the *Maryland* as well. The atmospheric chamber was outfitted with gauges and pressure tanks, lights, heater, telephone, a couple mattresses, sheets, pillows, and blankets.

If the specialized Navy divers could reach *F-4* at 300 feet, it would establish a new world record.

A few months before, Chief Gunner's Mate Stephen Drellishak had tested the new technologies and descended to 274 feet without a problem. He walked around for about 10 minutes on the sea bottom in Long Island Sound and said he could have gone deeper except the seabed was in his way. The five Navy divers were confident they would reach the *F-4* with no problem.

Drellishak's dive in Long Island Sound had set a new world record, beating the previous British Navy world record by 65 feet. Jack Agraz's Honolulu dive had eclipsed the British naval record as well and set a world dive record without pressurized gear at 215 feet. He'd done it on sheer determination.

A large force of supporting personnel prepared the dredge *Gaylord* for the renewed dive operations by April 14. A team of some 40 electricians, carpenters, steamfitters and mechanics readied the dive infrastructure and support equipment for the five specialized Navy divers, including the heavy steel decompression chamber, air tanks, and underwater lighting for night work. The five divers — Chief Gunner's Mates George Stillson, Frank Crilley, Stephen Drellishak, Fred Nielson, and William Loughman — prepared themselves to make history.

The diving operation was being directed by Stillson, who was in charge of the Navy diving corps, and monitored by Dr. G.R. French, Chief Medical Advisor. Stillson would remain on the surface at all times and not be doing any actual dives. That would be left to the other four divers. Stillson would direct all diving operations below the surface. Dr. French would manage the divers above the surface, monitoring their physical conditions as they worked at historic depths.

The scale of the operation had expanded dramatically in just two weeks since F-4 disappeared. Besides Lt. Smith's overall responsibility for the submarine's recovery, Naval Constructor Julius Furer was outfitting the two 600-ton pontoon scows that would be used to support the submarine once the boat was rigged by divers and ready to be lifted.

Before commencing actual dives, Drellishak and Crilley decided they wanted to test the decompression chamber on the deck of the *Gaylord*. Stillson and his technical crews had worked all day and into the night to ready the chamber.

Stillson opened the heavy steel door and Drellishak and Crilley stepped inside. The door was shut and clamped down hard. Stillson opened the chamber air valves, which emitted a loud rush of air. The air was being drawn from a dozen torpedo air flasks strapped to the *Gaylord*'s deck, each containing over 2,000 pounds per square inch of air pressure.

Stillson and French studied the external air pressure gauge that recorded the atmospheric pressure inside the chamber. It simulated deep water pressures. The needle on the mechanical gauge rose slowly at first, then accelerated. It hit 50 pounds then 75. Stillson leveled the pressure off when the needle registered 105 pounds on the dial, the equivalent of being 235 feet beneath the sea.

Drellishak and Crilley talked to Stillson by telephone from inside the chamber and said the air was sweet and pure but that the chamber was intensely hot. Crilley's voice sounded different when the air pressure reached its maximum level. It was a couple octaves higher. The two divers sat in the pressurized chamber for about 20 minutes, then the pressure was gradually reduced in stages, five pounds at a time.

Diver, believed to be Drellishak, readied to descend 300 feet to F-4. (Agraz Family Collection, Vallejo Naval & Historical Museum)

Rear Adm. Moore and Lt. Smith monitored the dive rehearsal from the deck of the *Maryland*, talking with Dr. French. Aware of the public perception, Moore asked French to order the divers to emerge with big smiles. The press were surrounding the site.

When the door was finally opened, Drellishak stepped out with the telephone in one hand and a screwdriver in the other. He was busy taking the phone apart. Crilley hopped out as well with a broad grin. His voice was back to normal. Neither diver felt any different than when they'd gone into the chamber. Drellishak lit a cigarette and proceeded to work on the phone receiver. Crilley was asked to splice a tube together. Dr. French watched the divers for five minutes, then inspected both for signs of the bends — decompression sickness. There

US Navy deep-sea divers conducting deep-sea diving tests, November 1914 in Long Island Sound, five months before F-4 disappeared; Left to right – GMC Fred Nielson, GMC Frank Crilley in dive suit and GMC Stephen Drellishak (Naval History & Heritage Command photo, courtesy of Jim Kazalis)

were none. They were ready to go deep.

Diving in rotation, Drellishak, Crilley, Nielsen, and Loughman would go down one at a time to work for 20-minute intervals, then return to the surface. It would be a long, tedious process. Despite the divers' optimism and eagerness, there were great physical and technical difficulties to overcome.

Frank Crilley was the first diver down the next morning, on April 14, 1915. He descended very fast, holding onto a wire from the *Gaylord*. As he glided past the 250-foot mark, he could see the ghostly *F-4* lying on its starboard side below him on the seafloor. Its bow was pointed toward shore as though it had been headed back to port. It was the first visual contact of the sub since Jack Agraz saw its vague shape far below him the previous week.

Frank knew that 21 men were sealed inside the vessel, just a few feet from where he stood on the sandy seafloor. He banged a metal tool against the hull, and his initial sense was that the sub had filled with seawater.

Crilley had reached the bottom at 305 feet in just five minutes. The deepest he'd ever been before that dive was 136 feet. When his dive was completed, it set a new world dive record. The crew above had spooled out more than 300 feet of line and hose to give Crilley plenty of slack for his movements.

With his cumbersome pressurized suit, heavy diving boots, and thick steel helmet, Crilley trudged along the sea floor to survey *F-4*. Using his new telephone, he asked to be hoisted onto the sub's deck. He walked on the boat's steel plate surface. He didn't talk much to the dive crew above. Stillson told him to save his energy for the return to the surface.

As Crilley peered through his helmet glass, the sea floor appeared smooth, like a white-sand beach. "When you look up, the water is a light green, but when you look down it's a deep clear blue," he said. "There are no weeds down here, no vegetation, no fish, nothing but white sand like the slope of a hill."

He saw two snare cables wrapped around the sub, testament to the relentless efforts by the *Navajo*'s skipper, Boatswain Metiers and his crew. Crilley did not report on any visual damages to *F-4* on that first dive. But he did observe that just beyond the stern, the ocean floor disappeared over an underwater cliff into an impenetrable void. The sub had landed at the edge of an abyss, the bow pointing toward the harbor. Had *F-4* missed that landing point and drifted down even 100 feet toward the open sea, it would have disappeared forever.

Crilley stayed on the bottom about 15 minutes then started for the surface. Dive director Stillson didn't want his divers in the deep water more than 15 to 20 minutes at a time because of the complex and lengthy decompression tactics required to return to the surface. The return trip took an hour and 45 minutes. The pace was deliberately slower to avoid developing the bends. Within the last 30 feet, Crilley waited 45 minutes to equalize the pressure.

He methodically climbed the Jacob's ladder that dangled 90 feet down into the sea from the *Gaylord*'s deck. He paused 15 minutes for every 10-foot section up the final three sections of the rope ladder. When he finally made it to the surface and climbed out of his pressurized suit, he felt good. But he was very cold. He could barely grasp a pencil to jot down his notes.

H-3

Conflict on the Beach

The unceasing roar of breakers on the Samoa Beach thundered along the surf line where *H-3* had run aground. Not enough of the boat protruded above water to permit rescuers to board. Seas engulfed the sub, sweeping the decks and crashing over the conning tower. The rescue effort was turning into a waiting game.

Station Keeper Lawrence Ellison studied the wave sets, the tide and the motion of the sub. The tide was rising, and Ellison could see the boat was being shoved toward shore. It had been riding higher in the seas since the captain had blown the ballast tanks. But there was little chance of rescue until the sub could be driven further onto shore and the tide shifted. Full ebb tide would leave more of the boat exposed, but that was still hours away, well into the night. Ellison would have to time the rescue to the beginning of the flood tide, just before sunset.

In preparation for the rescue, the life-saving crew readied the breeches buoy.

This was not the type of rescue that Ellison and his crew were used to. And there was no telling what the chlorine gas situation would be aboard. Ellison thought it might even be explosive. He tried to imagine a few thousand pounds of toxic chemicals in the midst of a rescue from a sealed vessel.

News of the submarine wreck had spread fast in Eureka, Arcata, Ferndale and other communities near the bay. The large crowd gathering on the beach had begun to exceed one thousand. Some people in the crowd became filled with impatient anxiety seeing the sub awash and tossed about in the breakers while the life-saving crew appeared to be standing around waiting, doing nothing.

Crowds gathered to witness H-3 trapped in the surf. This photo was taken after the sub washed closer to shore (Photograph by Emma Freeman, courtesy of Humboldt Bay Maritime Museum)

"There are men dying in that submarine and the lifesavers are just watching," was the word being spread in the crowd. Somebody shouted they should take the boat away from Ellison. But other people stood by the skipper and persuaded their fellow citizens to let the skipper make the call. Ellison knew his business. He could see there was no easy way to get the crew out, but he had a plan to take action when the flood tide started to turn.

To the south of his position, Ellison could see the *Cheyenne's* crew making their way up the beach. William Howe was out in front, followed by his officers, scores of crewmen plus medical staff. It had been a tiring, three-hour march across the dunes to the beach. The crew carried medical supplies, tents, clothes, food and other camp necessities.

As the crew of the *Cheyenne* made their approach, they could see an enormous crowd of citizens milling about on the beach. The crowd was growing by the hour. Ferries and private launches were carrying hundreds of people across the bay with every run. In the normally bustling Victorian farm town of Ferndale, 20 miles away, its main street was deserted. Shops had closed. Everybody wanted to see the spectacle.

Lt. Howe and his entourage of officers and sailors moved down the beach toward the crowd. He could see that the Coast Guard rescue crew from the Humboldt Bay Station was already on site with a surf rescue boat on the beach. But the rescuers appeared to be standing idle, looking out to sea, watching the sub. Like some of the critical onlookers, Howe's blood began to boil.

Howe was agitated the moment he arrived on the rescue scene. From his view, Ellison and his men appeared to be spectators, watching the sub getting hammered. Nobody was lifting a finger or moving gear to get a rescue underway. *H-3* had been in the breakers for over six hours. The crew undoubtedly had been and was continuing to be pummeled.

Howe got into an argument with Ellison right away. Howe felt the crew was in danger from chlorine gas and gear breaking loose inside the hull. He was worried about his men. He argued with the life-saving officer, and even suggested taking the rescue boat into the surf with a regular Navy crew. He was on the verge of taking the boat away from Ellison and running his own rescue. He had plenty of Navy men with him who were eager to go.

Aboard *H-3*, it was becoming impossible for Duane Stewart and the others to remain awake.

It was Jack Agraz again, Duane remembered. He slapped and punched them, going from man to man, exhorting them: "Come on, Sailor... keep awake. Keep awake and live!"

As soon as he would leave, they'd drop off again, holding onto whatever they could get a grip on subconsciously. Although the men liked having Jack visit them to make them stay awake, sleeping was easier than fighting it. They had no idea what time it was. They'd been sealed inside the sub for hours, with breakers rocking the sub every 15-20 seconds.

On one of his trips, Agraz told everybody the tide was rising and that was the reason they weren't pounding so badly. But the seas were still breaking over the boat. They couldn't open the conning tower hatch. When the skipper had ordered the ballast tanks blown, the sub had begun working its way toward the beach.

Coast Guard station commander Lawrence Ellison and his Humboldt Bay lifesaving crew; the boy is Lawrence's son; Werner Sweins is to the right of Ellison and Gustaf Christensen next to Sweins with his hand on Sweins's shoulder; then center to right, Tom McDonald, Ole Torgersen, Johan Knudsen and Paul Dichell. One crew member missing from photo (US Naval Historical Center Photograph, courtesy of Humboldt County Historical Society & Humboldt Bay Maritime Museum)

The next time Duane was slapped awake he noticed an increase in population up forward. The captain had sent several more men from the control room. Conditions there had become intolerable in that confined space with wisps of chlorine gas and carbon dioxide settling heavily at the bottom of the boat. They were trying to make Toad Blabon and Jim Anderson more comfortable.

The additional men created a problem. Duane had had enough rope chafing across his arms and chest so he gave up his position and his harnessing ropes to Nick Carter. Not that he had anything against Nick, Duane laughed to himself. He then squeezed in alongside Batlin Wyatt and one of the torpedo tubes. Here it was a bit easier. But still he couldn't get comfortable. So he took a place on the deck where he had a rail for his feet, and some pipes behind him to hold onto. He was pretty secure then and didn't slide around too much.

With more crew members up forward, it became necessary to valve in more air until they had used up both bottles. The added air pressure in the sealed compartment momentarily affected Duane's equilibrium. It made him feel dizzy and claustrophobic. Then they had to rely only on air from the ventilator, which somebody would open and shut when breakers weren't going over the outer deck. That relieved the air pressure build up.

Along with the other sailors on the horizontal lockers and torpedo skids, Duane tried to make himself stable, but he kept an eye on the torpedoes when he was awake. They made him nervous. Every time the sub rolled hard to port or starboard, the "one-ton fish" would lift and strain against those straps and then clang back into place when the sub settled on a more even keel. It didn't look good to Duane and the other sailors wedged into the compartment. In their condition, any potential danger was amplified.

On one of Jack's rounds, the nervous men called the chief's attention to the torpedoes. Jack paused and watched the torpedoes during a heavy roll, bracing himself with both hands. He told the crew the straps would hold. He reminded them that the fish were equipped with practice heads, containing no explosives. The crew already knew that, but just having Jack tell them again was reassuring, though, honestly, Duane was more concerned about getting crushed than blown up.

Ellison, the Coast Guard Station's commander, refused to relinquish the surfboat to Lt. Howe and his Navy team. He challenged Howe, demanding to know if Howe would take responsibility for any loss of life that might result from trying take crewmen off the sub in the breakers with a surfboat. He said the surfboat could never get close enough and that the tide was changing. Howe was adamant, but he wasn't a fool. He backed off his demands but insisted that the action begin. They needed to get the crew off the sub before sunset. Already he had decided to lay charges against Ellison when this whole ordeal was over, but he didn't say that on the beach.

The US Coast Guard was a new culture and a new idea for Keeper Lawrence Ellison. He'd spent most of his career with the US Life Saving Service, which had its roots in locally funded humanitarian efforts to assist distressed mariners. He was old school. The Life Saving Service had operated local, land-based lifesaving stations. Unlike the Coast Guard, it was not a military command organization.

President Wilson signed the Coast Guard Act of 1915, less than two years before H-3 went on the beach, merging the humanitarian-focused Life Saving Service with the more military-oriented Revenue Cutter Service, founded by Alexander Hamilton in 1790 and operated under the US Treasury Department. The United States didn't have a navy in Hamilton's era. The Continental Navy that had been created during the American Revolution had been disbanded due to war debt in 1785.

The Revenue Cutter Service was a fleet of small and fast sailing ships that were heavily armed for their size. They protected commerce along the seacoasts and later supported a re-emerging US Navy, funded by the Naval Act of 1794, which provided for the construction of six frigates, including the USS Constitution. The new Coast Guard, augmented by President Wilson, ended up with a military-based command structure, similar at the time to the US Navy.

Ellison was deeply irritated by the brassy Navy commander, but he wouldn't risk lives to satisfy anybody. He knew these waters. He'd been working the coastline for years and had commanded the Humboldt Bay Station for almost a decade, living every day in close proximity to the beach. He understood the nature of the breakers and the currents much more intimately than Lt. Howe. He knew the chance of getting sailors off the deck of the sub and into a surfboat in these conditions was poor at best, and the effort would likely end up in a disaster. He knew it had to be a breeches buoy, a line-based rescue system secured between the sub and the beach. It could be a treacherous ride for the crew but it would be more secure and predictable than jumping into a surfboat from the steel deck of a submarine trapped in the breakers.

Ellison also knew that Howe wasn't wrong, the rescue had to be done before nightfall. The sub had been pounded now for almost eight hours.

By four that afternoon, the submarine had moved a few hundred feet closer to shore, though the deck was still wave washed. The conning tower fairwater rose above the waves now, so they would attempt to secure a line on that high point.

Ellison called his Coast Guardsmen together and told his top surfman, Werner Sweins, that they were going to put him on the deck of *H-3*. Sweins was a strong and determined surfman and focused immediately on the task ahead. He listened intently to the plan that Ellison laid out, tugging at the ends of his walrus mustache. Their execution would have to be perfect at this point in the day. If they failed, the rescue would go into the night. Lt. Howe would probably not sit idly by if that was the case.

Howe directed his *Cheyenne* crewmen to set up a camp on the beach, using canvas tents and building a large bonfire. Medics from the *Cheyenne* were standing by, as were medical people from the Humboldt communities. A contingent of the Fifth District Naval Militia from Eureka had gathered on the beach, led by group surgeon Dr. Carl T. Wallace and Lt. A.B. Adams.

It wasn't long before conditions seemed as good as they were going to get. Ellison rallied his eight-man crew and gave the order: "Launch the surfboat."

As a big wave surged up onto the beach, the boat was sucked into the backwash. Navy men from the *Cheyenne* helped get the boat waterborne, running alongside it into the surf, gripping the side rails to propel the boat forward. Then the oarsmen took over. Gustaf Christensen of nearby Samoa was one of the surfmen. He immediately locked into a rhythm, along with Ole Torgersen, Johan Knudsen and the rest the crew. The sweep oar for steering was deftly handled by skipper Ellison. Werner Sweins readied himself on the point of the bow, concentrating on the submarine ahead, locking in his resolve to get aboard that boat. The fog had now lifted enough so the people on the beach could clearly see the action. The rescue was finally under way.

F-4

DANGER IN THE DEPTHS

Diver William Loughman was in a lot of trouble. He was 250 feet beneath the surface outside Honolulu Harbor in Mamala Bay, and his lifelines were ensnared in the undersea rigging. He was thoroughly stuck. This was the team's fourth dive and Loughman's first on the *F-4* recovery. He'd already been down an hour. His time was up, and he needed to get back to the surface. They were calling him on his helmet phone.

Loughman was very worried. He couldn't free his fouled lines. He'd already gone back down to the sub at 300 feet to try to undo the snarl. It didn't work. No matter what he did, he couldn't get more than 50 feet off the deck of *F-4*. The sustained pressure at that depth was starting to exact a toll, physically and mentally. In a crackly voice over the radio in his helmet, he called George Stillson, who was directing the operation from above and asked for help.

Stillson immediately went to Frank Crilley. Crilley wasn't supposed to dive that day, but he was next in rotation and had had the most rest. This would be the first time they had two divers in the water at those depths at the same time.

Crilley donned his dive suit and immediately went down the cable after Loughman. He worked for more than an hour to free him. He maneuvered up and down the cable in depths from 265 feet back up to 120 feet. An ocean surge sent a wave of tension spiraling down the cables, snapping them tight and almost knocking Crilley out.

Currents were also unpredictable down deep. They could spin a diver around in circles. More time was passing. Crilley had to be careful not to get ensnared in Loughman's cables. At one point, Crilley returned to the surface, taking very little time for decompression, to get a new line to attach to Loughman and immediately started back down the cable. Minutes later he was back to the trapped diver. This time Crilley was able to reset the lines and free Loughman. But Loughman was starting to fade after more than three hours under deep sea pressure.

On the surface, Stillson and Dr. French monitored the action intensely. They recorded depth intervals, minutes of exposure, decompression calculations. Despite his disorientation, Loughman began a slow and methodical decompression ascent. They brought him up to 100 feet and paused. He was receiving instructions through the phone in his helmet. Crilley stuck close to him. Loughman had been in deep water now for four hours. No man had ever sustained exposure at that depth. It was uncharted territory.

Over the diver phone, Dr. French instructed Loughman to stay at 100 feet. Loughman's mind was starting to break down from the effects of the narcosis. He stopped following Dr. French's instructions and began climbing the decompression ladder without pausing. In minutes he was at 60 feet, almost to the surface. He'd lost control of reason. He needed to get out of the water. Out of the dive suit. Get that claustrophobic helmet off his head. He pushed to 40 feet, then stopped and collapsed. He'd been under extreme pressure now for four and a half hours. He was no longer responding to calls on his phone.

They pulled Loughman to the surface. Crilley surfaced right behind him,

Frank Crilley on the Jacobs Ladder, diving for F-4 – (PigBoats.COM)

Chief Gunner's Mate William Loughman preparing to dive for F-4. He was trapped 250 feet under water for hours while working on the F-4 recovery and saved by Frank Crilley (US Navy, from Submarines at War, by Edwin P. Hoyt, 1983)

risking the bends himself. The crew used knives to cut off Loughman's diving suit, weights and clothes. He started to talk but lost consciousness. They
rushed him into the decompression chamber along with Crilley, Dr. French and
a surgeon, Dr. Garrison. Compressed air filled the chamber. Loughman was still
unconscious. He'd stopped breathing. His pulse faded. Then suddenly, as the
decompression chamber hit 75 pounds, he snapped back to life. He sat up, took
normal breaths and appeared rational. He'd been unconscious for almost three
minutes.

Though the decompression chamber saved Loughman, it harmed Dr. Garrison. In the first minutes after entering the chamber with the other three men, his
nose began bleeding and both his eardrums blew out due to the rapid increase
in air pressure Stillson had injected into the chamber to try to save Loughman.

Loughman remained in the decompression chamber for more than three
hours with Crilley and the two doctors. Loughman was chatty at first, in good
humor, telling Stillson and Crilley about the position of the cables below on F-4.
He appeared normal. But when they took the chamber down to 20 pounds, his
joints began aching violently. He kicked and screamed from severe pains all over
his body. He began to vomit. They took the pressure back up. The pains eased.
He was suffering from the bends —decompression sickness. It could be fatal. It
took them hours to stabilize him in that chamber. Crilley, Dr. French and Dr.
Garrison remained by Loughman's side sealed in the pressurized compartment
for hours before he was removed on a stretcher and placed in sick bay aboard
the Maryland.

At the end of the day, George Stillson told people that Loughman would fully
recover and be back to normal by the evening or next morning. He planned to keep
him in the diving rotation. But Stillson would soon realize that Loughman was far
from recovered. He went in and out of convulsions for days after the ordeal.

For the next 48 hours, in the sick bay of the Maryland, William Loughman
battled to survive. His joints ached profoundly throughout his body, blood vessels began to break down, causing internal hemorrhaging, his body temperature

plummeted, he lost his pulse, he continued to vomit, and was treated with mor-
phine and oxygen.

Although Frank Crilley also endured excessive underwater exposure, he
did not go through the catastrophic bends that Loughman experienced. Crilley
endured five hours of deep pain in his elbows, but that was it.

Frank Crilley's dive notes recorded by the surface team were scattered because of the emergency actions unfolding minute by minute. At one point in the
rescue, he descended from the surface to 120 feet in 60 seconds, then returned
to the surface two minutes later. Then he went down again. The medical doctors
on the surface lost track of Crilley's depths, time exposures and decompression
requirements in the chaos.

*USAT Sheridan transported William Loughman and wives and families of lost F-4 sailors to Mare
Island Hospital in 1915 (National WW1 Museum and Memorial)*

The event had been traumatic for all of the divers. First, for Frank Crilley.
He'd maintained a façade of determined stoicism during Loughman's rescue. But
after they took Loughman from the decompression chamber, he turned away as
the emotions caught up with him. Tears poured down his face. He knew what the
bends felt like. He was deeply grieving for his friend's suffering and reliving the

emotions that he'd felt during the rescue. Drellishak and Nielson also were drained. They had been engaged the entire time, helping manage the diving apparatus, from the time Loughman initiated his dive, to his time in the decompression chamber, and to his exit on a stretcher from the chamber hours later.

William Loughman's diving days were now over. The team was down to three divers. It would take Loughman three long months to fully recover his health. He had almost died during the rescue. In early May, he was transported across the Pacific Ocean to San Francisco aboard the United States Army Transport *Sheridan* to Mare Island Naval Hospital for the remainder of his recovery.

The same day Crilley saved Loughman, the surface teams managed to raise F-4 about 12 feet from its resting place and move it up the seabed slope toward shore. Loughman's efforts had helped that feat. It was a very small victory, but everyone hoped this was the beginning of bringing F-4 back to the surface.

Honolulu, Hawaii's Pacific Commercial Advertiser, May 8, 1915 edition (newspapers.com)

Despite the new dive technologies, the diver descents and working conditions were anything but easy. The physical toll from working on the sea floor 300 feet down added up and slowed recovery efforts. Fatigue and physical reactions to stress set in. Crilley, Drellishak and Nielson descended numerous times to install four large sling-like cables under F-4 so it could be winched upwards along the ocean bottom and closer to shore in shallower water for the final recovery.

But foul weather moved in. A series of powerful storms swept through the Hawaiian Islands, making it impossible to reset undersea rigging. The strain on the cables was tremendous when the dredge would ride up and over large ocean swells, then plunge on the backside. One cable sling supporting the sub snapped in the swells. Vessels returned to port. Between the weather, rigging setbacks and diver fatigue, the F-4 recovery was put on hold for three weeks.

During the desperate and laborious process of raising F-4, one of the German U-boats sank the passenger liner *RMS Lusitania* near Ireland on May 7, drowning almost 1,200 civilian passengers, including 128 Americans. Germany claimed the ship contained war supplies. The US debate on entering the Great War took on new urgency.

Three days after the sinking of the *Lusitania*, adversity struck again in the depths, when diver Fred Nielson got entangled in the underwater rigging, in an incident similar to Loughman's. Nielson had been passing a line through the lifting shackle at the sub's stern when he'd reached his maximum time exposure. He'd been as deep as 275 feet that day. It was time to surface.

When Nielson realized that he was caught in a tangle of four different lines, he started cutting the lines, working with his hands above his head. His dive suit filled with water. That extra weight doubled the amount of energy it would take for him to get back to the surface. He telephoned to Stillson that he was exhausted and wanted the shortest decompression time possible. He wanted to get out.

Stillson gave him the okay, but Nielson failed to mention that he was going back down deeper one more time before coming up to try to free a line. He just forgot. He would mention that to Dr. French the next day. About two hours after exiting the decompression chamber, his body revolted and he became extremely dizzy and began vomiting. He had to return to the decompression chamber before he was able to finally stabilize.

Drellishak had his problems, too, with constant deep-water exposures. The

day before Nielson's ordeal, after a 275-foot dive, Drellishak's heart started skip-
ping beats and he developed intestinal disorders. He did not stabilize until a day
later.

It was a long, tedious spring and summer in Mamala Bay. Recovery efforts
edged ahead slowly, with advances and setbacks. But the recovery teams and
leaders remained resolute in their mission to bring *F-4* up from the bottom.
Some just wanted answers for the crew and their families. The US Navy also
wanted answers, including why they'd lost a submarine.

One of Lt. Cmdr. Julius Furer's improvised, windless cable reels used to lift F-4 (Vallejo Naval &
Historical Museum, NavSource.org)

Daily accounts of progress were measured in feet. Sometimes the slings that
held *F-4* would break, sending the sub skidding back down the steep, sandy
floor. The crews struggled to raise the sub eight feet off the bottom one day, then
slide it 60 feet up the seabed slope the next. A few days later they would raise it
12 feet and slide it 10 feet. Everything was incremental. On their biggest day, they
lifted the sub 30 feet and moved it forward. It was a day in and day out process,
trying to drag *F-4* to the surface. They'd have to pause between big ocean storms

and swells when it was too dangerous to work above or below the surface. On one particularly turbulent day, a cable sling snapped, dumping the sub upside down onto the seabed.

Divers endured fatigue over the weeks of constant exposure in the deep water. They worked through rotations, but at one point, only one of the three remaining divers was able to put on a pressurized suit and go down to the sea floor. Big swells and surface storms interrupted progress for weeks at a time. Still the Navy crews kept grinding it out, moving F-4 up the underwater slope, like Sisyphus.

Julius Furer's steam donkey crews at work raising F-4 from the sea bottom (Pacific Fleet Submarine Museum at Pearl Harbor)

The divers were constantly having to repair broken cables. They swapped out the wire cable slings for heavy anchor chain to reduce the rate of breakage. But the heavy chains wreaked havoc on F-4's steel hull as the rolling seas sawed the chains against the sub, cutting into the steel. Lt. Cmdr. Furer was growing more and more concerned about the condition of the sub as they got it nearer to the surface. He thought it might get cut in half from the sounds of the divers' reports.

By late May, the divers and surface crews had raised F-4 to within 42 feet of the surface, but another storm rolled in that damaged the rigging and the sub.

Crilley, Drellishak and Nielson combined made 20 dives at this shallower depth. Crilley and Drellishak stayed underwater together for almost three hours one day trying to set the rigging. That was the longest work period underwater for the project, not counting Loughman's rescue.

Navy divers, George Stillson (left) and Fred Nielson with F-4 model and diving helmets in background (Vallejo Naval & Historical Museum and navsource.org)

The divers reported an enormous implosion in the forward port side of the boat and damage to the conning tower and dive planes, partly caused by the salvage efforts. Crilley and team tried to patch the gaping hole in the hull with a large canvas mat that the crew aboard the *Maryland* had fabricated on the spot. They planned to use the canvas mat to seal the hole, then pump in air pressure to force water from the hull so it could rise to the surface on its own. But the effort failed.

During the many weeks of work, the deep-sea dive team never took shore leave into Honolulu. They remained focused on their tasks. When they weren't toiling with the underwater rigging, they remained aboard the *Gaylord* or the *Maryland*. Besides staying focused on their momentous task and keeping their minds clear and alert, the divers were concerned what might transpire if they did go ashore. All of their underwater observations had to remain a guarded secret.

One of the divers said, "If we should go to shore and our identity found out, we would be asked a million questions undoubtedly. Because of restrictions we would not be allowed to answer them, and the many refusals would be unpleasant. So we are going to stay onboard and see Honolulu later."

The sheer complexity of the task to recover *F-4* continued to unfold. At almost every juncture of the salvage, the crews thought they were just a couple weeks away from bringing the submarine to the surface. The Navy thought they could drag *F-4* into shallower waters and then refloat it. That had failed. Now Julius Furer could see that they needed a new plan if they were ever going to bring the submarine to the surface without demolishing it in the process.

H-3

Leap of Faith

The crowds on the beach watched as the surfboat rose over each breaker, then plunged down the backside as the waves roared beneath the open, wooden-hulled boat. Some in the crowd called out encouragement. Others just stared intently at the action, saying nothing. Ellison manned the 16-foot tiller. His crew of eight pulled hard on 12-foot-long, heavy oars. Gustaf Christensen and the other oarsmen were giving it all they had. The sea boiled with white foam after each break. The bow of the surfboat would point to the sky as it rode the swells and then it would drop, sending spray over the crew. Werner Sweins held on tight in the bow, zeroing in his concentration on the round steel sides of the submarine they were closing in on. With oars in full stroke, the surfboat swung in near the sub, slipping in on the leeward side of the hull. Ellison steadied their position with the heavy tiller.

Crouched on the bow of the surfboat, Sweins held on, trying to time a jump onto the sub's wave-swept steel deck. It was nearly impossible since the sub's hull ballooned out several feet from the deck. Sweins had a line thrown over his shoulder that he needed to secure to the sub. His footing was precarious as the surfboat thrashed about in the turbulence. The messenger line was a few hundred feet long and was spooled into the boat. Having the line looped over his shoulder made the jump even more difficult.

Sweins made an exaggerated, gyrating leap toward H-3 at the exact moment the surfboat banged up against the sub. He landed hard on the edge of the steel deck, scrambled for a handhold, clawed his way up the slippery steel surface, and managed to tie off the line around a steel pipe on the sub's deck. In seconds, a breaker came roaring over the top of the sub and swept Sweins off the deck and into the surf between the sub and the rescue boat.

The crowd on the beach groaned as they lost sight of Sweins. Then he surfaced, treading water in his heavy wool pants and jacket. He'd managed to keep his grip on the line he'd tied off. He hauled himself toward the sub, hand over hand, through another breaker. With a tight grip, he clambered up the side of the hull, out of the surf, onto the deck. The hatch was sealed tight. Nobody knew he was on the boat.

No sooner had Sweins established a footing on the deck, another breaker hit. He was lifted off his feet and hurled back into the ocean. He again emerged from the breakers and pulled himself hand over hand back onto the sub. This time he got a firm grip on the conning tower rail. His progress raised cheers and groans from the townspeople at every turn.

With a wave of his hand, Ellison swung the surfboat around and headed for the beach. The surfboat trailed the line that Sweins had secured to the sub, paying it out steadily. As soon as the surfboat surged onto the beach on an incoming wave, the crew jumped out and ran the boat up onto the sand. They secured the end of the messenger line to the breeches buoy line and waited for Sweins to give them the signal.

Lt. Bogusch was in the conning tower when he heard thumping coming from outside. He saw a leg come up past the eye port. A man was kicking the metal housing. On closer look, he also saw a line leading shoreward. He raised the hatch cover and saw a weathered, tense face with a walrus moustache, looking down at him.

"How are you doing?" Sweins yelled.

"Rough," shouted the captain. "Get us out of here!"

Another breaker hit. The hatch went down again. Sweins hung on as he was engulfed by water. He clung to the conning tower superstructure. He waited for a lull in the seas before getting Bogusch to open the hatch again.

Werner Sweins had never rescued anybody from a submarine. His experiences had always involved rescuing people from boats that had decks. Or plucking people from the sea. That's what he was used to. This long cigar of a boat was foreign to him. It rolled unevenly in the breakers. Everyone was sealed inside, like canned sardines. And this tube was also filled with chemical gas.

Bogusch threw open the top hatch again. Sweins yelled over the sound of the surf, "Is there anybody on board that can help me haul out the breeches buoy line?"

Minutes later, Agraz emerged from the conning tower hatch and joined Sweins on deck. This was Jack's third time out on deck in the pounding surf. He was already soaked. He moved quickly. The salt air was a vast improvement from the atmosphere inside H-3. But the breakers remained a threat.

Both seamen gave it their all, hauling out the trolley line to the sub. Trailing all the way back to the beach through the breakers, the lines weighed a few hundred pounds. The breeches buoy harness would add weight to that once it was set up.

Sweins and Agraz pulled rhythmically. The lines, fixed on shore, slowly started to be drawn out toward the sub through the breakers. The men's hands were numbed by the 50-degree saltwater. The bristly, wound strands of the hemp line were hard and abrasive. The men kept pulling until the lines emerged from the surf and trailed up onto the steel deck.

Seas continued to pour over the deck. The two men periodically were forced to pause as they grabbed something solid to stop from being washed overboard. Werner struggled to secure the trolley line block and tackle to the highest point on the conning tower. He used special knots to secure it against slippage as the sub pitched and rolled.

On shore, Ellison and his crew and volunteers secured two large timbers used as shears to lift the rope trolley line as high as possible above the surface of the breakers. They secured that line to another block and tackle and reefed it down tight. They hoped the sub's movements would not break the line again. The block and tackle would absorb the motions. The breeches buoy was then rigged.

The long, outstretched line sagged into the breakers. Any passenger in the buoy would be dragged through the breakers. If the sub rolled in toward shore, slackening the line further, they might get dragged under water.

Breeches buoy illustration, from the 1885 wreck of the Malta on the New Jersey Coast; 31 years later, a breeches buoy was used on the H-3 rescue (Frank Leslie's Illustrated Newspaper, Dec 5, 1885, Archives of History LLC, New London, MN)

It took Werner Sweins, Jack Agraz and skipper Ellison's crew on the beach an hour to get the lines set up for the rescue attempt. Waves continued to break against H-3, but the boat was not swinging back and forth as wildly as it had earlier in the day. Sweins and Agraz climbed inside H-3, descending through double hatches into the control room.

The first two crew members Sweins saw were Toad Blabon and Jim Anderson, the two injured men. Sweins winced at the air quality inside the control room and said he would get the two injured sailors off first, then evacuate everybody else. Sweins could see some crew members fighting off drowsiness and nausea and others who were simply incapacitated by the ordeal, unconscious from the constant motion and exposure to contaminated air of the last nine hours. With waves coming at 15- to 20-second intervals over the past nine hours, the submarine would have been hit by more than 2,000 breakers at this point.

Sweins went topside and signaled to Ellison to send out more surfmen. He needed help. Taking a groggy and injured crew of 27 men up through a narrow hatchway and getting them into the breeches buoy harness would require more able hands. Ellison's crew launched the surfboat and rowed back out to the sub. The waves had started to settle down compared to the earlier sets. He sent three more rescuers to help Sweins. The men jumped from the boat and into the waves, hauling themselves up the line that Sweins had made fast earlier.

Scores of eager hands on the beach gripped the haul-back line and pulled as fast as they could. There were Coast Guard rescuers, Navy men and able-bodied citizens jumping into the action and pulling on the lines. The harness skimmed out through the breakers, sometimes dipping below the surface. They didn't have time to make further adjustments. The sun was going down. They didn't want to be forced to evacuate the crew in the dark. Sweins knew it was going to be a rough ride ahead for the men.

By 1700 hours, *H-3*'s crew had been sealed inside and tumbling around for the entire day. The crowd of onlookers still stood on the beach, and some had built an enormous bonfire from driftwood. Nurses and medical personnel were standing by. Navy sailors from the *Cheyenne* had made a large camp and mixed in with the locals. Conversations were in hushed tones.

All eyes were fixed on the sea and the intensifying activities around the conning tower. The breeches buoy had been trolleyed out to the sub. Two surfmen and a couple of the sub's crew worked around the conning tower hatch. Some of the spectators on the beach had field glasses, and they kept the others informed.

There were tense moments. The people with binoculars called out that a body wrapped in canvas was being removed from the sub. Had the gas been poisonous? Would there be more bodies? Someone else shouted that they would bring the living off the boat first. The living and the injured. The crowd remained anxious.

The first crewman out of the hatch was Toad Blabon. He was the "body" the people with binoculars saw and reported. Then Toad slowly untangled himself from the line that rescuers used to pull him up through the conning tower to the bridge. The canvas remained loosely wrapped around him. People could see that he was injured but all right. A second sailor appeared above deck, injured, but moving unassisted. That was Jim Anderson. His hand was bandaged as well. Sweins and Agraz helped Toad into the breeches buoy harness. Anderson would be next.

Toad received the same instructions that all the crew would get that December evening at sunset. "Hold your breath as long as you can. You'll be submerged part of the time."

With a wave of his arms, Werner Sweins signaled "haul away." A cheer arose from the crowd. The first man was off *H-3*. Toad Blabon was on his way to shore.

F-4

Unsung Heroes

Frances Pierard was left nearly destitute by the loss of her husband, Frank. She had the twins to raise on her own now. She had no job. The Navy would provide some money to the families, maybe $60. Adm. Moore's wife, Helen, had managed to raise several thousand dollars through her efforts in the Honolulu community. But that didn't create a future for the widows of *F-4*.

To raise some money for her and her twins, Frances agreed to auction off all of her furniture and household items in their modest home. The auctioneer, O.A. Stevens, had reached out to Frances, thinking the auction could help her and her girls. Frances had no way to know the auction would stir up an enormous emotional outpouring of support from people in the Honolulu community, mostly strangers.

Crowds came and bid wildly for the table, a few chairs, a carpet, a couch and other simple household items. The newspapers described it as a bidding frenzy involving people of different backgrounds and cultures. There were affluent people, workers and housewives of modest means. Items sold for many times their normal worth. A five-dollar chair could go for $12 or $14. When a person won a bid, they paid Frances and then gave the items back to be auctioned again. People had tears in their eyes when they called out and bid on two baby chairs that went for $22. Those were given back to Frances as well.

The auctioneer had prodded and challenged the crowd to keep bidding. Two women had stopped by the day before the auction and had given him $10 to buy something. Anything. "Go the limit," they'd said. Stevens bought something for $10 and then gave it back to be auctioned again. He noticed that many of the people there were poor as well. "It's from people like the ones we had, that haven't anything, that we always get the most," he said. "They really feel for the sufferers."

Frances received more than $300 that day, much more than the furniture was worth. Very few items were ever claimed by the winning bidders. And some people just stopped by and donated money without even bidding.

In late April, Frances Pierard made a difficult decision. With her twins at her side, Frances and her younger sister, Mae Lunger, packed their bags and planned to leave Honolulu. They could no longer bear waiting for F-4 to be brought back to the surface. The recovery had been going on for six weeks. Frank and Archie were inside F-4 and there was nothing they could do to change that. They had decided to return to the mainland to restart their lives. The four of them boarded the United States Army Transport *Sheridan* on May 12 and bid farewell to Honolulu. It was to be the same ship and voyage that was transporting injured Navy deep-sea diver William Loughman back to California as well as Margaret Ede and her two children.

During her final days in Honolulu, Frances had written a personal letter directly to Secretary of the Navy Josephus Daniels about her plight after the loss of F-4. Not only had she lost her husband and brother-in-law, Mae Lunger never recovered from the shock of the event. Frances would become the sole supporter of Mae and, eventually, Mae's newborn child. Daniels took the letter to heart and asked the president if he could extend assistance to the widows. President

Wilson signed an executive order, granting Frances Pierard and Frederick Gilman's wife full-time positions as seamstresses and flag makers at the Mare Island Navy Yard.

That day aboard the *Sheridan*, Frances carried a great basket of fresh flowers. The ship was bound for San Francisco. The ship's skipper, Captain Murphy, was well aware of the women's plight and the ill-fated *F-4*. As the ship's lines were cast off and the *Sheridan* began to move out of the harbor, the skipper asked the territorial harbor pilot, Captain J.R. Macaulay, to steer them toward where *F-4* lay below the ocean's surface. The salvage vessels had vacated their spot on the surface due to weather, leaving just a marker buoy directly above the sub.

Captain Murphy ordered the *Sheridan* to a full stop above *F-4*. They drifted there silently for 10 minutes. They could see its shape beneath the clear waters. Frances and Mae stepped to the ship's rail and cast great armfuls of fresh flowers onto the water above *F-4*. The flowers fluttered down the side of the ship and spread out delicately across the sea, directly above Frank and Archie and the rest of the crew.

On May 19, across the country, at an afternoon tea in Washington DC, eight affluent and influential young women sat around a table discussing the devastating fate of the wives, families and loved ones of the *F-4* catastrophe. The DC socialites decided on the spot to launch a major fund-raising event to support the families. Within 24 hours, they secured Polls Theater, the National Marine Band and Orchestra, film projection equipment, engravers, and the full support of Admiral of the Navy George Dewey.

In that single day, they also recruited Lt. Clarence Hinkamp, the foremost expert on US submarines, to present a film and lecture at the event on "The Submarine." The young socialites also reached out to the wives of the Secretary of the Navy — Addie Daniels — and Assistant Secretary of the Navy — Eleanor Roosevelt — and to scores of other ranking officials' wives and officers in the capitol.

All the theater box seats were sold out that first day, before the event was even announced. It was an enormous success. Adm. Dewey personally forwarded all the proceeds to F-4 families in Honolulu through the Navy Relief Society.

Julius Furer was determined, but realistic, about the monumental salvage task he'd taken on to bring F-4 back to the surface. With the rough seas and surging cable slings connected by anchor chains threatening to break up the sub, he realized he needed a completely new lift system to bring F-4 to the surface.

USS Maryland with six specialty pontoons arrives in Honolulu (Pacific Fleet Submarine Museum at Pearl Harbor)

Furer envisioned six enormous, cylindrical floating tanks, made from steel and sheathed with heavy timbers strapped together by metal bands, like coopers' bands around gigantic whiskey barrels. The huge 32-foot-long, airtight twin chambers would be flooded with seawater and submerged on either side of the sub, three to a side. Divers would trench channels beneath the sub and pass heavy chains under the hull to connect the floats through a piping system. Air

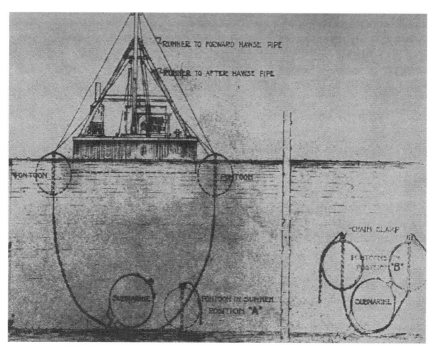

Illustration of the 1915 plan to raise F-4 with submerged pontoons and windlass-powered steam donkey (Bill Lightfoot, navsource.org)

Salvaging pontoons – Master Rigger Fred Busse standing in front of the Navajo. (PigBoats.COM, Ric Hedman)

would be pumped into the floats, lifting F-4 in a cradle to the surface. But these giant floats didn't exist. Julius Furer had to design them first, then build them.

All salvage work on the project was stopped. Julius Furer boarded the *Maryland* and sailed out of Honolulu to Mare Island Navy Yard in Vallejo, north of San Francisco, where the pontoon chambers would be fabricated. He would return to Honolulu two months later with his six giant flotation devices stacked up and strapped to the deck of the *Maryland*.

With the F-4 resting in 42 feet of water, Furer no longer needed the specialized deep-sea diving team. Stillson, Crilley, Drellishak and Nielson returned to the East Coast with all of their advanced gear. Furer would rely more on other Navy divers to set the final rigging in the shallower water. Jack Agraz and George Evans were two that spent long hours toiling under the sea, setting chains and cables beneath the sub and attaching the rigging to the enormous floats that Furer had brought to Hawaii.

⊂⋯⊃

The onerous task required heavy lifting and constant digging through the seabed to create channels beneath the submarine through which to pass the enormous chains. Numerous divers were involved in the effort. Agraz and Evans were soon joined by a new diver, recently transferred to the *Alert*. Gunner's Mate First Class John Henry Turpin donned a dive suit and became part of the underwater team setting the final rigging on F-4.

Turpin liked to go by the name Dick, but his shipmates nicknamed him Big Bill, because of his imposing size and strength. Originally from a small seaside neighborhood in Long Branch, New Jersey, he'd been in the Navy since 1896 and had seen a lot, some of it legendary.

Dick Turpin was a steward aboard the USS *Maine* in Havana Harbor in 1898 when it blew up and sunk, igniting the Spanish-American War. He was one of the 90 sailors who survived out of 350 crewmen aboard the *Maine* that night. He had been below deck in the ship's pantry when it suddenly heaved and erupted into an inferno. Before the *Maine* sank, Turpin was able to crawl out in darkness from below decks and jump into the bay, where he was picked up by a launch.

Between the dives to recover *F-4*, Jack Agraz and Dick Turpin undoubtedly shared stories from the turbulent times they'd experienced during their own naval tours in China. Turpin had been in the US Asiatic Fleet during the Boxer Rebellion in 1900, when the US Navy joined an eight-nation military expedition headed by several European countries and Japan. They marched into Beijing 20,000 strong to defend foreign interests against the nationalist Yihetuan Movement, which was backed by the Qing Imperial Army. The invading Western force prevailed and reimposed a ruthless, but temporary, order on China.

A decade later, Agraz also ended up in China during tumultuous times, as a member of the crew of the *USS Dale* steaming out of the Philippines to Japan and China. His skipper was Frank "Blackjack" Fletcher from Marshalltown, Iowa, who later became an admiral and would direct the battles of Midway and the Coral Sea in World War II. They'd been upriver on the Yangtze when the Chinese Revolution erupted in 1911. Jack had kept a journal about those events. His cryptic notes described a revolution unfolding around him, about rebels overrunning Chinese cities, a viceroy committing suicide, their ship carrying medical supplies upriver to Nanjing and Wuhu.

Jack's journal described Chinese gunboats alongside Japanese gunboats, gliding down the Yangtze, sometimes at night to avoid detection. The Dale anchored near naval warships from Italy, France, England and Germany, countries that had been struggling to maintain their possessions and influence in China since the Boxer Rebellion. Jack was still jotting down notes from his experiences in the Yangtze River near Wuhu when the 2,000-year-old Imperial Dynasty collapsed into chaos at the end of 1911. His last journal entry was in December, before they sailed back to the Philippines.

Both Jack Agraz and Dick Turpin had prevailed against the odds. Turpin seemed invincible and had a reputation that would follow him for years. In addition to being a strong diver, he had been a Navy boxing champion in sev-

eral weight classes and taught boxing at the
Academy. He was also famously aboard the
gunboat *USS Bennington* when its boiler exploded in San Diego Bay in 1905. Witnesses
were stunned at the magnitude of that blast,
which tore the ship apart and killed over
half its crew of 102 sailors.

Turpin walked out of that explosion,
too, as he had from the *Maine* seven years
before — but not before saving 15 shipmates. One at a time, he swam three officers
and 12 enlisted men from the burning wreck
to shore.

Eleven sailors aboard the *Bennington* received the Medal of Honor for saving fellow

*John Henry "Dick" Turpin, US Navy
diver (Puget Sound Navy Museum,
Bremerton, Washington)*

crew members. But Dick Turpin was passed over. He was one of only a few Af-
rican-American Navy sailors in 1896 and most likely the first black Navy diver.
The country was still heavily segregated in 1915 when Turpin was diving for F-4
with Agraz and Evans. Even Secretary of The Navy Daniels, FDR's mentor and
boss from North Carolina, was an avowed segregationist, as was Woodrow Wilson, the president of the United States.

The loss of F-4 had thrown chlorine gas and lead-acid batteries onto the
front pages of the country's newspapers. At the same time, the Germans had
deployed chlorine gas on the Western Front in trench warfare, with horrific results. During that long summer of efforts to recover F-4, Secretary Daniels said
he wanted to strengthen the Navy's capability above the surface — and below
the surface. He and FDR formed the Naval Consulting Board, enlisting Thomas
Edison to lead the organization. It would include experts from 11 engineering

and scientific societies, with Edison as chairman. Submarines would be a big part of Edison's concentration, especially batteries.

Later, it would come to light that the arrangement between the Navy Department and Edison had political and commercial benefits. The effort was orchestrated by Edison's chief engineer, Miller Hutchison, who said he came up with the idea for the Naval Consulting Board as a means to sell Edison submarine batteries to the US Navy. He and Edison thought if they worked inside the Navy, they'd have an advantage over competitors. And there was something in it for Secretary Daniels as well. By bringing in Thomas Edison, American folk hero, he could secure votes for President Woodrow Wilson in the upcoming, closely contested election of 1916.

Edison stood by his battery claims. His alkaline cells produced more energy than the sulphuric acid-laced batteries used in the subs and were smaller, lighter and easier to charge. And they had no chlorine gas risk. If successful, Edison's battery meant a sub could run farther under sea with less risk. Driven in part by the *F-4* loss and the chlorine gas threat, the Navy began experimenting with Edison's alkaline batteries aboard the older *USS E-2*, with further plans to build them into the *USS L-8*, which was the Navy's newest design. Edison's dream of powering submarines with his alkaline battery design was coming to fruition — at least that's what Edison believed.

H-3

ALL ASHORE!

When Duane Stewart woke up again, he was still in the torpedo compartment. Someone was manhandling him. Dazed, Duane struggled to focus. He'd lost consciousness. He felt himself being slapped, then shaken, but he couldn't respond. Then he got punched in the face. That snapped him out of his stupor.

A stranger in civilian clothes, soaking wet, had been pummeling him. Duane thought it was strange that there was a civilian aboard the boat in the torpedo room. Now he was yelling at Duane. "Come on sailor, can you stand?" It was one of Ellison's surfmen.

The drenched rescuer pried Duane's hands loose from the pipes he'd been gripping for hours. Duane had lost track of time. Then the man lifted him to his feet. He was dragged through the forward battery compartment and into the control room. Rescuers tied a line around his chest and under his arms to help them pull him up out of the sub through the two hatches in the conning tower. Strong hands in the tower and assistance from below moved Duane and the others up through the conning tower hatchway and out onto the bridge deck.

Then he found himself standing on the handrail of the conning tower, but he couldn't remember how he got there. He was staggering. Somebody smacked him in the face again. He was getting tired of being slapped. He could taste saltwater on his lips. Spray from another wave doused him. The fresh air felt good. He was still on the sub taking breakers, but from the outside this time.

Duane saw Nick Carter, his buddy, come up through the hatch, hoisted up with a line looped around his chest, under both his arms. They were carrying Nick, too. Sweins secured Carter in the buoy harness and told him to hold his breath as long as possible, that he might be underwater for a while. The surfmen waved their arms and the men on the beach hauled away the line and Carter was on his away. Duane hoped that he would be next. He was.

Duane's trip ashore was like a nightmare. He thought he remembered to hold his breath. Maybe he forgot. Maybe he hadn't heard them right. When he was placed into the rescue harness he slumped over and the men on the beach started pulling the line. Duane went off the H-3 deck and straight into the ocean. It was getting dark. Then he was underwater, getting pulled through the breakers. He swallowed saltwater at one point. The water was so shockingly cold that he was numb in seconds. He tried not to breathe. But he was coughing up saltwater. He seemed trapped in the waves for hours, though it was really only minutes.

Duane finally felt the sandy beach under his feet as he was dragged along by the breeches buoy line. He stumbled trying to get his feet under him. Then a swarm of hands and arms grabbed him and pulled him from the surf. He felt more drowned than alive. But he was grateful for the exposure of fresh, clean, sweet air and not the stinking smoke, gas and carbon dioxide of the past 10 hours.

The first four or five men taken off the sub experienced the worst rides of the evacuation. Civilians and sailors on the beach hauled the buoy line ashore. But because they were slow, they were practically keel-hauling the crew, subjecting them to long pulls underwater. Ellison could see the situation was bad and brought the horses over. They were hooked up to the back haul line. The horses were more powerful and faster. The rest the trips ashore went quickly.

As soon as each sailor hit the beach, the crowd reached out and unhooked him from the buoy harness. To a man, the half-drowned submariners were frozen and numb by the time they reached the shore. The seawater, inundated with deep water upwellings and northerly currents, was extremely cold in December on the Humboldt County coast. Hospital attendants cut the sailors' clothes off and discarded them in a pile. They were given vigorous rubdowns to restore body warmth and circulation. Blankets were thrown over their shoulders. The large driftwood bonfire was roaring, generating tremendous heat. The warmth was immediate and welcome.

Duane was stumbling around coming to his senses when he realized somebody had taken his belt, along with all his clothes. He found he was standing naked in the crowd, along with his shipmates. He didn't care about his clothes. But he wanted the belt back — his favorite. It was his razor strop, and he wasn't going to let anyone take it from him as a souvenir. He started cursing at everybody around him and yelling that somebody had stolen his belt. Later he would feel bad about how he yelled at his rescuers. The belt was quickly found and returned. Duane buckled it around his waist. He started to relax for the first time since H-3 hit bottom 10 hours before.

Duane remembered standing there by that big fire, naked with only that belt around his waist. He knew he probably looked pretty ridiculous.

He wasn't bare skinned long, though. Walter Pratt, the local lumber mill electrician, threw a blanket over him. Walter had stayed on the beach all day since he'd first heard the sub's distress whistle and discovered H-3 in the breakers that morning.

More blankets were coming. Wrapped up in them, the sailors huddled near the bonfire. Somebody handed Duane a cigarette and a cup of steaming coffee. "Man was that ever good. Even the cigarette," Duane recalled. "Funny, though, because I didn't even smoke."

Duane stood next to Nick Carter at the fire, warming his hands. Nick was also wrapped in a blanket and holding a cigarette and coffee. They started to laugh. The two of them stood side by side on Samoa Beach in front of that roaring fire. They were salty, gassed, and covered with acid. Their minds were fuzzy. Hundreds of people were around them. The sound of the breakers seemed far away, though they were right there. Both men could see H-3 leaning in the surf in the evening twilight, with the last of the crew exiting the boat.

All 27 men aboard H-3 were rescued safely by Ellison and the Humboldt Bay Coast Guard's surf crew. They had been taken off the sub one by one through the conning tower hatch, then pulled by the breeches buoy through the surf. Finally, just two men were left. Lt. Harry Bogusch closed the upper hatch and battened it down. Lt. Eric Zemke was right beside him. Zemke went into the breeches buoy first, then Bogusch. The skipper was the last man off H-3.

On shore, Zemke maintained a stoic attitude about the whole incident, at least publicly. "We rolled 75 degrees," he told a reporter. "Some of us kept a wary eye on the torpedoes overhead which threatened to break from their lashings." Zemke smiled and added, "One of the boys said he would have preferred to stay out at sea rather than ride that breeches buoy. That was some experience. I surely learned something today."

Carter looked out at the sub awash in the breakers and laughed. "Hell of a way to end up a cruise," he said. "First, they wreck you. Then they gas you. Then they try and drown you. Hell of a Navy!" He and Duane had a good laugh over that one, now that they were on the beach, with cigarettes and coffee, wrapped in those warm blankets by the fire.

The townspeople of Samoa helped crew members recuperate. They took some of the men to their own homes to get cleaned up and have a warm meal. Maybe even a drink. Walter Pratt invited Duane and Nick to his modest home near the mill, where his wife was preparing dinner. Duane would forever remember the hospitality and the wonderful meal Mrs. Pratt prepared.

Lt. j.g. Harry R. Bogusch on Samoa Beach, December 1916 (United States Naval Institute)

When Bogusch stepped out of the breeches buoy, completely soaked, he carried a leather satchel with a few belongings. He looked around a little stunned by the crowd on the beach as the sun set — throngs of local citizens, timber workers, sailors from the *Cheyenne*, the life-saving crew, his crew, newspaper reporters, telegraph agents, medical personnel, kids, and mill workers. He was devastated that he'd put the sub on the beach and caused all this commotion — a catastrophe. It was just his second command. But above all else, he was proud of his men.

That night aboard the *Cheyenne*, anchored in Humboldt Bay, Bogusch told Howe, "Were it not for the courage and perfect discipline of my men, we would not all be here tonight." Howe knew that Bogusch was bearing a personal responsibility about the whole calamity, but he didn't judge the young captain. Howe respected Bogusch's knowledge and ability as a submariner. He'd leave the judgment to the regional commanders.

When Bogusch retired for the evening and lay in his bunk on the tender, he replayed the day's events in his head again and again. His second command. Now his sub was on the beach. Thank God no lives had been lost. He knew there would be repercussions from the Navy, an investigation. He would accept whatever outcome those findings determined. But his mind was also harnessing all he'd learned in Hawaii the previous year, struggling for months to bring *F-4* back to the surface. He still had to get his own submarine off the beach. It hadn't been damaged much. He planned to go back aboard *H-3* the next day to retrieve some items. He and Howe were already discussing what their next move would be to save *H-3*.

The day after Lawrence Ellison's Coast Guardsmen rescued the *H-3* crew, local speculation began about what would come next. Could they salvage the submarine, or would it be added to the growing list of vessels in the graveyard off the Humboldt coast?

Lt. Howe wanted action. He wanted to get a line on board *H-3* and pull it back to sea as soon as possible. The Navy Department also wanted to get the spotlight off the fact that they had an expensive submarine on the beach.

Howe had the *Cheyenne* onsite, and the Navy fleet tug USS *Arapaho* was already on its way up the coast from San Francisco along with the US Coast Guard Cutter *McCulloch*. With the *Cheyenne*, he'd already pulled *H-3* off the rocks at Point Sur the previous year, so he figured it was doable. He just needed to get a line from the sub to a ship in the ocean — no easy task.

The next morning Howe and his entourage rowed ashore from the *Cheyenne* and walked back over the dunes to the beach where *H-3* was hard aground. Seventy-five sailors from the sub and *Cheyenne* were bivouacked in tents in the dunes, standing watch over the sub. The crowd was again starting to build, with hundreds of local people arriving by the hour.

H-3 remained stuck in deep sand, in about the same position as the previous evening, with breakers swirling around its half-buried hull. Ellison and a few of his Coast Guard crew were at the site, gathering up their life-saving gear from the previous day's ordeal. Ellison's surfboat was still on the beach. To Howe's dismay, Ellison's crew had removed the breeches buoy lines from shore that were secured on the submarine.

Jack Agraz and a local citizen on the Samoa Beach with H-3 in background (Agraz Family Collection)

Howe went to Ellison and ordered that he take a surfboat of Navy sailors out to the submarine and re-attach lines. Howe needed those lines on the sub to pull in a larger tow line. Right away, Howe and Ellison became embroiled in another heated conflict. Ellison stood by the Coast Guard mantra that they were in the business of saving lives, not salvaging marine assets. Howe was consumed by frustration. The two skippers stood there arguing their cases to each other in the midst of the crowd of locals who continued to come to the beach to gawk at the submarine.

Without fanfare, Jack Agraz took a line, stepped into the surf and swam out to the sub while the skippers continued to argue. He secured a small line to the submarine, then swam back to shore through the breakers, which weren't as powerful as they had been the day before. The crowd was transfixed by Jack's easy manner. A reporter approached Jack on the beach and asked if he was enjoying the fact that the whole crew had shore leave. Jack laughed. "I'd rather be in Honolulu diving for F-4, than here on the beach today," he declared. "I like diving."

William Howe was at his wit's end trying to reason with Lawrence Ellison. As commander of the Humboldt Bay Coast Guard Station, Ellison might have been doing his duty by the book, but Howe was about to go beyond the book. He sent a wireless message to the 12th Naval District headquarters in San Francisco and requested that Ellison be placed under his command. The *Cheyenne's* officers on the beach were frustrated by Ellison's stubborn adherence to the code of conduct, though Ellison and Sweins' efforts the previous day had earned the respect of all the enlisted sailors.

In the early years following the Coast Guard merger of the Life Saving Service and Navy-oriented Revenue Cutters, there was significant confusion about ranks and position. Life Saving Station Keepers possessed skills and knowledge equal to junior officers in the Navy or the Revenue Cutter Service, but were compensated at the rate of an enlisted seaman. It would take several years to sort out the tangled alignments of command, but in 1916, the Coast Guard Rescue station commanders, like Ellison, were temporarily ranked as Warrant Officers of the Treasury Department; there was no direct correlation of ranks between the Coast Guard Life Saving crews and the Navy at that point.

In response to Howe's request, Ellison received an immediate wire from his regional commander, Captain Searles, skipper of the *USCGC McCulloch*, which was en route to Humboldt Bay, to report to Lt. Howe, commander of the H-boat flotilla. From that point on, Ellison did everything Howe requested, without fail.

Howe wanted to get four Navy sailors on the deck of *H-3* to set a block and tackle to receive the larger tow line. He asked for volunteers and had 70 sailors step forward. He chose four — three from the *Cheyenne* and Jack Agraz from *H-3*. Ellison's crew rowed the surfboat out through the waves and came up alongside the sub. Breakers still washed over the hull. Jack was the first man off the surfboat and onto *H-3*'s deck.

The next two sailors made it onto the deck fine, but the last had bad timing. Just as he leapt from the surfboat, a breaker buried the deck of *H-3*. In one fluid motion Jack wrapped an arm around a steel stanchion on the sub, then swiped out with the other to grab the sailor just as the breaker hit, saving the crewman from getting washed off the deck and into the sea. People on the shore cheered.

The *Arapaho* and *McCulloch* had arrived and were standing by farther offshore. They were joined by a private salvage ship from San Francisco, the *Greenwood*, and a destroyer, the *USS Truxtun*, aboard which Rear Adm. William Banks Caperton was taking an account of the operations. The *Cheyenne* pulled anchor in Humboldt Bay and sailed out to join the other ships.

The coastal fog drifted in and out, at times obscuring visibility and halting the operation. A series of efforts to float lines ashore or out to the ships came up empty. In one bungled attempt, a line that was floated in from Ellison's power launch outside the breakers was secured to *H-3* by Bogusch and his men but had not been fastened to the *McCulloch*. Bogusch ended up with the whole line on the beach and nothing attached to the other end. In another, a line from the beach was placed aboard a small dory and floated out with the tide to the *Cheyenne*. It disappeared in the fog, and the line was pulled back to the beach — minus the dory.

Although he was young, Bogusch — along with Jack Agraz — had a comprehensive understanding of the tasks at hand to move a sub after the months they'd spent engaged in the *F-4* recovery. As days wore on, crowds continued to trek to the beach to watch the rescue efforts. On Sunday, December 17, three days after the initial wreck, the local newspaper estimated that 3,000 people made the trip to the beach to watch the ships trying to get a line on the sub.

Navy setting lines to pull H-3 off the beach (USN photo courtesy of Vallejo Naval & Historical Museum)

Ultimately, Bogusch and several *H-3* crewmen rowed one of Ellison's surfboats through the breakers and managed to bring a small line to the *Arapaho*, which transferred it to the *Cheyenne*. Through a series of graduated line size transfers, the *Cheyenne* ended up with a 10-inch hawser connected to *H-3*. Howe was ready to go. Local waterfront men who were watching the whole rigging episode doubted they'd ever be able to drag the sub back out into the ocean.

Much to Howe's mounting frustrations, the enormous 10-inch-diameter tow line secured to the sub snapped when he powered up the *Cheyenne*. A steel eye that linked the hawser to the *Cheyenne* had shattered, which they later determined to be due to a faulty casting. The line ended up washing ashore in the breakers, still attached to the sub. The next day, seas kicked up and the line could not be secured again. The five rescue ships were forced to move farther offshore to avoid deeper breaker lines, which had begun to form. Over the next few days, storm waves moved *H-3* more than 300 feet through the breakers, mostly toward land. The crew found they could wade out to the sub now in shallow water at low tide and unload provisions.

Bogusch maintained a determined attitude through the whole ordeal even when reporters peppered him with questions about the likelihood of ever pulling the sub back into the ocean. "If the *H-3* were an ordinary vessel, I too might have doubts about pulling [it] off the beach," he said. "But [it's] a submarine of entirely different build. [Its] bottom curves from bow to stern and when the pull is made, it should slide over the sand easily ... [it's] as strong as steel and [its] peculiar build can make [it] capable of great resistance."

Behind the public salvaging effort, William Howe pressed ahead with charges for dereliction of duty against Lawrence Ellison, despite Ellison's compliance with all of Howe's commands since having been ordered to do so. An investigation began. A top regional Coast Guard investigator arrived in Humboldt Bay at the same time Rear Adm. Caperton arrived off the harbor entrance. Rumors started flying that Ellison would be court-martialed on the spot. That proved untrue. However, the Navy officers were gathering facts, conducting interviews, and planning a judgment.

F-4

An Ominous Reckoning

Recovery of F-4 in Honolulu Harbor in August 1915 (PigBoats.COM, Courtesy of Ric Hedman)

At midnight on August 30, five months and six days after *F-4*'s final dive, the Navy hoisted the stricken submarine from the water. It was positioned onto the submerged Inter Island Dry Dock, a privately owned floating dry dock in Honolulu Harbor. The sub was positioned over the submerged dock along with the six giant flotation pontoons that Julius Furer had designed to lift the sub off the ocean floor. The final operation of bringing F-4 out of the water had taken hours to execute.

Seawater cascaded off the massive dry dock as it slowly rose from the water. Air was being pumped into the dry dock chambers to displace the seawater. Divers were still at work under the boat adjusting rigging right up to the final minutes. Agraz, Evans, Turpin, and the rest of the crew had spent long hours preparing the rigging for this moment.

Illustration of the final lift during the salvage operations. The artist has cleverly superimposed an actual photograph of the above-water scene with his illustration of the below-water scene. All of the salvage efforts to this point had rolled the F-4 nearly upside down, and this is how it was put into the dry dock. Note: This illustration shows it rolled onto its port side, when in actuality it was rolled to starboard. (Kerrick, Military & Naval America, via Bill Lightfoot and Navsource.org)

Night lighting created shadows of the emerging hull works, and the illumination of the wet, steel hull at midnight made it appear like a ghost ship surfacing from the deep.

Crowds on the pier had been gathering for hours. There were Navy officers in white uniforms accompanied by women, Navy sailors in working blue dungarees, Japanese men and women, business owners, Hawaiian workers, sailors from the *Maryland* and the F-boat flotilla. Cars would come and go late into the night

as new onlookers arrived for a glimpse. But only a few Navy personnel were allowed near the dry dock.

Those on the dry dock experienced a haunting sight. As the sub emerged
from the water they could see a gaping dark hole surrounded by crushed and
torn steel on the port side of the boat's hull. *F-4* was lying on its starboard side,
almost upside down when it emerged from the water. The port side implosion
looked large enough to walk through. There was also damage to the conning
tower and dive planes.

The recovery of *F-4* had taken so many months that pre-scheduled Navy
command rotations had changed leadership in Hawaii by August 1915. Rear
Adm. Clifford J. Boush had replaced Rear Adm. Charles B. T. Moore as commandant of the Naval Station at Honolulu. Moore retired from the Navy. Lt.
Kirby B. Crittenden took over the *F-4* salvage effort and F-boat flotilla command
from Lt. Charles Smith, who had been promoted to lieutenant commander and
assigned to a destroyer. Ensign Harry Bogusch was promoted to lieutenant junior grade and given command of *F-1*. Crittenden had been in the public eye
earlier when *F-4* disappeared, countering the provocative claims by retired submariner Jimmy Howell.

At midnight, Julius Furer, Boush and Crittenden entered *F-4*. The three officers walked through the breached hull into the boat. A few other Navy submariners accompanied them, including Bogusch. They stood together, flicking
their lights throughout the central control compartment and shining them into
the deeper recesses of tangled machine works, filling the space with an eerie
luminescence.

There was no sign of the crew. Not a single element of human presence or
remains was visible. The compartment was in shambles. The bulkheads and overhead were littered with debris piled on top of more debris. When the boat was
unintentionally inverted at one point during the salvage, most of the battery cell
plates had tumbled from the suspended battery tanks onto the sub's overhead
and then crashed back to the inner deck when it was righted. Once on the dry

dock, F-4 again lay hard over on its port side, with its contents in total disarray.

The Navy maintained guarded secrecy around the recovered F-4. Only a tight group of personnel directly involved in the recovery were privy to viewing the sub or studying its condition. Nobody was allowed to talk about it. At least not until the Navy had a full understanding of what went wrong aboard F-4.

Maneuvering the pontoons and F-4 remains to Quarantine Dock Honolulu. They were waiting for the dry dock to be ready. (PigBoats.COM, Courtesy of Ric Hedman)

The next morning a gruesome discovery began to unfold. As the debris field inside the hull was removed, scattered remains of six crewmen were found in the main battery-control room. The remains of the other 15 were found in the engine room, and all likely died swiftly and violently when the engine room's watertight door collapsed under extreme pressure, instantly flooding the entire compartment.

As the recovery crew cleared debris from around the shattered engine room door and moved inside the compartment, the stench was overpowering. The recovery crew had to use large blowers to disperse the putrid air from the compartment before they could enter. A macabre picture emerged, piece by piece, bone by bone, mixed into the debris field of metal plates and few human belongings.

Only three personal items were recovered — a pocket book containing $71.10 in two $20 gold coins, three $10 gold coins, a one dollar bill, and a dime; an officer's hat in the central compartment; and a shoe with an initial on it. Everything else was rubble or muck.

F-4 in the Inter-Island Company dry dock in Honolulu. (PigBoats.COM, Ric Hedman)

Navy inspectors would eventually uncover the remains of Gunner's Mate First Class George Ashcroft, believed to be stationed at the torpedo room door, but forced up against a forward bulkhead, apparently blown back by an enormous underwater force. Inspectors also found remains of Machinist's Mate Second Class Charles Wells and Electrician's Mate Second Class Frank Herzog, in proximity to the electrical control panels in the battery-control compartment. Machinist's Mate First Class Ivan Mahan was also identified. The remains of the rest of the crew were beyond recognition.

Harry Bogusch was involved in the clean out and assessment of F-4's operational condition for the review board. He would be the recorder of data and notes, detailing the findings aboard the submarine. He and others spent two weeks going through the vessel, checking every valve, the dive plane controls, circuit breakers, engines, gauges, electric switch boards and every control panel in the boat. Those settings frozen in place would become the evidence of the final moments aboard F-4 and what it might have been like.

F-4 was stricken from the Navy Register as an active vessel on Aug. 31, 1915.

In mid-September, two weeks after F-4 was dry docked, a Honolulu newspaper released a front-page story that claimed a battery explosion had sent F-4 to the bottom. The newspaper article claimed Naval electricians had discovered all four main battery circuit breakers blown out as a direct result of the explosion. That corroborated a Barbers Point Lighthouse keeper's claim at the time that he heard an underwater explosion after F-4 submerged. But this wasn't the Navy talking. Somebody had leaked bits and pieces of the Naval findings that had found their way onto the front page of the paper. The Navy's official report wasn't scheduled to be released for another month.

A week later, the newspaper updated the story with a new disaster theory, about possible faulty Kingston valves, hedging their claims now as "logical conclusions" that may be based on "insufficient" knowledge. The media speculation raised the ire of the Navy, which remained silent ahead of the official findings.

The newspaper described an elaborate scenario of "possible system failures" focused on batteries, Kingston valves and circuit breakers that ultimately led to the loss of F-4. The article also suggested that the sub then drifted down into the depths, hitting an underwater rock formation that punched a hole in its side — the hole that the Navy commanders walked through once the sub was in dry dock that night. It was front-page, sensational speculation. And that's all Jimmy Howell needed to hear.

Four days after the article was published, Jimmy Howell spoke again at the

Commonwealth Club in San Francisco. He had not rescinded at all his opinion that the F-4 had been lost due to skipper error. "There was no other reason for the sinking of F-4," Howell claimed at the luncheon, "than absolute inexperience on the part of the commander. ... I take no stock in the explanation that F-4 sank through battery trouble or any other trouble."

Navy personnel inspecting the crushed F-4 hull. View is the port, forward side of the inverted sub. Remains of the conning tower are directly behind where the personnel are standing (USN photo courtesy of Scott Koen and navsource.org)

Howell went on to praise the F-boat design and criticize Navy plans to make the F-boat obsolete and end its service. He also described how one of his early dives had failed, but fortunately the boat had grounded on an undersea ledge just 60 feet below the surface. Otherwise, he said, he would have faced a similar fate as F-4.

"It's just like aeroplaning," Howell said. "If you don't know [your position] in a downward draft, you may not have enough space left to recover before hitting the earth. A submarine can easily get enough momentum to carry it beyond the depth of control, and that's what happened to F-4."

Howell's assessment would ultimately be proven completely wrong.

The Hawaiian newspaper story faulted mechanical systems and not the captain's seamanship. The newspaper claims were made despite the Navy's statement that all of the sub's surfacing mechanisms were in working order when they inspected them after bringing F-4 into dry dock. The Kingston valves were found to be functioning normally. Every valve in the boat was correctly set to surface. The automatic, pre-set emergency blow system that is activated to force the sub back to the surface at a set depth was also working and in perfect repair. Nothing seemed conclusive.

H-3

Saving *H-3*

The Mare Island Navy Yard in San Francisco Bay sent veteran marine salvager Captain Thomas P. H. Whitelaw to survey *H-3*. Whitelaw was one of the most savvy and famous marine wreckers in the world. He became known as the "The Great Wrecker of the Pacific" for all the ships he'd salvaged over the years, from tall-masted sailing ships to steel steamers. Whitelaw was a civilian. He'd come from a poor Scottish family, apprenticed himself to the British Navy when he was 12 years old and ended up in San Francisco as a teenager with 25 cents in his pocket. He'd read the Greek classics, was a self-taught philosopher and went on to amass a fortune in real estate, mining, ranching, and marine salvaging.

The Navy wanted Whitelaw to help figure out what to do with *H-3*. Whitelaw arrived off the Humboldt Coast with his salvage ship, the SS *Greenwood*, loaded with tons of salvage equipment. He looked over *H-3* sitting high on the beach, sunk in the sand, and declared that it would be cheapest to pull it back out to sea but that such an effort would pose enormous challenges. Moving it over land to the bay would be far more costly, but a more certain outcome. He estimated the cost of moving the sub overland at more than $75,000.

Whitelaw had his salvage ship standing by off the coast and offered to pull the sub from the beach. The Navy Department set hard terms, which Whitelaw rejected. "We were prepared to pull H-3 from the beach at that time," he said. "However, we were not given our own way in the matter. I had instructed the ship's master not to stand any closer than 200 yards from shore." The Navy men wanted him to anchor in the breakers. He refused and was told he might as well return to San Francisco.

A month after wrecking on the Samoa Beach, H-3 was washed farther ashore (Photograph by Emma Freeman, ibiblio)

While being interviewed on the beach that day by a local reporter, Whitelaw also had gotten wind of the charges being levied against the Humboldt Bay Coast Guard skipper, Lawrence Ellison, by Lt. Howe. "Any man who can save the lives of every man aboard a vessel placed in the position of H-3 when she was stuck and in such a surf as she was in, deserves the highest praise and commendation rather than criticism and demand for investigation of his conduct."

With that comment, Thomas Whitelaw pulled anchor and sailed back to San Francisco to relay his assessment to the US Navy.

James D. Fraser was among the crowd on Samoa Beach the day *H-3* wrecked. As James studied the sub's position and its size and shape, he began thinking how he could save *H-3*. In his mind, he could see it being dragged over the sand dunes and re-launched in Humboldt Bay. But Fraser wasn't in the Navy. He didn't think like a Navy man, nor was he a salvager.

Fraser and his partners ran a construction firm, the Mercer-Fraser Company, based across the bay in Eureka. They had a lot of experience engineering and completing industrial projects. Seemingly insurmountable odds were no deterrent. He was the company president and known to be an original thinker with an irrepressible nature. He and his late business partner, Harrison Mercer, had taken on gigantic projects in the region since the 1870s, like building the jetties into Humboldt Bay and building railroad trestles, tunnels, bridges and wharves to connect the region's timber economy to San Francisco.

In 1893, Harrison Mercer moved a 100-ton, two-story Queen Anne-style Victorian home across Humboldt Bay. They jacked it up in the town of Arcata at the north end of the bay, pulled it down to the wharf in one piece, with the roof on it, the brick chimneys towering, all the windows and doors in place and all the gingerbread trim decorating its facades and bay windows. They put it on a barge and towed it several miles down the bay to Eureka, where it was reset on a new foundation.

After the 1906 San Francisco Earthquake, Fraser opened a Mercer-Fraser office in San Francisco. They rebuilt part of the city's seawall and drove 3,000 pilings into the bay to build a wharf at the Panama-Pacific Exposition site. Mercer-Fraser was geared up to take on large projects.

Fraser also understood how to log the ancient redwoods. Old-growth redwoods were larger and heavier than the submarine. They were also long and cylindrical, similar to H-3. Loggers moved those giant trees around using steam donkeys on skid roads. That's what James Fraser was imagining for the H-3 as he stood on the beach thinking. The trick would be to get the sub out of the sand. It weighed 800,000 pounds and was sunk 10 feet into wet beach sand, which had suction like quicksand.

The headquarters of the 12th Naval District in San Francisco Bay was becoming impatient with the stalled salvage efforts and began to weigh all options. Should they pull H-3 out into the open ocean or move it across the peninsula to Humboldt Bay? One plan suggested digging a canal over a mile long and floating the sub across the peninsula into the bay, but the cost of a canal would be prohibitive.

The Navy called for bids to salvage the sub. James Fraser submitted an $18,000 bid to move the sub over the sand dunes and refloat it in Humboldt Bay. Six other salvage companies from as far away as San Francisco submitted bids as well. Fraser's bid was the lowest by far. The Navy concluded that Fraser might be out of his league trying to move H-3 for such a meager sum.

The Navy admirals decided to go for sheer power, which would be the cheapest solution in their view. They declined Fraser's bid. They ordered the cruiser USS Milwaukee to steam north from San Francisco Bay along with the Cheyenne — which had earlier returned to San Francisco — and the Navy fleet tug USS Iroquois. They would use the three ships to pull H-3 off the beach.

The Milwaukee weighed 10,000 tons and had tremendous horsepower, though its design was obsolete. The Navy used it primarily as a training ship. It recently had been outfitted with a machine shop and was intended to be repurposed as a tender for the Pacific submarine fleet and surface torpedo boats. After the loss of F-4 in 1915, the Navy wanted larger, more capable support ships for the submarines as the underwater fleet expanded. This would be the Milwaukee's first major support mission.

F-4

The Long Road Home

The day after *F-4* was brought to the surface, Assistant Secretary of the Navy Franklin D. Roosevelt wasted no time releasing a preliminary statement, mostly condemning the basic design flaws of F-boats, but released nothing specific about what happened aboard *F-4*. That would come later.

The statement laid out the premise that responsibility for controlling a dive lay solely with the commander, not the technical systems aboard the boat. That statement would add fuel to Jimmy Howell's claims of skipper error. FDR also announced that an in-depth review of the recovered *F-4* would be coming in a few weeks. Recently appointed Rear Adm. Boush, Lt. Cmdr. Furer and Lt. Crittenden, the new flotilla commander, would lead that review. Lt. Bogusch, recently given the command of *F-1*, would be the recorder.

On September 9, a lone bugler sounded taps at the Honolulu Naval Station. Hundreds of servicemen stood solemnly at attention. Flags were at half-staff. A wire from Washington DC had come in just hours before, ordering that the remains of the 21 sailors be placed aboard the *USS Supply* and brought back to the mainland. Until that wire, everyone assumed the crew would be buried in Honolulu. A large funeral procession had been anticipated. The wire from the Navy Department canceled those plans. The departure would be unannounced. The Navy did not want to create a public spectacle.

Flag-draped coffins of F-4 crew (Agraz Family Collection)

Admirals and generals surrounded by their ranking staffs, the governor of the Hawaiian Territories and the mayor of Honolulu with their own civil entourages paid final respects. Hawaii was still a US territory and wouldn't become a state for another 44 years. Three battalions of Coast Artillery formed long uniformed lines and columns that spread out across the station grounds. Scores of US infantry personnel from the Hawaiian Department of the US Army were present. The crews of *F-1*, *F-2*, *F-3*, and the *Alert* stood close by their fallen fellows, laid to rest in eight flag-draped caskets. Four caskets contained individual sailors who had been identified: Frank Herzog, George Ashcroft, Ivan Mahan and Charles Wells. The other four caskets held the unidentifiable remains of the seventeen others. They were to be placed in Arlington Cemetery in Washington DC

After a prayer, the contingent began to march. An Honor Guard in blue uniforms and white caps marched four abreast, 12 deep in four companies. Caskets were hoisted onto the shoulders of 48 pallbearers, all crew members of the other F-boats. Submariners together at the end. They marched from the Naval Station, across Allan Street to Pier Three, where the *Supply* was tied up, waiting to depart.

Rather than hoisting the caskets aboard the ship with a boom, the pallbearers closed rank and carried each one up the gang plank and placed them inside the ship.

Final march of the eight coffins on September 9, 1915 in Honolulu. (PigBoats.COM, courtesy of Pacific Fleet Submarine Museum)

Only the few civilians who happened to be on the streets that morning caught a glimpse of the final departure of the lost crew from *F-4* aboard the *Supply*.

The *Supply* had entered the harbor a few days before and lost power while approaching its mooring slip. In almost a final blow to morale, it plowed into the other three F-boats, damaging them all to the point that none was operational. The captain of the *Supply* had dropped two heavy anchors when power was lost on approach, but the anchors failed to take hold and the ship rammed the subs. The F-boats were left in fan-shaped disarray, tangled at their sterns and bows pointing out in every direction. They would all have to be dry docked and repaired. Some of the damage was significant. Hawaii was left without a single combat-ready submarine.

That incident forced the Navy to expedite the removal of F-4 from the dry dock. They needed to repair F-1, F-2 and F-3 for duty. The Great War had already reached the Eastern Pacific, with Japan capturing German-controlled territories in China and other Asian regions. The Japanese Navy was pursuing German and Austrian ships at sea. That was why the German cruiser *SMS Greier* — and its collier — claimed engine problems and had taken refuge in Honolulu Harbor. Japan and the United States were allies at the time. Japanese cruisers were frequently passing by and anchoring around Hawaii.

Unceremoniously, the dry dock was submerged and F-4 slipped silently back into Honolulu Harbor still tethered to Julius Furer's six floatation pontoons. The Navy didn't want to give up the boat but didn't know what to do with it and needed to make room for repairs on the other three subs. They considered rebuilding F-4 for training service but scuttled the idea. It had been a tomb for 21 sailors. No one would want to go under the sea in it again. But cutting it up for scrap was too dismissive of its pioneering legacy and the crew's sacrifice. F-4 remained in the harbor, hanging from Furer's pontoon chains for weeks. With no answer from the Navy Department, the local command chose to sideline F-4, towing it up the coast into Pearl Harbor, releasing it from the flotation pontoons without fanfare and allowing it to sink in a shallow, vacant corner of the bay. At the same time, a flotilla of four K-boats were dispatched to Hawaii from the West Coast to permanently relieve the damaged and near obsolete F-boats.

Later in September, the crew's long, circuitous road to a final resting place passed through Vallejo, California, on its way to Washington DC. The remains of the four F-4 sailors that had been identified were returned to their families, and a moving funeral was conducted for two of them — Ivan Mahan and George Ashcroft — at the Mare Island Naval Cemetery near San Francisco Bay.

Mahan's wife, holding their baby, who was born after the sub went down, stood with Ashcroft's wife, Mary, George's mother, and his two sisters. A large contingent of Marines, Navy officers, and crew from the *Maryland*, *Cheyenne*, *Annapolis*, *Cleveland*, and *Iris*, as well as destroyers and submarines, were present. As the caskets were lowered, there was a roll call of all the *F-4* crewmen, followed by rifle volleys. In the following days, the cortège made its way across the country. Frank Herzog was eventually buried in Salt Lake City, Utah, and Charles Wells near Norfolk, Virginia.

1915 F-4 funeral procession during the Fifty-Year Celebration of the end of the American Civil War in Washington DC (PigBoats.COM, newspaper photo)

The remains of the other 17 *F-4* crew went on to Arlington by train. Enormous crowds had gathered in Washington DC to recognize the 50th anniversary of the ending of the American Civil War. Veterans of the Grand Army of the Republic, described in a newspaper account as "gray and worn with age" had come to the U.S. capital for one last hurrah.

President Woodrow Wilson, a Virginian, encouraged veterans from both the Union and the Confederate armies to attend. An estimated quarter of a million people were in the capital for that event, including more than 20,000 veterans of the Civil War from across the country. They marched down Pennsylvania Avenue.

In the midst of that enormous throng, nearly the whole crowd witnessed the passing of the caissons carrying the flag-draped remains of the F-4 crew, on the way to Arlington National Cemetery. The veterans of the Union and Confederate armies stood in respect and saluted as the procession of lost sailors passed by.

The final small, white burial stone that was put in place in Arlington unceremoniously read, "Seventeen Unknown US Sailors, Victims of USS F-4, March 25, 1915."

Absent were the names of the F-4 crew, the recognition of their service, their commitment to pioneering the early underwater trials of the submarine, and what it had cost them. This was the first American sub to be lost in the modern Navy. After driving front-page articles from coast to coast and overseas for months, after all the heroic actions to save the crew, after recovering the vessel from depths never before achieved, the crew were cast into anonymity.

❦

Nobody can ever know the exact chain of events that occurred aboard F-4 when it made its final dive that day in Mamala Bay. After an exhaustive study, the results of the Naval Board of Inquiry were released on October 6, 1915. The report numbered 175 pages and exceeded 70,000 words. The board had examined the boat for weeks, valve by valve, bolt by bolt, gauge by gauge, its control positions, batteries, plane positions, circuit breakers, crew positions and metal structures, and it provided a briefing. It was signed by the review board staff: Rear Adm. Boush, Lt. Crittenden (commander of the 1st Submarine Division), and Lt. Cmdr. Julius Furer, whose innovations and pontoon design raised the vessel. Lt. Harry Bogusch was the inquiry's recorder of record.

What actually transpired on the F-4 that day cannot be known, but it can be imagined. Based on the inquiry board's report, here is what probably happened:

It began as a routine maneuver, with a planned submerged run. The running dive would mark more than 150 dives under Ede's watch. When Ede ordered the dive sequence to begin, he instructed crewmen to open the ballast tank vents and Kingston valves, flooding the ballast tanks and giving the boat the needed negative buoyancy to submerge. He ordered the planesmen to take the sub down to periscope depth and level it off, 30 feet beneath the surface. Then as F-4 entered deeper water farther off shore, he directed the planesmen to take it down to a cruising depth of 60 to 70 feet for the remainder of the run.

The two planesmen were standing at large control wheels on the port side of the control room. Those wheels adjusted the positions of the fore and aft dive planes, easing the boat down to the ordered depth. The bow planesman kept a close eye on the large, glass-faced depth gauge, adjusting his planes to reach the ordered depth the captain had indicated. The stern planesman studied a bubble gauge, which indicated the fore and aft angle of the boat. He adjusted his planes to keep the boat at the proper dive angle, leveling it as they reached the ordered depth.

A third crewman operated F-4's trim and drain manifold, working in a precision sequence with the planesmen, to adjust how much water was in the amidships trim tank and how much in the forward and aft trim tanks. His job was to achieve neutral buoyancy, making the planesmen's jobs easier. A helmsman steered the submarine on its course.

Ede rang up two-thirds on the engine order telegraph, then called back to make turns for five knots. This was a good submerged speed to balance battery reserves but still have enough momentum to maintain depth and course control. Ede locked in on that five-knot underwater speed for the entire submerged run.

Suddenly, things started to go terribly wrong for Ede and his crew.

The stern planesman saw it first. It was subtle — a persistent downward angle on the bubble gauge. The boat was out of trim and getting heavier forward. He turned the wheel to give rise to the stern planes to regain a level attitude. Then the bow planesman saw it. The depth gauge began to creep slowly downward. He immediately put rise on his planes to counter it and called to Ede to request more speed from the motors to help push the boat back on cruising depth.

Now the trim operator, alerted to the angle of the boat, saw it. He quickly opened valves and began pumping water from the forward trim tank to the aft trim tank to help the planesmen and to bring the boat back into proper trim. It had little effect. F-4 kept gliding downward.

From his command station in the center of the boat, Ede rang up a full bell to power out of the unintended descent. He was now on high alert. At his order, electricians immediately twisted their rheostats to the right, increasing power to the electric motors. The boat's twin propellers began thrashing the water madly with increased power. But their added turbulence stalled the propulsion as they cavitated badly.

The boat was not responding. Ede had never trusted the new test propellers installed on F-4 five weeks before. He'd thought they compromised the sub's performance under water by not taking a strong bite. They were designed to be more efficient at slow speed in order to extend battery life, but they lacked thrust. He'd made a note of that a few weeks before F-4's final dive. The submarine builder would later contest that claim.

Now Ede could feel it, the lack of thrust was making the sub harder to control as the propellers spun at higher revolutions, generating more turbulence and cavitation, reducing the water flow over the stern planes. He had to take further action.

Back in the engine room, Chief Nelson immediately sensed the skipper was struggling to control the boat as the descent continued. All of his misgivings about the condition of the boat raced to the forefront of his mind. Nelson's darkest premonitions were being realized: He dreamed the previous night that F-4 went to the bottom with the whole crew.

F-4 passed through the 100 foot mark.

Ede either ordered the ballast tanks blown or the automatic pre-set emergency blow system, the plow, activated on its own. He had to make an emergency surfacing maneuver. He'd never done one before, because he'd never had to. The

Kingston valves were opened as crewmen pulled hard on the long steel levers and compressed air roared into the ballast tanks, trying to force seawater out against the rapidly increasing deep water pressure. By now, everyone on board knew that it was a full-blown emergency.

What Ede and the entire crew of F-4 didn't realize in the first minutes of that dive was that deep inside the boat, below the battery wells, corroded rivets and plates had let loose. Sulfuric acid had been trapped in the bilges beneath the batteries for months, undetected and had slowly eaten away at the surrounding metal. Thomas Edison's claim would prove correct, that sulfuric acid in proximity to ballast tanks created a significant risk that could result in a catastrophic outcome.

Seawater had begun to enter the boat, slowly at first. Nobody knew it was happening. The intrusion was deep inside the hull, beneath the forward battery well. The crew had no visibility into that part of the boat while it was at sea.

At the start of the flooding, the sub was only 60 to 70 feet below the surface, but the pressure had increased enough that weakened rivets had sprung and seams separated. Incoming seawater in the forward battery well not only made the boat heavier overall, but it shifted weight forward, making the sub angle downward. The deeper they went, the more the pressure increased, which increased the rate of flooding.

As the boat sank deeper, the increasing water pressure reduced the effectiveness of the main ballast tank blow system, greatly slowing the rate at which the tanks were being emptied. The intensifying sound of compressed air struggling to purge seawater reverberated throughout the boat as Ede attempted to bring F-4 to the surface. The crew responded by attempting to pump the forward bilges, but the bilge suction strainers were clogged with sealant used to make the rubber lining of the battery well watertight. That action failed.

In full emergency mode, Ede rang up a flank bell, ordering the battery into series line up, jamming every amp he could into the motors. The forward battery well was now flooded, and water began bubbling up over the forward walking deck of the battery-control room, gathering at the torpedo room bulkhead. From his forward station, Gunner's Mate George Ashcroft shut and dogged down the door to the torpedo room. But the weight of the water was slowly dragging the boat down, and the power of the motors could not overcome it.

In a last, desperate attempt to drive the boat to the surface, Ede changed tactics and ordered all back full. Since they couldn't correct the down angle, he was going to try to back the sub to the surface. The sudden reversal caused the propellers to cavitate again, losing thrust. F-4 continued down. The motors whirled at maximum power, with all available amperage thrown into the effort. F-4's crew was trying to claw their way back to the surface. But the boat's electrical systems were pushed into overload.

Circuits began to burn, and breakers blew. The flooded forward battery was arcing and burning. Within moments, an explosion occurred caused by hydrogen gas buildup. All the main breakers went at once. The motors immediately quit. The Hawaiian newspaper story got that part right.

F-4 was without power. They drifted downward with increasing speed, now past 200 feet. They were taking on more water. They were out of control, headed for the bottom.

It's impossible to know how large the explosion was, but even though it was contained inside the hull, it might have weakened the structure. Overpressure from the explosion overwhelmed the crew, stunning Ede and his control room watchstanders into senselessness. Every crew member in the battery-control room was bleeding from the ears and nose from the concussion. Even the five men in the engine room felt the impact if the engine room door was open at that point.

Ede's earlier, incendiary statement in his letter to his brother was now playing out, 200 feet under the sea. "If the whole boat should suddenly vanish in smoke, I do not think that I'd be terribly surprised," he'd written.

Ten additional men entered the engine room. It was possible that Ede remained at his captain's station in the battery-control room, along with Ensign

Timothy Parker, but ordered 10 men into the engine room, possibly even when the motors were still running, in an effort to place more weight in the stern of the boat to regain control. Or it could have been a mad dash of survivors escaping the hydrogen blast and chlorine gas forming in the battery control compartment. With saltwater overflowing the forward battery wells, chlorine gas clouds engulfed the entire control room.

Shattered engine room compartment door of F-4 (PigBoats.COM, Courtesy of Ric Hedman)

F-4 continued dropping. Every crew member knew he was going to the bottom. This was it. Everyone could hear sounds of metal compression, a structural groaning through the whole boat. Riveted, metal seams began to strain, as F-1's crew experienced in 1912 when Jimmy Howell took them down to 283 feet. The hull began to warp out of shape. The deeper they went, the intensified pressure outside the boat compressed its structure, increased its weight versus buoyancy, and further reduced any chance to survive what was coming.

Then the final seconds occurred in a sudden series of violent events.

The hull near the overhead torpedo room loading hatch started to deform, bending inward. It was the weakest point of the hull. Suddenly rivets began

breaking loose, shooting across the compartment like bullets. Then the hull rup-
tured as *F-4* slammed onto the bottom, 306 feet down.

Original 1915 Arlington Cemetery F-4 headstone (PigBoats.COM)

The hull structure gave way at the top on the port side of the torpedo loading
hatch. The ocean thundered into the torpedo room. The implosion was so great
that it instantly blew the watertight iron door completely out of the forward bulkhead where George Ashcroft was stationed and sent it hurtling 50 feet across the
control room, hitting the engine room bulkhead full force. The compartment
flooded instantly. The six sailors in the compartment were gone in a second, including Alfred Ede, if he'd remained at his command station.

William Nelson and the other 14 men in the engine room felt the shock wave
of the implosion. A deep rumbling and vibration followed, as hundreds of tons
of seawater raged into the damaged hull, filling the boat.

They had only seconds to comprehend the final outcome. Only seconds to
live. Time slowed. A gigantic force on the other side of the bulkhead was ripping
their boat apart, through rivets, steel plates and compartments — until there was
just one barrier between them and eternity.

They saw the engine compartment door leading to the flooded battery control room bulge inward as the ocean exerted its massive force against the only remaining bulkhead. Hinges flexed inward. Fifteen men faced their own destruction. Perhaps a final glint of life passed before them. The bulkhead door shape began to distort. Slowly at first. Then suddenly, the iron door exploded into the engine compartment. A roar of green turbulence behind it. Then silence. *F-4* lay still at the bottom of the sea. The crew was gone.

The whole disaster, from the first sign of trouble to the final collapse, was estimated to have taken only minutes. It had been rapid and horrific. The crew knew what was happening at every turn, but they were powerless to stop it. There had been no hope for rescue, even before Charles Smith, Harry Bogusch, Jack Agraz and the flotilla realized *F-4* was missing that morning.

H-3

By Land or By Sea!

USS Milwaukee running sea trials in San Francisco Bay, California (ibiblio.org)

The *USS Milwaukee* set sail from San Francisco Bay immediately upon receiving orders to recover *H-3*. The ship's veteran captain had been on scheduled leave and missed the *Milwaukee*'s emergency departure. By Navy protocol, command fell to the ship's second ranking officer, Lt. William Newton. William Newton knew *H-3* intimately after having run it onto the rocks at Point Sur and onto a mudflat in San Diego harbor. He had never commanded a ship the size of the *Milwaukee*.

Three o'clock in the morning. January 13, 1917. Peak tide on the Northern California coast. The night sky over the ocean off the Samoa Peninsula was illuminated by search beacons and deck lights of large naval vessels assembled off the Humboldt County coast. The *Milwaukee*, *Cheyenne*, and *Iroquois* were in position several hundred yards off Samoa Beach. Navy crews were preparing to pull the *H-3* submarine off the beach.

The ships were positioned outside the breaker line. They'd spent the last week gearing up, setting tow cables, arranging logistics. Harry Bogusch, Eric Zemke and Jack Agraz were on Samoa Beach with their crew, monitoring developments via two-way communication managed by Duane Stewart, the *H-3* radio operator. It had been a month since Bogusch put *H-3* into the breakers at Samoa. It was still stuck in about 10 feet of sand far up on the beach.

The Navy had gone for sheer power. The *Milwaukee* alone had over 22,000 horsepower, more than the entire West Coast tugboat fleet combined. More than 700 Navy sailors were on board the three ships. They were under orders to pull the sub back into the open ocean.

Once onsite, Lt. Newton and Lt. Howe devised a plan to cable together the three ships and pull *H-3* off the beach. The *Milwaukee* would be backed in close to the surf line, setting port and starboard anchors off its bow and securing a 24-ton steel cable more than 1,000 feet long, floated by logs, bridled to the bow of *H-3*. The crews had worked for a week to get the massive cable in place. The *Cheyenne* and *Iroquois* would connect tow lines to the bow of the *Milwaukee* and throw their horsepower into the tow, keeping the *Milwaukee* pointed due west, straight out to sea.

Bogusch, Ellison and the mayor of Eureka, Elijah Falk, all had serious misgivings about the whole plan. Elijah Falk was not just a politician; he was a timber industry icon and had built more industrial sawmills than just about anybody in the region. He well understood the task at hand.

Bogusch respected the veteran Humboldt Bay Coast Guard skipper. Ellison knew the waters and had managed to save every one of Bogusch's men in the rescue. Bogusch and Ellison went together to meet the two commanding officers of the salvage effort and express their concerns, but Newton especially was adamant about going ahead as planned.

The planned exercise was risky. A sailor from the *Milwaukee*, Seaman H.R. Parker, had already died as a crew of eight were trying to get a line to the sub. The ship's lifeboat, in which they were riding, was hit by a 20-foot breaker that flipped the half-ton boat on top of the crew. Sailors from *H-3* who had been on the beach waiting for the line waded into the breakers to assist the men who swam for shore. Parker didn't make it.

Jack Agraz on Samoa Beach, center looking down with cap (Agraz Family Collection)

There was speculation in the news that the *H-3* crew had refused to take a boat off the beach to get the line, forcing the *Milwaukee* to launch a lifeboat into the outer, more dangerous, surf line. Jack Agraz took issue with a reporter who dared ask him the question. "I was willing to take a boat out through that surf," Jack responded. "And I'm willing to bet of the 75 men camped ashore at least 50 of them would have volunteered to come with me."

Boatswain's Mate Second Class J.B. Roth from the *Milwaukee*, who was at the tiller of the lifeboat and whose shoulder was severely injured when the boat landed on him in the surf, backed up Jack's claim. He had seen all the risks that Jack had taken to help the submarine crew get through their ordeal, and he knew about Jack's exploits in Hawaii with *F-4*. "There is not a man on the beach who would not go through the breakers with Agraz of the *H-3* in charge," Roth said. "Likewise, there are no quitters in our crew."

Howe had his doubts about Newton's plan as well. He questioned the tides. He preferred to wait another week when a king tide was predicted, raising sea levels higher that night than the average high tides. Maybe by then, the *Milwaukee*'s veteran captain would be back aboard to supervise operations.

Newton chose not to wait. He commanded the *Milwaukee* and the overall recovery mission. He had the seniority. Howe agreed to go along with the plan. The previous day they'd managed to move the sub about a foot toward sea, then backed off to wait for the next day's slightly higher tide.

❈

At peak tide, 0300 hours, Newton was on the *Milwaukee*'s bridge. He ordered the boiler room crew to bring up the power. The ship's enormous triple-expansion, twin steam engines started to rumble as the shafts turned. The crew could vaguely see the bonfires on the beach through the fog, but not the sub. The 24-ton steel cable to the sub stretched tight in the darkness, under hundreds of tons of load-bearing tension. Newton was determined to bring that sub off the beach.

H-3 began to move. Then everything started to go wrong for William Newton and the crew on the *Milwaukee.*

Howe didn't realize that Newton was going to initiate the tow at that moment. The *Cheyenne* had backed over its own tow line in the dark, and one of the ship's powerful propellers severed the line. The *Cheyenne* wasn't even tied off on the *Milwaukee* when Newton powered up the cruiser. A strong northerly coastal current began to slowly drag the ships south, angling toward the beach in the darkness. The two bow anchors that the *Milwaukee* had dropped in the sand did not hold. The sub was still mired deep in the sand and was not moving.

The *Iroquois*'s chief boatswain, Frank Bruce, acted next as his tugboat was being pulled toward the beach in the dark by the currents. From the deck of the *Milwaukee*, the silver flash of axes under the spotlights could be seen as the *Iroquois* crew cut the lines to avoid being pulled into the outer surf line. The *Milwaukee* was suddenly on its own and tethered by the steel cable to *H-3.*

On board the *Milwaukee*, the situation quickly became dire. Lt. Harvey Haislip, who had commanded the lifeboat that flipped in the breakers, felt the first solid impact of the sea bottom from his aft cabin. Haislip was still recovering from his ordeal of being flung into the ocean when the lifeboat flipped. He'd washed up on the beach half alive. Harry Bogusch had pulled him from the surf.

Haislip could hear the ship's engines pulsing from his bunk. Then the 10,000-ton ship touched bottom. The rudder caught the first impact. It sent a subtle but chilling tremor through the ship. It was the last sound anyone wanted to hear at sea. Haislip ran from his cabin to the bridge. Newton wasn't there.

"The bridge except for one man at the wheel, was deserted; the engine telegraphs were set at stop," Haislip later said. "Everyone had gone aft, the helmsman told me, to get rid of the hawsers. The compass showed that we were not heading straight seaward but had swung to [the south]."

Newton had been slow to react. Once the situation started to unravel he disengaged the engines and left the bridge to supervise cutting the tow cable at the ship's stern. The cable was jammed tight with the weight of the submarine sunk deep in the sand, tethering the ship to the beach. Currents gripped the *Milwau-*

kee, moving it south, creating enormous tension on the 24-ton cable.

Off the port side, the sound of breakers was getting louder, but they couldn't see them in the darkness and fog. They were in the grip of the southerly current, drifting into the outer surf line. The swells were running up to 20 feet high. Just the white water was visible when the waves toppled toward the shore.

Sailors struggled mightily to cut the massive cable. The steel strands were each four to six inches thick. They couldn't do it fast enough. They pounded at steel rigging pins with sledgehammers. Used hacksaws and axes to cut through the thick, steel cables. It was tedious and slow. Tension was mounting. They had acetylene torches in the machine shop. But for some reason, they weren't on deck. Nobody went to get them.

In the final moments, the crew managed to unshackle the enormous weight of the tow cable, and Newton ordered the gunnery crew to unbolt and jettison the big, six-inch deck guns to lighten the ship. Tons of armaments were cast into the sea. Then Newton ordered a last-ditch effort to power out of the current, calling for full-ahead on the steam engines, then full astern, to pivot the massive ship, unleashing bursts of 20,000 horsepower. But it was too late. The *Milwaukee* lifted, then hit bottom again.

Duane Stewart was on the beach that night, near the sub, in charge of a temporary radio transmitter providing communications from the beach to the *Milwaukee* when he received a message from the ship's radio operator who said, "Stand by for an S.O.S."

Five minutes later William Newton sent out a solemn, understated radio transmission from the bridge of the *Milwaukee* just before 0400 hours: "Stay clear. We're in the breakers, beyond help."

Newton undoubtedly felt his gut wrench as the ship's hull began to scrape hard against the seafloor. Here he was. Crashing onto the beach. At night. Again. Tethered to the cursed sub. Though instead of Big Sur, Newton was drifting into the break with hundreds of men aboard, plus a cat and a dog, the mascots of the engine room gang.

Hundreds of Sailors line the rails of the Milwaukee as US Coast Guard and Navy volunteers begin to evacuate the crew (Photo by Emma Freeman, US Naval Historical Center/ibiblio.org)

The coastal sea currents had become an ancient siren for Lt. Newton, luring his vessels onto the beaches of California. Each wave lifted and moved the *Milwaukee* farther toward the shoreline. Each breaker dropped it harder onto the seabed. By 0410 hours the ship was solidly stuck and starting to list 20 degrees westward. It was breaking up in the darkness. The $7.5 million vessel now rested sideways on the beach in the breakers with 438 crewmen aboard. Now the Navy had almost $8 million of equipment washed up on the Samoa Beach. The scale of the disaster had snowballed.

As the sun rose that morning, Harry Bogusch and Jack Agraz stood on Samoa Beach at the edge of the heavy surf. They studied the ghostly outline of the *Milwaukee*, heeled over on its starboard side in breaking seas. Towering waves thundered as they hit the cruiser broadside, lifting it and wrenching it toward shore. Its four gigantic smokestacks and twin masts pointed toward the western horizon at a 20-degree angle. The ship looked to be threatening to roll over on its side. Its angle prevented the crew from launching lifeboats.

Bogusch and Agraz and the other rescuers jumped into the fray to get the sailors off the *Milwaukee*. There had to have been a lot of "what ifs" in Bogusch's mind that day in the surfboat. What if he'd waited for the fog to lift before trying to run the Humboldt Bar? What if *Milwaukee*'s seasoned captain had not missed the ship's departure in San Francisco Bay, inadvertently turning over the ship's command to William Newton? What if the communication about when to initiate the tow had been clear?

Bogusch was a good submariner. All of his peers knew that. He had been close to the top of his class at Annapolis, but because subs were a new technology in the early 1900s, they were rife with problems and limitations. By 1917, nearly half the subs on the Pacific Coast had been on the beach at one time or another. Every dive was a training maneuver. Every problem incurred a lesson. The sea was educating Bogusch harshly.

Four hundred and thirty-eight US Navy sailors were stranded aboard the ship in the breakers. At sunrise, rows of men stood anxiously at its port rails wearing life jackets. The ship's starboard guns and ventilators languished in the seas. Just a few hours before, black smoke had billowed from those four stacks. Now those stacks were dormant. The engines were dead. The massive steel hull had fractured. The boilers had taken on eight feet of seawater. The boiler room crew was struggling to contain the seawater to avert a massive boiler explosion that would have blown the ship to pieces along with the hundreds onboard. Rescuers on the beach were preparing open surfboats, and Ellison's Coast Guard rescue team was readying a breeches buoy to evacuate the crew.

At dawn, mill whistles at the Hammond Lumber Company on Samoa Peninsula blew loudly, signaling that the *Milwaukee* was on the beach. There had been so much skepticism among local people about the Navy's plan that it had been arranged that the mill whistles would signal if things had gone wrong. The steam-

The surfboats that Harry Bogusch, Jack Agraz and the Coast Guard deployed that day faced heavy surf (Photograph by Emma Freemen, Humboldt County Historical Society)

powered whistles echoed across the bay into the towns of Eureka and Arcata. Droves of citizens started making their way toward the disaster.

Humboldt County spectators watching the wreck of the USS Milwaukee and subsequent rescue operations on Samoa Beach on January 13, 1917 (US Naval Historical photograph; NH46158 ibiblio.org)

Bogusch gave the command, then he and Agraz and the other rescuers ran hard alongside the open surfboat into knee deep water, launching the boat into the breakers. Bogusch pulled on the steering oar in the stern for all he was worth. Eight sailors pulled in unison, long hard strokes, their backs to the bow. They rowed headlong into the northern Pacific surf.

Jack caught glimpses of approaching waves over his shoulder as the men heaved on the oars. The heavy surfboat rose sharply over the tops of the combers, then plunged. The salt air ripped through Bogusch's senses. It had been six years since he'd been with a team of rowers, back at Annapolis in 1911. But those were placid waters, and the Naval Academy crew boat was sleek and ultra-light, built for sport. This was survival.

As the men rowed into the seas that morning, their memories harbored all the events that had led up to the wreck of the enormous ship. Fog could be so dense on this coastline, the currents and breakers unpredictable. Commanding H-3, Bogusch had learned that hard lesson just 30 days before. The sub's silhouette was hauntingly visible in the distance that morning, washed up high on the beach in the breakers with a severed tow cable attached to its bow. Now the *Milwaukee* was on the beach, and they needed to save hundreds of sailors before the ship broke apart. Sailors rappelled on lines secured to the deck down the side of the ship and jumped into the surfboat.

Harry Bogusch and Jack Agraz were once again fully engaged in another historic naval event unfolding around them.

❧

Lawrence Ellison thought he'd seen just about everything when he found a submarine on the Samoa Beach a month before. Now he had a 10,000-ton warship in the breakers with more than 400 men aboard. It would be the largest shipwreck ever on California's North Coast.

Ellison's Coast Guard team sprang into action. They worked feverishly to set up the breeches buoy, then began to take sailors off the ship by early afternoon. It was a 10-minute ride to shore. The first sailor — the *Milwaukee*'s Coxswain, T.S. Decker — had the ride of his life and likely prompted second thoughts by the entire crew watching from the rails.

Decker climbed into the harness and jumped off the rail of the listing ship. He dropped 20 feet and plunged beneath the breakers. Then the ship jerked and pitched farther away from shore, instantly tightening the breeches buoy line almost to the snapping point, flinging Decker 30 feet into the air then dropping him hard, back into the breakers. But he remained in the harness.

The evacuation of the ship was only about getting the sailors off safely. They were told to leave all possessions behind, except the cat and dog from the engine room. Even the ship's purser left $90,000 in cash in the ship's safe. They would have to come back later for that. Bogusch and Agraz and the other crewmen fought the surf that day to make numerous trips with the surfboat to pick up sailors from the *Milwaukee*. One of those trips they had the spaniel and tomcat from the engine room. Ellison's crew kept a steady pace of evacuation, until every sailor was safely on the beach by evening. The rescue had taken more than 12 hours to complete.

H-3 and Milwaukee (background) wrecked on Samoa Beach (ibiblio/PigBoats.COM)

Later that evening, a group of *Milwaukee*'s sailors, primed for a night out on the town, showed up in a Eureka restaurant with the tomcat in their arms. They didn't want the cat to be lost in all the chaos, so they'd carried it with them that night around town. They made the cat the guest of honor for the evening, and it

Breeches buoy taking sailors off the Milwaukee (Photograph by Emma Freeman - US Naval Historical Center-ibiblio.org)

ate at the table in the restaurant with them.

Under Ellison's leadership, not a single injury or loss of life had occurred on the two rescues. In the space of 30 days, his US Coast Guard crew from the Humboldt Bay Station had saved 465 US Navy sailors, a cat and a dog. The one, tragic loss of life was Navy Seaman H.R. Parker, who had perished on the ill-fated launch of the lifeboat from the *Milwaukee*.

But the Hoodoo itself, the *H-3*, still lingered in the twilight, stuck fast in the deep sands of Samoa Beach. The Navy needed a new plan.

A day after the wreck of the *Milwaukee*, the Navy signed a contract with Mercer-Fraser Company to take *H-3* over the peninsula by land to Humboldt Bay. James Fraser stuck by his original quote of $18,000 to deliver the sub over the dunes to the bay in 90 days. It was the same plan the Navy had rejected a month before. There were still people in the Department of the Navy who thought it was a mistake to turn a submarine over to a local contractor, but the Navy had run out of options.

The *Milwaukee* was a total loss. *H-3* was still high up the beach, stuck in the sand but in good condition. The national press was all over the incident. The Navy had left millions of dollars of equipment on the Samoa Beach.

After the loss of the *Milwaukee*, Harry Bogusch, Eric Zemke, Jack Agraz and most of the *H-3* crew boarded a local tow boat in Humboldt Bay and rode out over the Humboldt Bar to meet Lt. William Howe and the *Cheyenne*. Howe had chosen to wait a couple miles offshore instead of risking another incident on the notorious bar crossing. A skeleton naval crew remained on the Samoa Beach to watch over the transit of *H-3*.

With its entourage of exhausted sailors, Lt. Howe and the *Cheyenne* began the journey south toward San Francisco Bay.

In a race against tides, Mercer-Fraser's crew of construction workers and timbermen jacked up *H-3* from its entombment in 10 feet of beach sand using shovels, a pile driver, tree jacks and large wooden bracing timbers. It was a slow and arduous process lasting many days. They built a massive timber-framed cradle around the sub as it was suspended above the sands over the incoming tides, with two enormous, 80-foot logs several feet in diameter lashed with cables to each side of the sub. They worked between tides. The preparation took over a month. At a low tide, they set the cradled sub back onto the beach on wooden rollers and used the mechanical steam donkeys with cables to pull the heavy load up away from the surf, just ahead of the day's returning tide.

Local construction firm, Mercer-Fraser Company, dug H-3 out of 10 feet of sand and built a lifting frame around it (Humboldt Bay Maritime Museum)

James Fraser ingeniously used engineering concepts he'd learned from building trestles and wharves and from relocating buildings. He combined the methods of the local lumberjacks and the railroads to move the submarine by constructing a three-rail wooden track of large-dimension timbers bolted together that followed the rolling contour of the sand dunes for more than a mile toward the bay. Like a railroad, he kept the grade under five percent.

The giant logs that cradled H-3 rode directly on top of the wooden rails as donkey spools winched the load along. Fraser skidded the sub about 500 feet a

James Fraser (center of the photo) standing in front of H-3 as it moves along his improvised rail system, pulled by steam donkeys. (Naval History and Heritage Command - NH-53856)

James Fraser (far right) stands with the Mercer Fraser salvage crew, Navy personnel and local citizens aboard the re-launching of H-3 into Humboldt Bay in April 1917 (Naval History and Heritage Command - NH-53858)

day on those rails. They finished the project within budget, one week ahead of the 90-day contract deadline. On April 20, he delivered *H-3* back into the water, this time in Humboldt Bay, with no damage from its overland transit.

H-3 was recommissioned in April 1917 in Humboldt Bay after James Fraser handed it back to the Navy to great local fanfare. It was towed across the Humboldt Bar and down the coast to San Francisco by the Navy tug *Iroquois*.

In The Wake

Epilogue

Edison's Battery Explosion

Two days after the wreck of the *USS Milwaukee*, Thomas Edison's alkaline battery aboard submarine *E-2* exploded while the sub was in the Brooklyn Naval Yard for maintenance. Edison's batteries had been tested extensively aboard *E-2* and were being designed into the new *L-8*, one of the Navy's most advanced submarine designs at the time. Battery performance had been exceptional; boats could stay under water longer, cruise farther, re-charge faster, and eliminate chlorine gas risk.

Then one afternoon during a re-charging test on *E-2*, a blast ripped through the interior of the sub, killing four and injuring 10. An investigation was not conclusive but determined the blast was an explosion of gases, most likely hydrogen; however, it was never officially stated. The Navy canceled the *L-8* alkaline battery installation. It later dropped Edison's batteries from the submarine program altogether because of the undetermined cause of the *E-2* explosion, ending Edison's dream of powering submarines with his alkaline batteries.

USCG's Ellison Prevails

Lawrence Ellison, the US Coast Guard Keeper of the Humboldt Bay Rescue Station, stood before a United States Government Court as they reviewed all the interviews, accounts and actions of the Coast Guard involving the wreck of the *H-3* and *Milwaukee*. Ellison had been accused of incompetence by Lt. William Howe, commander of the *Cheyenne* and H-boat flotilla. The court found Ellison not guilty, and he was exonerated of all charges. After reviewing his actions and conduct, he was recommended to receive a commendation for superior performance and outstanding efforts in saving so many lives.

Founding of the Naval Submarine School

In the winter of 1917, after the loss of *F-4* and grounding of *H-3*, the newly established Naval Submarine School in New London, Connecticut, mustered its first class of enlisted sailors. The school and submarine base at Groton, Connecticut, under Cmdr. Yates Sterling Jr., was founded June 21, 1916, and is still in existence. Graduates from this school take their first step toward being recognized as a qualified submariner.

Demise of the *Milwaukee*

The USS Milwaukee on Samoa Beach 1917 — a total loss (NavSource.org, contributed by Robert M. Cieri)

The *Milwaukee* joined the Pacific Graveyard of Ships. The Navy built a railroad trestle out to the *Milwaukee* from the Samoa mill and salvaged much of its equipment and guns that summer but left the ship to the sea. It slowly disintegrated over time, and its steel superstructure was cut up for scrap in the following years. Its metal bulkheads are still visible at minus tides.

FATE OF THE SISTER BOATS

After the loss of *F-4*, the three remaining F-boats were transferred back to the West Coast as training vessels. On December 17, 1917, a year after *H-3* wrecked on Samoa Beach, *F-3* rammed *F-1* during a practice run in dense fog off the California coast near Point Loma due to poor weather, poor seamanship, and missed communications. *F-1* sank in over 600 feet of water in seconds, ironically in the same vicinity that Jimmy Howell had taken *F-1* down on its record, 283-foot dive in 1912. Five crew escaped, 19 went down with the boat, never to be recovered. Three of the crew who were lost had been on *H-3* when it wrecked at Samoa Beach — Clyde W. "Batlin" Wyatt (who had come down hard onto a case of eggs in the after battery compartment of *H-3* with Duane Stewart), Ray E. Scott and Guy R. Stewart. The remaining *F-2* and *F-3* boats were decommissioned and scrapped in 1922.

In 1920, *H-1* ran aground and sank at Baja California, Mexico, searching for the entrance to Magdalena Bay. It was abandoned, with the loss of four crew members, including the captain, who perished trying to save his men. The remaining *H-3* and *H-2* boats sailed to the east coast in 1922 and were decommissioned. Both subs were scrapped in 1931.

DOLPHINS - 1924

In June 1923, Captain E.J. King, commander, Submarine Division Three, suggested to the Secretary of the Navy that a distinguished insignia for "qualified submariners" be adopted. He submitted a pen and ink drawing of two dolphins alongside a submarine. The suggestion was enthusiastically passed along through Naval departments, and various design iterations evolved. However, the actual origin of the Dolphins design is credited to William C. Eddy, a cadet in the Naval Academy in 1922, when he was on the Class Crest Committee and submitted a "bows on" photo of the USS 0-2 submarine, adding two dolphins on both sides of the boat. That concept made it up the ranks.

In March of 1924, Theodore Roosevelt Jr., acting Assistant Secretary of the Navy and eldest son of Teddy Roosevelt, accepted the Dolphins design — two dolphins on the bow planes of a submarine. That basic design is still used today, though there have been iterations of style.

At first, only qualified submariners on subs could wear the insignia. If they were transferred to a surface ship, they could no longer wear Dolphins. After years of varying uniform dress codes and rules, submarine officers were authorized in 1950 to have gold-plated pin-on Dolphins and enlisted submariners, sterling silver Dolphins. Both had embroidered options.

F-4 Salvage Pontoons — 1915-1940

Julius Furer's incredible feat of raising F-4 to the surface from 306 feet down established a new engineering design that would be used numerous times to recover submarines over the next 25 years. Two of Furer's original pontoons were used again in 1925-1926 as supplemental equipment to assist six larger pontoons built to salvage USS S-51 (SS-162). The six larger pontoons built to Furer's original design, were later used for the S-4 salvage in 1928 and again in 1939 for the salvage of the big fleet boat Squalus (SS-192)

F-4 LEGACY – 1915-1940

New USS F-4 Arlington Cemetery Memorial in 2000 (PigBoats.COM)

For 25 years, F-4 languished just beneath the surface of Pearl Harbor in Magazine Loch, near the Submarine Base. Finally, in 1940, the Navy decided to bury F-4. Its rusting, abandoned form was barely visible in the shallow, murky waters of Pearl Harbor — a haunting reminder of what had transpired 25 years before. The Navy dug a deep underwater trench next to the boat and pushed F-4 into the void and covered it over. It would remain there under 10 feet of mud, eternally submerged beneath the bay.

Then there was the matter of the crew cast into anonymity at Arlington Cemetery.

That had never sat right with submariners who knew the story. Or anybody else who had ridden the emotional rollercoaster of the event at the time. But over the years, the F-4 saga was mostly forgotten. Two World Wars came and went. Even those who knew the story and would go to Arlington to search for the small headstone could never find it. The cemetery was vast and records incomplete.

But in 2000, a group of Navy veterans could be seen canvassing the cemetery for weeks and weeks, looking for the F-4 crew's burial spot. Their actions were eerily reminiscent of the flotilla searching the waters off Honolulu Harbor 85 years before, dragging cables, diving, looking for F-4. The Navy searchers were from U.S. Submarine Veterans, Inc., led by Chaplain and Rabbi Richard Mendelson.

Their mission is "to perpetuate the memory of shipmates who gave their lives in the performance of their duties, that their dedication, deeds, and supreme sacrifice be a constant source of motivation toward greater accomplishment."

Even with the help of Arlington historians, it took the group months to find the small headstone of the F-4 crew. They were shocked at what they discovered. "It was dirty, deteriorating and entirely too small for the 21 victims of the F-4," Mendelson said. "We left the cemetery speechless. I looked back at the hill where they were buried and then to our group. There was not one dry eye. ... How sad it is that these submarine pioneers gave their lives for us and we have never acknowledged their sacrifice or existence."

Mendelson and his peers researched the National Archives in Washington DC to get a list of the crew members and then sought out relatives. They organized a full military memorial ceremony at the rediscovered gravesite, with a Navy Honor Guard, a drum and bugler, and a veteran's color guard.

The group convinced Arlington Cemetery to create a larger, more detailed headstone with the names and ranks of all 21 sailors from F-4 to replace the original, anonymous stone, and they arranged for a permanent memorial display of F-4 at the National Navy Memorial in Washington, DC.

Richard Mendelson and his group weren't done yet. With the new marker in place, they wanted to save the century-old headstone for a museum. But cemetery law requires that headstones being replaced had to be sent to a rock crusher and destroyed. After much negotiating on Mendelson's part, Arlington Cemetery agreed to turn over the F-4 headstone to the Navy's Pacific Fleet Submarine Museum, at Pearl Harbor in Honolulu, near F-4's burial site. It is the only headstone ever transferred from a national cemetery. In 2021, the museum became home to the original headstone and a dedicated memorial to the pioneering submariners of *F-4*.

JACK AGRAZ – 1879-1934

Jack Agraz second from left, others unidentified (Agraz Family Collection)

Jack Agraz served 16 years in the Navy before retiring in 1920. After serving on *H-3*, Jack was chief gunner's mate aboard the armed merchant ship *SS Col. E.L. Drake* during the Great War. He was awarded the Navy Cross for heroic actions when he fired on and hit a German submarine that was stalking their ship. In 1919, Jack disappeared into Europe for a few months on a naval assignment on the Italian front, where he was injured by a large shell fragment that shattered his knee and led to his retirement. In 1930, Jack married his cousin Bertha Corona. They had two children and resided in Santa Cruz, California. Jack Agraz passed away suddenly at his Santa Cruz home on July 6, 1934.

HARRY R. BOGUSCH — 1887-1934

Following a Board of Inquiry of the *H-3* accident, Lt. Harry Bogusch was court martialed for "improperly hazarding the vessel under his command," but he was immediately reinstated as a lieutenant with a recommendation of clemency because "he is a young officer of unusual ability and promise." Bogusch lost a few promotion points, but those were later reinstated as well. After the *H-3* incident, he transferred into Naval Aviation and eventually rose to command a seaplane squadron in the Pacific Fleet. His squadron received honors for performance aboard the aircraft carrier *USS Lexington* in 1928. He also led squadrons on tours and war games into Central America, along the West Coast, and the Mexican Coast. His numerous long-distance flights cited in newspapers across the country occurred at the time when Charles Lindbergh and Amelia Earhart were establishing flight records. He survived a seaplane crash in the Pacific, escaping the wreckage before the plane sank. He was transferred to Washington, DC to the Navy's Bureau of Aeronautics. Harry Bogusch passed away suddenly at his East Coast home on September 7, 1934, just 60 days after Jack Agraz passed away at his West Coast home. Harry Bogusch is buried in Arlington National Cemetery.

CREW MEMBERS OF F-4 AND H-3

HEROES ALL OF THEM—GONE BUT NOT FORGOTTEN.

THE ILL-FATED U.S. SUBMARINE F-4.

IN AFFECTIONATE REMEMBERANCE OF OUR BELOVED SHIPMATES
WHO ACCIDENTALY LOST THEIR LIVES DURING SUBMARINE EXERCISES OFF HONOLULU HARBOUR.
MARCH 25TH 1915 BELOVED BY ALL THEIR SHIPMATES. R.I.P.

F-4 CREW – 1915	H-3 CREW – 1916	
George T. Ashcroft, GM1	Jack Agraz, GMC/chief of the boat	W.C. Senst, EM1
Clark C. Buck, GM2		Duane F. Stewart, EM1
Ernest C. Cauvin, MM2	Jim M. Anderson, EMC	Guy R. Stewart, MM1*
Harley Colwell, MM1	T.H. "Toad" Blabon, GM1	J.P. Traino, Oiler
Walter F. Covington, MM1	C.L. Brown, MM2	G.C. Walker, EM2
George L. Deeth, EM1	J.J. "Bobby" Burns, GM1	G.W. Wells, MM1
Alfred L. Ede, LT(jg) (CO)	Harry R. Bogusch, LT(jg) (CO)	Clyde W. "Batlin" Wyatt, MM1*
Frederick Gilman, GM1		
Aliston H. Grindle, EMC	T.H. Carter, EM3	Eric F. Zemke, LT(jg) (XO)
Frank N. Herzog, EM2	W.E. "Doc" Carter, EM3	
Edwin S. Hill, MM1	H.G. Fosket, MM2	*Died on F-1 sinking
Francis M. Hughson, MM1	Steve Galazitas, MMC	
Albert F. Jennie, EM2	A.G. Grassell, GM2	
Archie H. Lunger, GM2	L.K. Johnson, MMC	
Ivan L. Mahan, MM1	L. Peterson, GM3	
Horace L. Moore, GM1	E.F. Rodgers, Coxswain	
William S. Nelson, MMC	W. Robinson, GM3	
Timothy A. Parker, ENS (XO)	J.B. Rollins, EM1	
Frank C. Pierard, GMC	Tom Scarvin, MM1	
Charles H. Wells, MM2	R.F. Schmidtbauer, MM1	
Henry A. Withers, GM1	Ray E. Scott, EM2*	

Frank W. Crilley – 1883-1947 – Crilley was awarded the nation's highest military award, the Medal of Honor, and the Coast Guard Silver Life Saving Medal for the rescue of William Loughman during the *F-4* salvage. He later worked on the salvage efforts for *S-51* (SS-162) in 1926 and on the *S-4* (SS-109) in 1928. He was awarded the Navy Cross for his work on the *S-4*. In 1931 he served as the second officer and master diver on the civilian submarine *Nautilus* during an Arctic expedition. In 1939, he returned to submarine salvage, this time assisting in the rescue of 33 men from the sunken *Squalus* (SS-192) and eventually working on the subsequent salvage. Frank Crilley is buried at Arlington National Cemetery.

Julius A. Furer – 1880-1963 – After the tremendous engineering feat of salvaging *F-4*, Furer rose steadily in US Navy ranks to become one of the most renowned Naval engineers of his time. He was awarded the Navy Cross for his contributions during WWI. He designed subchasers and modernized battleships, and held Naval attaché posts in Europe and South America. He was promoted to the rank of rear admiral at the start of WWII and coordinated scientific research and development between civilian and military agencies. He came out of retirement in 1951 and produced the study, "Administration of the Navy Department in World War Two" for the Naval History Division. Julius Furer is buried at Arlington National Cemetery.

William B. Howe – 1883-1968 – After his service on the *Cheyenne*, Howe was promoted to commander in 1920 and was given command of the destroyer *Worden* (DD-16). In 1923 he taught at the Naval War College and in 1925 was appointed as the commanding officer of Naval Station Tutuila in American Samoa. During WWII, he worked the Office of the Chief of Naval Operations, OP-16 Naval Intelligence Branch.

Charles A. Lockwood – 1890-1967 – Lockwood was an ensign on *A-2* in the Philippines when *F-4* disappeared. He had a brilliant career in the Navy and

submarines, eventually rising to the rank of admiral and being appointed as commander, Submarine Force, Pacific Fleet, during WWII. A highly capable and
personable officer, he was universally respected by those who served under him,
and he was instrumental in developing and executing the war-winning submarine strategies and operations. He was awarded the Distinguished Service Medal
three times, in addition to the Legion of Merit. He served as the Naval Inspector
General after the war. In retirement, he became an author, writing such historical
works as *Hell at 50 Fathoms* and *Tragedy at Honda.* He also worked as a technical
consultant on numerous movies and television shows.

William F. Loughman – 1884-1959 – Though Loughman never fully recovered from the near-fatal encounter he had while diving on *F-4*, he went on to
have a long and successful career in the Navy as a diving supervisor. He was
awarded the Navy Cross for his extensive efforts salvaging the submarines *S-51*
and *S-4*, working alongside Frank Crilley.

William F. Newton – Lt. Newton was scheduled to be court-martialed for
wrecking the *Milwaukee* on the Samoa Beach. But with the United States entering the Great War in 1917, Navy witnesses were scattered afar. The case was
dropped. Despite his misfortunes involving *H-3*, Newton was recognized for
having made significant contributions to the advancement of the early Pacific
submarine fleets and programs.

Charles E. Smith – On a previously scheduled duty rotation, the Navy transferred Smith from his command of the Pacific submarine flotilla in Hawaii in
1915, just before *F-4* was brought to the surface. He went on to a distinguished
career, commanding the destroyer *Greer* (DD-145) and the fleet oiler *Kanawha*
(AO-1). He retired from the Navy as a captain.

Duane Stewart – Stewart served on several different ships after the *H-3* disaster, including a subchaser in WWI. After a long career in the Navy, he retired as radioman chief petty officer (RMC). In civilian life, he ran a radio compass station at Pt. St. George, California. Fifty-five years after the grounding of H-3, Stewart spoke at a summer meeting of the Humboldt County Historical Society at the Samoa Cookhouse on Humboldt Bay, one mile from the site of the H-3 accident. Though originally from North Dakota, he retired in Crescent City, California, just north of where H-3 hit the beach. He wrote a 50-page manuscript describing what happened that day inside H-3.

John Henry "Dick" Turpin – 1876-1962 – Turpin served on the *Cheyenne* as well as the *Alert* and 10 other Navy ships. In 1917, he was promoted to chief gunner's mate on the cruiser *USS Marblehead*, making him one of the first African American chief petty officers in the US Navy. He retired from active duty in 1925. As a civilian, he worked as a master rigger and diver at Puget Sound Navy Yard in Bremerton, Washington. In 2020, an attempt to retroactively award Turpin the Medal of Honor for his rescues during the *Bennington* explosion failed due to the inability to locate living witnesses. A local congressman and social historian in Kitsap County, Washington, succeeded in officially changing the name of Bremerton's US Post Office to the John Henry Turpin Post Office.

Eric F. Zemke – 1888-1975 – Eric Zemke went on to get his own submarine command aboard the *R-7* (SS-84) and *L-1* (SS-40). He was awarded the Navy Cross for heroic actions during WWI. He retired as a captain.

GLOSSARY

INDIVIDUALS APPEARING IN THE STORY

Jack Agraz CGM – Chief of the boat, chief gunner's mate and diver for *F-1* in Honolulu and then for *H-3* on the West Coast; senior enlisted man on the sub, reports to
the commanding officer

Lt. j.g. Harry R. Bogusch – Ensign and, later, lieutenant junior grade (Lt. j.g.) and commanding officer of *F-1* in Honolulu in 1915 and commanding officer of *H-3* on the
West Coast in 1916

F-4 - 1915

Lt. Charles E. Smith – Lieutenant and commander of the Hawaiian F-boat flotilla
(*F-1, F-2, F-3, F-4*) and sub-tender *USS Alert*; also commanding officer of *F-1* before
turning over command to Lt. j.g. Bogusch in 1915

Lt. j.g. Alfred Ede – Lieutenant junior grade and commanding officer of *F-4* in Hawaii

Lt. j.g. James Howell – Lieutenant junior grade and former commanding officer of *F-1*
when stationed in California

Lt. Cmdr. Julius Augustus Furer – US Naval Architect, Constructor and Engineer,
Pearl Harbor, Hawaii

George Evans CMM – Chief machinist's mate and diver on *F-3* in Hawaii

Josephus Daniels – US Secretary of the Navy in 1915

Franklin D. Roosevelt – Assistant US Secretary of the Navy in 1915

Frederick W. Metiers BMC – Chief boatswain's mate and skipper of the *Navajo*

John Henry Turpin GM1 – Gunner's mate first class and diver on the *Alert*

George D. Stillson CGM – Leader, US Navy deep-sea dive team 1915 assigned to *F-4*
recovery

Frank W. Crilley CGM – Diver, US Navy deep-sea dive team 1915 assigned to *F-4* recovery

Stephen J. Drellishak CGM – Diver, US Navy deep-sea dive team 1915 assigned to
F-4 recovery

William F. Loughman CGM – Diver, US Navy deep-sea dive team 1915 assigned to
F-4 recovery

Fred C. Nielson CGM– Diver, US Navy deep-sea dive team 1915 assigned to *F-4* recovery

Dr. G.R. French– Chief Medical Advisor, US Navy deep-sea dive team 1915 assigned
to *F-4* recovery

H-3 - 1916

Duane Stewart, EM1 – Electrician's mate first class and radio operator on *H-3*

Lt. j.g. Eric Zemke – Lieutenant junior grade and executive officer on *H-3*; reported to
the commanding officer

Lt. William Howe – Lieutenant and commanding officer of the Pacific H-boat flotilla

(H-1, H-2, H-3) and sub tender USS *Cheyenne*

Lt. William F. Newton – Former commanding officer of H-3; designated commander of USS *Milwaukee* and H-3 salvage effort

Jim Anderson, CEM – Chief electrician's mate, H-3

T.H. "Toad" Blabon GM1 – Gunner's mate first class

Steve Galazitas, CMM – Chief machinist's mate

Lawrence Ellison – US Coast Guard warrant officer; keeper of the Humboldt Bay Life Saving Station in Northern California

Werner Sweins – US Coast Guard surfman, USCG Humboldt Bay Station, California

Walter Pratt – Chief Electrician at Hammond Lumber Company at Samoa, California

Submarine Terms

Ballast Tanks: A series of chambers in the lower portion of boat — in a U shape — below and to the side of the battery tanks, used to adjust the sub's buoyancy, allowing it to stay on the surface or to dive. To dive, seawater is flooded into the tanks through the Kingston valves at the bottom of the tanks while vent valves are opened at the top of the tanks, allowing the displaced air to escape. To surface, the top vents are kept shut, the Kingston opened, and high-pressure air is blown into the tanks to push the water out. Ballast tanks are fully flooded for submerged runs and or completely emptied for surface runs.

Battery Compartment: The compartment of the boat that contains the submarine's storage batteries, housed underneath a walking deck inside the hull. The F-boats contained just one large battery compartment that included all the batteries and the control room. The H-boats had two battery compartments on either side of the control room, separated by watertight bulkheads and doors: the forward battery compartment, forward of the control room; and the after battery, aft of the control room. Above the walking decks in the battery compartments were electrical panels, the gyroscope, crew berthing and messing spaces, the galley, and a primitive, open toilet.

Battery Tanks: The lead-lined compartment below the walking deck in the battery compartments. This is where the lead-acid battery cells that provide lighting and submerged propulsion power for the electric motors are kept.

Bridge: A platform on top of the conning tower fairwater that provides a watch station for the officer of the deck and the lookouts. Some boats had a steering station on the bridge, which is outside of the pressure hull and free floods when the boat dives.

Conning Tower: A small, vertical and round watertight steel compartment that rises from the submarine's outside deck and is attached to the pressure hull directly above the control room. On F-4 and H-3 the tower contained a periscope station and glass deadlights to see out. A watertight hatch separates it from the control room below, and another hatch in the overhead allows access to the bridge which is open to the sea. Two steel ladders provide access between the three decks.

Control Room: This compartment, located in the center of the boat, contains all controls for diving and surfacing the submarine, controls for adjusting ballast, a steering station and controls for adjusting the boat's speed through the water.

Dive Planes: Forward and aft adjustable, horizontal control surfaces outside the bow and stern of the submarine, used to change the boat's depth or up and down angle, similar to an airplane

Gyrocompass: A nonmagnetic compass, based on a fast-spinning device that can determine true north based on the rotation of the earth. This was the cutting edge of navigation in 1915 and 1916.

Helm: The wheel or steering wheel that guides the rudder

Kingston Valve: A large, heavy valve that closed off the bottom of the ballast tanks. When opened, it allowed seawater to enter the tanks, displacing air and making the boat heavy enough to dive. A ballast tank vent valve also had to be opened to allow the air to escape when seawater flooded the tanks. Kingston valves were mechanically controlled by long steel levers.

The Plow: This was a slang term in 1915, not widely used in the Navy, that refers to an automatic emergency surfacing system in the early boats. The captain would set an automatic air pressure discharge system to force seawater out of the ballast tanks at a predetermined depth (usually not more than 100 feet). If the boat descended below that level for any reason, the system would engage and force seawater from the ballast tanks and the boat would automatically surface.

Props: The vessel's propellers

Rudder: A vertical plane used for steering the boats to port and starboard

Shaft: The subs drive shafts that connect motors to propellers

Signal Bell: Air-powered, underwater communication device used in 1915 and 1916, audible up to four miles underwater.

Trim Tanks: Smaller tanks located at the forward and aft ends of the boat and amidships. The seawater volume in these tanks is constantly being adjusted by the captain to maintain neutral buoyancy while submerged and to help keep the sub on an even keel.

Ventilators: Stationary vents that rise up from the submarine deck, used to capture fresh air and ventilate the boat on surface runs, but that are shut or removed for dives.

SUBMARINES AND SHIPS IN THE STORY

Submarines

USS A-2 (SS-3) – USS Adder

USS E-2 (SS-25) – USS Sturgeon

USS F-1 (SS-20) – USS Skate

USS F-2 (SS-21) – USS Barracuda

USS F-3 (SS-22) – USS Pickerel

USS F-4 (SS-23) – USS Skate

USS H-1 (SS-28) – USS Seawolf

USS H-2 (SS-29) – USS Nautilus

USS H-3 (SS-30) – USS Garfish

USS K-7 (SS-34)

USS L-8 (SS-48)

Other Vessels

USS Alert (AS-4)

USS Arapaho (AT-14)

USS Bennington (PG-4)

USS Buffalo (AD-8)

USS Cheyenne (BM-10)

USS Dale (DD-4)

USS Iroquois (AT-46)

USS Maine (BB-10)

USS Maryland (ACR-8)

USCGC McCulloch

USS Mohican (Tender)

USS Navajo (AT-52)

USS West Virginia (ACR-5)

USAT Sheridan

USS Truxtun (DD-14)

RMS Lusitania (UK)

SS Greenwood

SMS Greier (Germany)

Izumo (Japan)

Naval Historians and Advisors

TN(SS) Richard C. Hedman, USN (Ret.)

From his home state of Washington, mostly spent in the Seattle area, Ric joined the Navy in 1964 and spent a year in Submarine School at New London in Groton, Connecticut. He was assigned to the pre-commissioning crew of the submarine USS Flasher (SSN-613) and served on numerous patrols across the Pacific Ocean. After four years active duty, he transitioned to the Navy Reserve and was assigned to the Submarine Reserve Unit in Seattle. During this period, he performed temporary duty on the diesel submarine USS Cusk (SS-348). He is Qualified on Submarines.

In civilian life in the Puget Sound region, Ric engaged in yacht repair and the biotech industry while also developing a passion for the early history of the submarine service. He began producing a small web page, culminating in the creation of PigBoats.COM, co-founded with author and historian David Johnston. Ric has collaborated with numerous authors on submarine history matters, serving as a technical advisor on approximately a dozen books and manuscripts. He is a member of the local Seattle Base of the United States Submarine Veterans, Inc. and has been its Base Commander on three occasions. Ric resides in Mountlake Terrace, Washington.

DCC (SS/SW) David L. Johnston, USN (Ret.)

A native of Dexter, Michigan, Chief David Johnston enlisted in the Navy in September 1983. Over the course of a 21-year career, he served on the submarine USS Darter (SS-576) and five other surface ships, including the USS Forrest Sherman (DDG-98). His overseas deployments include the western Pacific, the Persian Gulf, the Red Sea, and the Gulf of Aden. He has been on staff with four Navy Operational Support Centers and the Supervisor of Shipbuilding in Bath, Maine. He retired from active duty in August 2019 and is Qualified in Submarines and Surface Warfare.

David is the author of the Visual Guide series of articles concerning US submarine identification, and two of his articles on submarine history have been published by the Naval Submarine League in The Submarine Review. He is a team member with the Lost 52 Project as a research historian, an editor of the project's quarterly newsletter, and co-founder of the website PigBoats.COM. He has been a contributor to the US Naval Institute's Proceedings magazine and is also a volunteer photo analyst and researcher for Navsource.org. David resides in Norfolk, Virginia, with his wife, Theresa.

Acknowledgements

In compiling this story, I received invaluable assistance from numerous people who provided source material, advice, and editorial assistance along the way. First, this story emerged from the original manuscript by Duane Stewart and from the diary and photos of Jack Agraz. A sincere posthumous recognition to them and great thanks to John Agraz and Jeanette Quick for their family archive contributions.

Before the Dolphins Guild would not have achieved such in-depth detail, authenticity, and photographic imagery without the contributions of Ric Hedman and David Johnston, who co-founded the website PigBoats.COM, historic archive on US submarines from 1900–1940. Both Ric and David served on submarines in the Navy and read through the story to advise on technical accuracies, terminology, historical context, submarine operations, as well as Navy protocol relating to F-4, H-3 and other naval vessels of the era. They also provided open access to their photo archives that illustrate this story.

Much gratitude as well to my longtime friends and posse of willing readers of yet another manuscript. Their commentaries and critiques ultimately helped shape this story through numerous versions. Many thanks to Robby Jarvis, Margot Genger, Regina White, Connie Peterson, Randy Bakke, and Page Read. Page is also a retired naval officer from diesel submarines. He was ensign on the *USS Corporal (SS 346)* and Lt. j.g. on the *USS Trout (SS 566)*. His input influenced fine points in the story as well as the title concept and cover details.

Special recognition to Sarah Bellian, Museum Curator at the Pacific Fleet Submarine Museum at Pearl Harbor, which houses an extensive exhibit and collection of F-4 archives. Sarah met with my editor when she was in Hawaii visiting the museum and provided access to scores of documents and photographs for the project.

My appreciation as well to Cory Platt for his archival assistance at the Humboldt County Historical Society and to Don Hofacker at the Humboldt Bay Maritime Museum for their contributions. And to Sara Stahl for uncovering John Henry Turpin in the F-4 story, and to Megan Churchwell of the Puget Sound Navy Museum for providing Turpin's photo and other background material. Also, to the many photo archive sites that allowed access to their imagery. They are listed in the bibliography and individual photo credits.

To Renée Davis for her book design, creative ideas, and layout contributions, and to Jack Harmon for providing comments on the story, humor, and an alternative view to everything under the sun.

Finally, my deepest thanks to Katie Sanborn, my editor of the last 30 years — a friend, fellow bicyclist, intellectual sounding board and research advisor since our paths first crossed in San Francisco in 1990. I can always count on Katie to tell me if my story needs more work. Besides her editorial contributions, she researched and verified numerous sources in this project and spent a day — March 25, 2022 — in the Pacific Fleet Submarine Museum in Pearl Harbor, exploring F-4 archives. Coincidentally, that was the exact day that F-4 disappeared 107 years before. Knowing the story, she felt chills, standing before the preserved uniform of Lt. Alfred Ede and the original USS F-4 gravestone marker from 1915, on display in the museum.

BIBLIOGRAPHY AND SOURCE MATERIAL

SOURCE MATERIAL

Agraz Family – Courtesy of John Agraz and Jeanette Quick; Jack Agraz's personal diary from his years in the US Asiatic Fleet, family photographs, family history, newspaper archives, and personal Naval documents, from the early 1900s.

California Naval History; California's Ships: *USS Alert, USS Cheyenne* sub-flotilla tenders; www.militarymuseum.org

Humboldt Bay Maritime Museum, Samoa, California; Photographs of the *USS H-3* and *USS Milwaukee* wrecks; story details and Humboldt Bay historical commentary

ibiblio: A collaboration of the School of Information and Library Science and Information Technology Services at University of North Carolina at Chapel Hill; a collection of collections, including millions of archived items; historical photos of *F-4* and *H-3* submarines and events. ibiblio.org

Pacific Fleet Submarine Museum at Pearl Harbor, Honolulu, Hawaii; historic photos and documents on loss of *F-4*; Sarah Bellian, Museum Curator; www.bowfin.org

PigBoats.COM – *Through the Looking Glass: U.S. Submarine History from 1900-1940*; Ric Hedman and David Johnston; historical photographs, submarine details, personal stories, anecdotes and technical archives on early US Navy submarines and submarine crews from 1900-1940, including F-Boats and H-Boats. pigboats.com

Walter Pratt, Chief Electrician at the Hammond Lumber Company at Samoa mill: Eyewitness to the Samoa Beach life-saving developments; Pratt later recounted details to Duane Stewart

Duane Stewart EM1, USN – Crew member of the submarine *H-3*; Duane wrote a 50-page manuscript about what happened inside *H-3* during the trip down the Pacific Coast and subsequent wreck on Samoa Beach at Humboldt Bay on December 14, 1916.

BOOKS

Bartholomew, Capt. Charles and Milwee, Jr., Cmdr. William *Mud, Muscle and Miracles: Marine Salvage in the United States Navy*, Dept. of the Navy, 2nd ed. 1992, 1st ed. 1990; Naval History and Heritage Command; U.S. Navy divers, *F-4* data history.navy.mil

Beach Jr., Edward L. *Run Silent, Run Deep*. New York: Henry Holt & Co., 1955

Christley, Jim; Bull, Peter (illus.). *US Submarines 1900-35*. Oxford, United Kingdom: Osprey Publishing Ltd., 2011

Thomas A. Edison Papers: *The Year of Innovation; Edison in World War I*; Rutgers, School of Arts and Sciences; edison.rutgers.edu

Hillman, Raymond W. *Shipwrecked at Samoa, California: The Loss of the Navy Cruiser*

U.S.S. Milwaukee, Launched 1906, Lost 1917. Pride of the River, 1994

Hoyt, Edwin P. *Submarines at War: The History of the American Silent Service.* New York, Stein & Day Publishers, 1983. – Notes on Jack Agraz on the *F-4* and service in the Philippines

Irving, Leigh H. *History of Humboldt County, California – With Biographical Sketches*, Los Angeles: Historic Record Company, 1915

Lightfoot, Bill. *Beneath The Surface: World War 1 Submarines Built in Seattle and Vancouver.* Washington State: Green Board Press, 2005 – In-depth technical details about the construction and operations of the Navy's early era Pacific submarine fleet

Lockwood, Charles A., Vice Adm. USN (retired); Adamson, Hans Christian Colonel, USAF (retired). *Hell at 50 Fathoms.* Chilton Company, 1962 – Extensive details on the *F-4* loss and *H-3* recovery

Masters, David. *Divers In Deep Seas: More Romances of Salvage.* London: Eyre & Spottiswoode, 1938 – A story about Jack Agraz

Powers, Dennis M. *Taking the Sea: Perilous Waters, Sunken Ships and the True Story of Legendary Wrecker Captains.* New York: AMACOM Books, 2009

PERIODICALS

"100 Years Ago Today: *USS E-2* explodes in dry dock" *USS* Flier Project: The Stories Behind History, January 15, 2016

"Corroded Rivet Sent *F-4* Submarine to the Bottom" *New York Sun*, October 28, 1915

East Oregonian, Pendleton, Oregon, June 15, 1916

Carranco, Lynwood. "Maritime Fiasco on the Northern California Coast, by – California History" *The Magazine of the California Historical Society*, Volume 60, Issue 3 (October 1981)

French, Dr. G.R.W. "Diving operations in connection with the salvage of the *USS F-4*" *The United States Naval Medical Bulletin*, Volume 10 (1916), US Government Printing Office, University of Chicago (digitized April 20, 2011) – US Navy Assistant Surgeon's *F-4* dive notes on Crilley, Drellishak, Loughman, and Nielson.

Harris, Alfred W. "Last Dive of the *F-4* Sub" *Sea Classics* Vol. 48, No. 6 (March 1973) Challenger Publications Inc.

Hawaiian Gazette Honolulu, Hawaii, March 1915 to September 1915

Honolulu Star Bulletin Honolulu, Hawaii, March 1915 to June 2020

The Humboldt Times Eureka, California, December 1916 to June 1917

The Library of Congress, *Chronicling America: Honolulu Star Bulletin; Hawaiian Gazette*

Los Angeles Times, Los Angeles, California, March–June 1915

"Nevada Then and Now" *Pahrump Mirror*, Pahrump, Nevada – Alfred Ede
www.pah.stparchive.com

The Oregon Daily Journal, Portland, Oregon, March 28, 1915

The Oakland Tribune, Oakland, California, June 27, 1929

The Pacific Commercial Advertiser, Honolulu, Hawaii, March 1915 to September 1915

The San Francisco Chronicle, San Francisco, California, December 1916 to March 1917

The San Francisco Examiner, San Francisco, California, March 28, 1915; newspaper photo of F-1 crew with Lt. Jimmy Howell and Lt. j.g. Harry Bogusch on the bridge

San Jose Mercury Herald, San Jose, California, September 20, 1920

Our Navy magazine, August 1937; First Submarine Disaster, by John Bunyan Atkins

Stevens, Peter F. "Death in the Depths" *Hawaii Chronicles – Island History from the Pages of Honolulu Magazine*, University of Hawaii, 1996; Story of the F4, reprinted from November 1990

"Socialite Fundraiser for F-4 Families" *Washington Times*, May 16, 1915

Washington Herald, Washington, DC, October 17, 1915; Edison believes his alkaline battery will revolutionize submarine construction

"What Sank the F-4" *New York Tribune*, New York, NY, April 11, 1915

White, Sondra. "The Sinking of the USS F-4" eNewsHawaii, March 25-26, 2000 militaryhonors.sid-hill.us/history/f4-hist1.htm

Newspapers.com: Access to more than 100 F-4 and H-3 articles and personal stories from newspapers across the country (Hawaii, California, Michigan, Nebraska, New York, Oregon, Utah, and Washington) www.newspapers.com

California Digital Newspaper Collection: Articles on F-4 and H-3 and associated personnel www.cdnc.ucr.edu

HUMBOLDT COUNTY HISTORICAL SOCIETY MATERIALS

Anthony, Douglas. "The Wreck of the USS *Milwaukee* and the Submarine USS *H-3* – Senior Seminar Paper" University of California Press, November 29, 1989

Humboldt County Historical Society. Collected writings of local historians, historical columnists, and photographs of the USS *H-3* and USS *Milwaukee* wrecks

McCormick, Evelyn. "The *H-3* Submarine" *The Humboldt Historian*, February–March 1979.

McCormick, Evelyn. "A Colossal Mistake: How the USS *Milwaukee* Got Stuck in Humboldt" (Eyewitness) for the *Times Standard*, November 24, 1996 – Courtesy of Humboldt County Historical Society

"Radio Man of Submarine *H-3* Recalls Terrors of Grounding 21 Years Ago" *Humboldt Times*, April 3, 1938 – Duane Stewart interviewed by *Humboldt Times* reporter

Rohde, Jerry. "Decking from the Disaster: A Memorial to the USS *Milwaukee*" *Humboldt Historian*, Spring 2013

Duane Stewart interviewed 46 years after the wreck by Humboldt Historian Andrew
      Genzoli for his weekly column called RFD, *Humboldt Times*, December 15, 1962

NAVY SOURCES

Moore, C.B.T. *C.B.T. Moore to the Secretary of the Navy, April 19, 1915.* Letter. U.S. Naval
      Station, Hawaii. Pearl Harbor. *Pacific Fleet Submarine Museum*

Moore, C.B.T. *C.B.T. Moore to the Secretary of the Navy, April 26, 1915.* Letter. U.S. Naval
      Station, Hawaii. Pearl Harbor. *Pacific Fleet Submarine Museum*

Moore, C.B.T. *C.B.T. Moore to the Secretary of the Navy, June 15, 1915.* Letter. U.S. Naval
      Station, Hawaii. Pearl Harbor. *Pacific Fleet Submarine Museum*

Haislip, Capt. Harvey, U.S. Navy (retired). "The Valor of Inexperience," U.S. Naval
      Institute Proceedings – officer aboard the USS *Milwaukee*

"Report on Loss of Submarine F-4" *United States Naval Institute Proceedings.* U.S. Naval
      Institute, Annapolis, *Maryland*, Vol. 41, No. 6 (Nov.-Dec. 1915, Whole No. 160)

"Loss of the USS F-4" The Submarine Force Library and Museum, Groton, Connecti-
      cut, *USSNautilus*.org (March 25, 2014) www.ussnautilus.org/category/submarine-
      history

"Loss of the *Turtle* in 1776 at the Battle of Fort Lee" The Submarine Force Library and
      Museum, Groton, Connecticut, *USSNautilus*.org (Sept 7, 2017)
      www.ussnautilus.org/category/submarine-history

Army and Navy Register. *The U.S. Military Gazette,* Army and Navy Publishing Co.,
      Washington, DC, Volume 57 and Volume 59 (1915), Volume 60 (1916)

NavSource Naval History. Photographic history of the U.S. Navy NavSource.org

Puget Sound Navy Museum – John Henry Turpin photo and background –
      pugetsoundnavymuseum.org

Bright, Alexander and Palmer, Elijah "Before Chief Turpin: Other African American
      Chief Petty Officers" Hamptons Roads Naval Museum, February 18, 2021 (an of-
      ficial museum of the United States Navy, reporting to Naval History and Heritage
      Command, Washington DC) – hamptonroadsnavalmuseum.blogspot.com/

Annapolis Year Books – 1911, 1912, 1913

United States Navy Memorial, United States Naval Academy; Lt. Ede and Ensign
      Parker www.navylog.navymemorial.org

U.S. Naval Academy Virtual Memorial Hall – F-4 Officers: Alfred Ede and Timothy
      Parker usnamemorialhall.org/index.php/USNA_Virtual_Memorial_Hall

OTHER RESOURCES

Goodman, William. "Below The Surface: United States Submariners Identity During
      World War Two" Texas State Graduate Council of Texas State University,

www.digital.library.txstate.edu

Wikipedia: *USS H3 (SS-30, USS Garfish); USS F4 (SS-23, USS Skate); USS Milwaukee (C-21); HMS Bedford (1901);* Naval Act of 1794; Bushnell's *Turtle* (submersible); *H.L. Hunley* (submarine); Imperial Russian Navy; John Henry Turpin, GMC Wikipedia.org

"History of the Submariner's Dolphins" About Subs aboutsubs.com

Cipra, Dave, ed. "A History of Sea Service Ranks & Titles" Commandant's Bulletin 5-85 (1985), US Coast Guard, Washington DC

Columbia River Maritime Museum; photograph of a breaker on the Columbia River Bar from 1895; Astoria, Oregon – www.crmm.org

"President Roosevelt Underwater for Three Hours In *Plunger*" Theodore Roosevelt Center at Dickinson State University; Dickinson, North Dakota theodorerooseveltcenter.org

National Park Service – nps.gov/articles/franklin-delano-roosevelt-assistant secretary-of-the-navy.htm – Franklin D. Roosevelt, Assistant Secretary of the Navy

Illustration: *Life Saving Station Crews Use Breeches Buoy to Rescue New Jersey Shipwreck Malta.* Frank Leslie's *Illustrated Newspaper*, December 5, 1885, Archives of History LLC, New London, Minnesota

Soundings – Real Boats and Real Boaters. Horse Drawn Surf Boat. American Red Cross Collection, Library of Congress soundingsonline.com

"U.S. Navy World War I Enlisted Rates" Uniform-Reference.net uniform-reference.net/insignia/usn/usn_enl_wwl.html

United States Navy Submarine Tenders *USS Wyoming* and *USS Cheyenne.* TenderTale www.tendertale.com

Olson, Kenneth J. *Fighting from Below: Diary of a WWI submariner* Boston, Massachusetts: Period Americana, 2019

Internet Archive – archive.org

National Archives – archives.gov

About the Author

Jon Humboldt Gates is a fifth-generation native of Northern California and the Pacific Northwest. His great-great-grandparents came West by wagon train during the California Gold Rush in 1849, and his grandfather was a miner in the Klondike Gold Rush, near Dawson City, in 1900. Jon, who has lived most of his life in Humboldt County, the San Francisco Bay Area and the Pacific Northwest, has been a travel writer, historian, musician, story teller, business journalist, and co-founder of the international market research firm OTR Global. He and his wife now live near the Columbia River in Oregon.

Other Works

Firestorm
A personal narrative: Vignettes from the epicenter of the 2017 Tubbs Fire –
one of the most destructive wildfire in California history
Moonstone Publishing

Falk's Claim
The Life and Death of a Redwood Lumber Town
Moonstone Publishing

Night Crossings
A half-century of maritime encounters with rogue waves in the night while
crossing California's notorious Humboldt Bar
Moonstone Publishing

Soviet Passage
Travel stories and photography from a solo journey across Russia and Siberia in 1984
Summer Run Publishing

Lost Nations (CD)
The Timezone Band
Russian-American worldbeat music collaboration in 1991
Moonstone Publishing

Lost Nations (MP3)
The Timezone Band
Reconstruction and mixtranslation by Bill Laswell
M.O.D Technologies, New York, NY